READING MARGINALLY

Feminism, Deconstruction and the Bible

BIBLICAL INTERPRETATION SERIES

VOLUME 21

READING MARGINALLY

Feminism, Deconstruction and the Bible

BY

DAVID RUTLEDGE

E.J. BRILL
LEIDEN · NEW YORK · KÖLN
1996

The paper in this book meets the guidelines for permanence and durability of the Committee on Production Guidelines for Book Longevity of the Council on Library Resources.

ISSN 0928-0731
ISBN 90 04 10564 6

TO JACQUI GODDARD

CONTENTS

ACKNOWLEDGEMENTS

This text began life in its present form as a PhD thesis, written at The University of Edinburgh, Scotland, between January 1990 and April 1993, and during that time I received assistance from a number of sources whose support it is a pleasure to acknowledge. First of all, I wish to express sincere thanks to my supervisors: I am indebted to Dr. A.P. Hayman for his encouragement, his availability, and for his skilful and painstaking supervision of the bulk of the material presented here; also to Professor J.C.L. Gibson for his helpful and constructive critique of specific points and chapters, and to Dr. A.G. Auld. I wish also to express my gratitude to Professor A.M. Gibbs and Professor E. Ruth Waterhouse of Macquarie University, Sydney.

Financial support was made available to me by the Faculty of Arts, The University of Edinburgh, from January 1990 to the end of 1992; without this generous assistance, which is gratefully acknowledged, my research would not have been possible.

Special thanks are also due to Professor Robert P. Carroll of The University of Glasgow, whose advice, assistance and encouragement have been invaluable during the revision stages of these chapters.

In the fourth chapter of this book, I note with admiration some of the exegetical techniques of Rabbinic commentary on the Hebrew Bible, wherein the primary biblical text is surrounded in its margins by interpretative discussion, argument and counterargument. I would like to (and maybe in a subsequent publication, shall) weave acknowledgements around and through my text in a similar manner, in order to indicate at various points the various debts of thanks owed to a great many people. My grateful "midrash" would include, first and foremost, my family: my mother and father Janet and Philip Rutledge, my sister Lisa and my brother Jonathan. It would include Anne Morrison, without whose imagination and support this work would not have been completed. It would include friends in Edinburgh from the Muirhouse Community: Diane Armstrong-Robertson, David Jasmine, Caroline King, Xiang Yang Li, Mathias Ross, Sujatha Ross, Elaine Stewart, Don Stubbings and Zamantha Walker. I would also thank Carolyn Butler, for advice, encouragement and argument over lunch in the early stages of this study, and Mary Moffett, for the whole idea in the first place.

In Sydney, the long and demanding process of revision has been greatly assisted—made more of a challenge and more of a pleasure—by the support of Niamh Stephenson. Her ideas and her willingness to engage critically with various aspects of the rewrite have been invaluable; I acknowledge her contribution with love and gratitude, and look forward to collaboration on future projects. I am thankful also to Maddie Oliver for her advice and encouragement.

I would like to make special mention of Sophie Goddard, who for many years has offered support, criticism, correspondence, literary diversions and invaluable friendship.

Thanks are also due to friends for assistance of various kinds. They include: John Baron, Stewart Boydell, Victoria Buckley, Genevieve Corish, Katy Cronin, David Dawson, Martin Derkenne, Elizabeth Fullerton, Dorothy Goddard, Simon Goddard, Todd Gray, John Henderson, Victoria Hollingum, Richard Johnson, Mick Joyce, Justine Lange, John Livingstone, Maria Lock, Felicia McCarren, Don McLean, Chris Moore, Sonal Moore, Wendy Moran, Diana Olsson, Mark Pearse, Nicolas Rasmussen, Christine Stanford, Richard Stanford, Lucy Tod, Eduardo Ugarte, Toni Williams, and Meron Wilson.

INTRODUCTION

It has become customary to begin any discussion which deals at any length with deconstructive critical theory by meditating upon the function of introductions.[1] For there is a strange paradox inherent in the phenomenon of the introduction, a paradox at work both in the introduction's production and in its reception. Anybody who has written a reasonably lengthy piece of work knows that the introduction is usually written after everything else has been completed, and it is then placed at the beginning of the discussion as "a gesture of authorial command",[2] a kind of preparatory summary which in effect tells the reader not only what is about to be read, but also *how* it is to be processed and understood. Such information, however, is only of limited value while the main body of the text remains unexplored, not only because the introduction paradoxically calls upon a certain level of familiarity with the work under discussion, but also because the introduction in turn cannot really be understood or evaluated until that work has been read. To read a preface to *Don Quixote*, for example, is to begin to formulate a skeletal reading of *Don Quixote* itself; once the main text has been assiduously worked through, this pre-reading can be assessed and adjusted, and thus the *Quixote* becomes a preface to its preface—an elegant reversal, whose ironies would surely not have been lost on Cervantes.

Such introductory musings are often irresistable to scholars of deconstructive literary criticism because they conveniently and immediately open onto a key strategy in the work of Jacques Derrida: that of questioning the distinction between text and commentary. Perhaps Derrida's most notorious claim is that there is no such thing as a stable, authoritative master-text against which its interpretations can be measured; rather, the meaning of any text resides precariously and elusively in the play (an important Derridean term) of

---

[1] Cf. Derrida (1981a), pp.359; Norris (1982), pp.xixiii; Spivak in Derrida (1976), pp.ixxiii. Cf. also Burnett (1990), p.52.

[2] Norris *op. cit.* p.xiii.

those innumerable readings. Gayatri Chakravorty Spivak, in her introduction to Derrida's *Of Grammatology*, writes that

> two readings of the "same" book show an identity that can only be
> defined as a difference. The book is not repeatable in its "identity":
> each reading of the book produces a simulacrum of an "original" that
> is itself the mark of [a] shifting and unstable subject....The preface, by
> daring to repeat the book and reconstitute it in another register, merely
> enacts what is already the case: the book's repetitions are always other
> than the book. There is, in fact, no "book" other than those ever-dif-
> ferent repetitions....[3]

The paradox of introduction/primary text has been expounded in
various ways and contexts. Jorge Luis Borges invokes it when he
suggests that Kafka is as much a literary precursor of Robert
Browning as vice versa; when the two authors are compared, he
says, the way in which Kafka's work illuminates that of Browning
means that the twentieth-century novelist provides the "introduction" to subsequent readings of the nineteenth-century poet.[4]
Fred W. Burnett, in a similar fashion, points out that the relationship
between modernism and postmodernism is distinguished by the way
in which "[e]ach concept is the condition for the other",[5] that it is
only our (historically) postmodern perspective that enables us to
understand or even to perceive modernism—and rarely has there
been a concept less extricable than modernism from our interpretations of it. Elsewhere, Derrida argues (as we shall examine in
greater detail further on) that in philosophical discourse, the
"centre" of argument has no self-validating claim on truth, that it
can only be determined as central by prescribing the marginal;
marginality thus becomes the *necessary condition* for centrality, the
centre of the centre.[6]

It is this last formulation that is most readily expressed in so-
cial/political terms, and which thus has the most immediate bearing
on the subject of this book. For if feminist theological criticisms of
traditional mainstream Judaeo-Christian religion can be said to be

---

[3] Spivak, in Derrida (1976), p.xii.
[4] Borges: "Kafka and His Precursors" in (1989), pp.234-36.
[5] Burnett *op. cit.* p.252.
[6] Cf. Derrida: "Structure, Sign and Play in the Discourse of the Human Sciences"
in (1978), pp.278-93.

legitimate—that is, if women are accorded marginal or secondary status in the overwhelming majority of biblical texts, and if this marginal status has long been reflected in patriarchal religious institutions and practice, and if feminist biblical interpretation subsequently has been accorded marginal or secondary status in official biblical-critical discourse—then the insights offered by Derrida and deconstructive criticism enable it to become apparent that feminism's "marginality" is in fact not a result *of*, but the necessary condition *for* patriarchy's centrality. It is only a short step from this realisation to the point where the issues at stake in the feminist struggle can be seen not so much as issues of truth and propriety as ones of influence and power, in particular the power of those at the centre to determine where the margins lie and who inhabits them. Traditional biblical scholarship—reflecting the patriarchal leanings of Church and academy—has long sought to sideline feminist concerns on the grounds of what is and is not relevant to what the bible has to say. A deconstructive response to this involves arguing that "what the bible has to say" is no more than what patriarchal scholarship would have it say, and that the authoritative status claimed by male-oriented readings of biblical texts is not grounded in "real" or authentic meaning, but in the institutional power to devalue interpretative approaches which (like feminism) contradict established orthodoxy. Furthermore, where patriarchal discourse cites objective Truth as the overarching master-text to which it alone provides the sanctioned commentary, deconstruction interrogates both the hierarchy and the distinction at work in such a claim. The text/commentary dichotomy is first reversed by demonstrating that determinations of truth actually function as legitimising commentaries on patriarchal power, and the dichotomy is then questioned at a deeper level by showing that both the power-structure and its ideological buttresses rely fundamentally on each other for their identity, and also that they form part of a larger network of social codes and conventions. My main intention throughout the course of this book is to argue that this kind of strategy is indispensable to feminist readings of biblical texts.

But why *feminist* readings? In the following chapter I will argue that feminist theory and criticism are important because they deal first and foremost with gender differences, and gender is a crucial issue for any explicitly politically-oriented approach to biblical texts. This still, however, leaves the question of whether or not it is desirable for a male writer to speak "on behalf of" women—if that is what I am doing. In a 1991 essay entitled "The Problem of Speaking for Others", Linda Alcoff discusses how the act of speaking for another person or group can compromise the power of that person or group to speak for themselves, especially if the speaker speaks from a position of privilege or authority, on behalf of the oppressed. On the other hand, a retreat into individualism, based on the decision that from now on I will only "speak for myself", takes insufficient account of the fact that what I say and how I say it, and indeed the "I" that speaks in the first place, are all inseparable from a complex matrix of communal causes and effects.[7] I do not wish to go so far as to claim that since "I" do not exist as a unified subject, then "I" happily cannot be held responsible for such authorial transgressions as speaking on behalf of others—although this kind of leap into postmodern outer space has its obvious strategic advantages. What I would claim is that feminism has, since the 1960's, broadened in scope and significance to the point where it now constitutes a discourse—or a range of discourses—which impinges upon so many aspects of cultural life that *not* to speak of feminism is difficult, to say the least, for anyone interested in gender issues. So while I have no particular interest in arguing the toss over the exact or definitive relationship between men and feminism (e.g. whether or not a man can "be a feminist"), I am suggesting that feminism exists as a discourse which has, to an extent, constructed me as a speaking/ writing subject, and so within which I consider myself to be a legitimate participant. As a participant *in* feminist discourse, rather than as a commentator *on* it, I would therefore hope to position myself as one "speaking with and to, rather than speaking for, others".[8]

---

[7] Alcoff (1991), p.21:

> It is an illusion that I can separate from others to such an extent that I can avoid affecting them. This may be the intention of my speech....but it will not be the effect of the speech, and therefore cannot capture the speech in its reality as a discursive practice. When I "speak for myself", I am participating in the creation and reproduction of discourses through which my own and other selves are constituted.

[8] *Ibid.* p.23.

The issue of who is speaking for whom could perhaps be sidestepped by abandoning the term "feminist" altogether, and substituting some kind of negative reference such as a-sexist or counter-patriarchal; not because feminism should be understood as an exclusively negative or reactionary practice, but because such formulations might serve to divert attention away from the problematics of representation and onto the task at hand: the deconstruction of patriarchal ideology in biblical texts. My main argument throughout this book is that if feminist biblical interpretation is to engage with patriarchy—as it inevitably must, given the nature of the society from which both the bible and biblical religion have emerged—and if patriarchal power is a social construct rather than a Divine order, then feminist "deconstruction", in at least a broad sense of the word, is not so much desirable as absolutely necessary. I have offered above what perhaps amounts to a gross oversimplification of a deconstructive perspective on patriarchy, but it should suffice to indicate in general terms (terms which will shortly become more specific) how and why the necessity of deconstruction in feminist exegesis stands. The questions which these opening remarks raise are, of course, numerous. Is feminism no more than a commentary on patriarchy, with no definitive qualities of its own? Do texts possess definitive qualities, or are these always supplied by the reader? What is the author's role in the production of meaning? Does marginality automatically guarantee "deconstructive" legitimacy in interpretation, or are there hermeneutical constraints? Perhaps most importantly, if the meaning of a text is a product of the society in which it is received, what use does this insight have for those—feminists and others—who read the bible in search of truth? The following discussion should be read not necessarily as an endeavour to come up with conclusive answers to these prefatory questions, but as the attempt to provide (in the manner of all primary texts) a satisfactorily extensive introduction to them.

This book takes the following form: in chapter 1, a discussion of sexism (particularly sexism in what I have, for the sake of brevity, chosen to call "Judaeo-Christian" religion) leads onto an examination of various existing feminist biblical-critical responses to the bible's patriarchal concerns. The appropriation of the Old Testament prophetic tradition, "depatriarchalizing" reading strategies, the search for a women's history behind biblical narratives: these are assessed in an argument which focuses finally on the rhetorical criticism of Phyllis Trible and her reading of the Garden of Eden story in Genesis 2:4b-3:24. This reading (and the methodology behind it) is criticised for its heavy reliance on a concept of the text's intrinsic or authentic meaning. The subject of essentialism or definitive signification having been broached, chapter 2 looks at this issue in the light of patriarchal dualism and the concept of the essential Female. I outline Linda Alcoff's argument[9] that neither radical ("cultural") feminism, with its valorisation of "definitively" female characteristics, nor hardline poststructuralist feminism, which can too easily relativise gender issues out of discursive focus, provides a useful alternative to patriarchal-dualistic determinations of woman, and I put forward Alcoff's concept of "identity politics" as the achievement of a satisfactory middle ground where the tensions between essentialism and relativism are allowed to operate fluidly and creatively. Essentialism in biblical interpretation is then re-examined and criticised as a restrictive approach to exegesis which has much in common with the logic of patriarchal oppression.

Relativism in biblical interpretation receives both more specific and more extended treatment, as chapter 3 presents deconstructive criticism and the work of Jacques Derrida as providing a usefully non-deterministic understanding of writing, reading and meaning. After an introductory outline of some important Derridean terms and gestures (logocentrism, *différance* and so on), the discussion turns to the relationship between deconstruction and feminism, arguing that both Derrida's call for an explicitly "sexualised" approach to reading and deconstruction's ultimate concern with the politics of interpretation can well serve feminist-critical interests. I then turn to consider various arguments against deconstruction, first examining the case (put forward by such critics as Robert Alter) that politics and reading should not mix, and that modern literary theories of interpretation transgress the proper boundaries of respect for the literary text.

Chapter 4 continues the case "against" deconstruction by bringing up an issue central to this book: that of whether or not decon-

---

[9] Cf. Alcoff (1988).

struction is an inherently atheistic programme which goes fundamentally against the grain of religious faith. I first consider the relationship between deconstruction and metaphysics, suggesting that rather than "destroying" such metaphysical determinations of truth as God, deconstruction in fact first relies on their structures and postulations for its efficacy, and then reconfigures them, seeking not so much to deny truth as to "resituate" it.[10] It is therefore not unthinkable that the deconstructive-feminist reader of the bible and the religious reader of the bible can be one and the same individual. I then go on to look at aspects of the Judaeo-Christian theological tradition which evince turns of thought or belief congruent with ideas now called deconstructive. After a brief detour touching on medieval Christian mysticism and contemporary black American theology, the discussion arrives at Rabbinic midrash; the controversy over whether or not Rabbinic hermeneutics prefigures deconstruction is examined, and I argue that if the temptation to paint the Rabbis systematically as early deconstructionists (or modern literary theorists as latter-day Rabbis) is resisted, we can see that midrash does, in many if not all instances, show us a species of biblical criticism which is at once informed by respect for the integrity of the biblical text, underpinned by a positive theology and nascently, if inconsistently, deconstructive.

The chapter closes with a comparison between the aims and intentions of Rabbinic hermeneutics and those of feminist exegesis; I suggest that the marginal perspective historically adopted by (or forced upon) both Jews and women has given rise to a strong similarity between Judaic and feminist understandings of identity, difference and truth, a similarity which indicates that those feminists who wish to experiment with deconstructive criticism of biblical texts could benefit greatly from the close reading of midrash. The fifth and final chapter consists of a reading of the Garden of Eden story in Genesis 2:4b-3:24, a reading not intended to be taken either as definitively deconstructive or as definitively feminist, but which suggests one of an innumerable number of possible outworkings of deconstruction in feminist exegesis.

---

[10] Cf. Lentricchia (1980), p.174.

This study is, essentially, of an introductory nature, which means that I have in many places sacrificed depth for breadth, and this has necessitated a number of generalisations, condensations and omissions. I have, for example, made rather free use of Stanley Fish's term "interpretative communities" while relegating the important and extremely relevant work of Fish himself to only the most occasional of footnotes. I have, perhaps more seriously, on the whole neglected to make more than a passing mention of the work of such French feminists as Hélène Cixous, Luce Irigaray and Julia Kristeva, writers whose cultural/philosophical links with Derrida are strong, and whose insights might well be expected to have considerable relevance to the subject under discussion. The principal reason for their marginal role in this thesis is that their work is (like Derrida's) complex, rigorous, and requires extensive discussion; piecemeal appropriation of isolated ideas would inevitably result in distortions and shallow generalisations. I have, therefore, opted to treat the French feminists as constituting a major field of study in themselves, one whose relationship to feminist biblical interpretation invites further attention. In doing this, I have unfortunately done little to narrow the much-criticised gulf between Anglo-American and French feminist discourse. Ironically, this exclusion (in tandem with a similar curtailment of discussion concerning Derrida's philosophical forebears and sympathetic contemporaries) has also resulted in a more-or-less constant reversion to Derrida as the founding or exemplary practitioner of deconstruction, a reversion which contradicts both the notional autonomy of *feminist* criticism and the extreme scepticism with which deconstruction is meant to treat origins and authoritative "presences".[11] This contradiction is noted further on, but not to any final degree resolved; it provides, perhaps, an appropriate point of entry for the deconstructive reader of the following pages.

---

[11] Cf. Felperin (1985), p.43.

CHAPTER ONE

FEMINISM, RELIGION AND THE BIBLICAL TEXT

In the introduction to this book, I have acknowledged that men, when they speak at length of feminism, inevitably raise uncomfortable questions concerning motives and propriety. On one hand, it makes sense to say that the field of gender studies can only benefit from cross-fertilisation, and that to make feminism exclusively the discursive province of women (and men's studies exclusively that of men) is to perpetuate gender determinism, a sexual ghetto mentality, mutual suspicion and misunderstanding, and a thousand other unwelcome phenomena which rightly belong back in the bad old days of uncontested patriarchy. On the other hand, it is plain that patriarchal attitudes, while contested, are proving more difficult to shift than the first optimistic proponents of Women's Liberation might have hoped. Regardless of the material and social gains made by many women in many fields, and the increasing sophistication of feminist theory, it remains the case that patriarchal culture, as a power structure with its institutions, ideological currencies and apparatuses of control, still constitutes a formidable matrix of oppression for many others (or so it appears in Western society; it is important to bear in mind that "patriarchy", like "feminism", is a white European construct which does not translate unproblematically across into other cultural contexts[1]). And so it is appropriate that the musings upon feminism of a

---

[1]   Cf. Butler (1990):

> The notion of a universal patriarchy has been widely criticised in recent years for its failure to account for the workings of gender oppression in the concrete cultural contexts in which it exists. Where those various contexts have been consulted....it has been to find "examples" or "illustrations" of a universal principle that is assumed from the start. That form of feminist theorising has come under criticism for its efforts to colonise and appropriate non-Western cultures to support highly Western notions of oppression, but because they tend as well to construct a "Third World" or even an "Orient" in which gender oppression is subtly explained as symptomatic of an essential, non-Western barbarism [p.3].

genetic representative of the oppressing class should be regarded as
ideologically problematic, rather like the kind of earnestly socialist or
anarchist press article which occasionally emerges from the living
room of a wealthy suburban appartment.

It seems necessary, therefore, to begin with some kind of explanation as to why the aims and interests of this study should be centred
around feminist hermeneutics. I do not wish to attempt any systematic
definition of feminism; such a definition would have to take into account liberal feminism, radical feminism, black feminism, Marxist,
Jewish and Christian feminism, and so on. If a definition were to be
offered, it would be more appropriate to speak of "feminisms", given
the diversity of women's experience and political activity. This study,
however, as a literary-critical work, is less directly concerned with
women's experience than with the fruits of that experience as evi-
denced in feminist critical theory, and so my answer to the question
"why talk about feminism in the first place?" has to do with the way
feminism works, a kind of model which it provides, rather than with
the day-to-day struggle of women against patriarchy (although of
course one grows out of the other, and I do not believe there is an
identifiable point at which feminist theory cleanly separates from
women's experience[2]).

The explanations of "patriarchy" put forward in the present discussion are to be understood as (Western) culture-specific, and as distinct from a more general notion of
"sexism".

[2] The theory/experience opposition is, ironically, one often upheld by feminist
writers who elsewhere denounce dualistic constructs. Feminist antipathy to theory
rests primarily on the association of abstract, rationalistic thought with male-dominated systems of power and control, and patriarchal society's privileging of the ra-
tional/spiritual over the intuitive/physical. According to this view, theory is

> a way of denying the centrality of women's experience, a way of removing the control of
> the meaning of our lives from individual women and telling us what we should think
> [Weedon, 1987, p.6].

But it is not necessary to see theory as an irredeemably "patriarchal" practice (which
is not, all the same, to say that theory presents no problems for feminism—cf. the
opening discussion in chapter 3). To theorise is to generalise, to establish models
from patterns of experience which can be helpful or even essential to an
understanding of how the individual functions in society; if there is no theory without
experience, it could also be said that experience has no meaning without some kind of
theory. Chris Weedon sees the theory/experience problem as existing at a
social/political rather than an ethical/ideological level:

Sexism and Religion

The particular strength of feminism in the sphere of religion is that it offers a critical paradigm which has its roots firmly planted in the so-cial/political, and yet which is, at the same time, widely applicable *as a paradigm* in considering and criticising other forms of oppression apart from the patriarchal. In his book *Domination or Liberation,* Alistair Kee looks at the ambivalent role played by Western religion in social and political oppression, and it is no accident that Kee takes issue first with the oppression of women. He writes:

> I begin with this area of domination....because it is the most extensive, running throughout recorded human history, across most if not all known societies, and directly affecting more than half of the world's population. Domination on the basis of gender is so pervasive because it is present everywhere in addition to other forms of domination.[3]

Kee goes on to point out that this results in a particularly acute form of oppression for women in societies already suffering the experience of domination on the basis of race, class or economic status: "rich people can dominate poor people....but poor men can still dominate poor women".[4] Similarly, Rosemary Radford Ruether sees the subor-dination of women as the most basic form of social oppression, an oppression so deeply-ingrained and long-lived that even the "subvers-ive memory" of freedom is denied:

> Unlike subordinated races who have preserved some remnants of an al-ternative culture from a period prior to their enslavement, the subordi-nation of women takes place at the heart of every culture and thus de-

---

To dismiss all theory as an elitist attempt to tell women what their experience really means is not helpful, but it does serve as a reminder of the importance of making theory accessible and of the political importance of transforming the material conditions of knowledge production and women's access to knowledge....rather than turning our backs on theory and taking refuge in experience alone, we should think in terms of transform-ing both the social relations of knowledge production and the type of knowledge pro-duced [p.7].

[3] Kee (1986), p.1.
[4] *Ibid.* p.1.

prives women of an alternative culture with which to express their identity over against the patriarchal culture of family and society.[5]

But here, with the presentation of women as "the first and oldest oppressed, subjugated people",[6] whose domination "takes place at the
heart of every culture", we have a universalisation of feminist concerns which, as I have mentioned, is not without its problems. Exactly
what constitutes power, domination and resistance differs from culture to culture, and while it would be absurd to argue (for example)
that the practice of ritual genital mutilation and the institution of universal suffrage differ only conventionally on any global scale of
women's experience, there still remains a bewildering range of perspectives on an innumerable variety of social practices which makes it
difficult, and arrogant, to try to determine confidently the nature of
patriarchy and women's subordination in each and every cultural
context.[7] At the same time, however, if we are talking about discrimination, or the awareness of difference which is necessary for any pattern of domination/subjugation, then sexual difference does assume
major significance. Even a racially homogenous, classless society will
be made up of women and men, and so its members will differentiate
among themselves according to gender if to no other criterion. This
means that gender, the "bifurcation of sexed bodies" which
constitutes "an irreducible cultural universal",[8] raises issues of Self
and Other, of identity and difference, which engage human society at
a level of significance which cuts across cultural boundaries. What
gender differences *mean*, the ways in which they inform social roles,
hierarchies and practices, is a more complex and culture-specific
question. But I would argue that sexism, or the devaluation of the
perceived status of women in favour of the status of men, in its
"genderedness" lies very close to the heart of the Self/Other crisis
from which spring all forms of discrimination.

---

[5] Ruether (1986), p.22. As far as the possibility of access to a "lost" women's religion or religious history is concerned, Ruether seems to share a certain scepticism with
those who believe that "the story of the pre-patriarchal women's religion seems more
like the *in illo tempore* of an attractive myth than real history" (p.24).

[6] Ruether (1979), p.51.

[7] One is put in mind, for example, of women in traditional Japanese and orthodox
Jewish societies, who occupy positions of "power" of a kind unrecognised or marginalised by conventional liberal-feminist definitions of the word.

[8] Grosz (1994), p.160.

The dualistic psychology of sexism in Western society is well-documented; androcentric thought conceives the male/female opposition as paradigmatic of any number of other binary distinctions—mind/body, heaven/earth, spirit/matter, reason/instinct, order/chaos, and so on. The former term is valued as male-identified over and above the latter, which is held to represent the "female" realm, and so in a society dominated by this kind of thinking, the female stands for all that is most dark and dangerous in the human psyche—that which must be controlled. The theological perspective is significant: Sallie McFague, among others, sees this way of structuring reality as partial evidence of man's (i.e. men's) fundamental sense of alienation from a distant, transcendent God:

> At the heart of patriarchalism....is a subject-object split in which man is envisioned over against God and vice versa. God, as transcendent being, is man's superior Other and woman in this hierarchy becomes man's inferior other....man, alienated from God, has projected the pattern of subject-object dualism down the line with woman—as man's most significant human "other"—the chief repository of his alienation.[9]

This pattern of alienation, then, works not just at a general social level, but "at the level of man's being: it is ontological warfare in which women are the first victims".[10]

I would say, therefore, that the case against sexism as one of the forms of discrimination most urgently in need of redress is a strong one—and that feminism, in directly addressing the issues of sexism and sexist oppression, could well be dealing with a root form of the psychic/social malaise which gives rise to other forms of discrimination and subjugation such as racism and classism. The importance of feminism, then, should not be underestimated, particularly in the area of religion, where there is (or should be) a profound commitment to a "healing" of society and to the cessation of oppression and injustice— feminist theology may, in at least some of its forms, constitute a paradigmatic theology of liberation, and feminist biblical hermeneutics may serve to illuminate and throw into sharp relief a message of wholeness and social responsibility not only critical to the Judaeo-

---

[9] McFague (1982), p.148.
[10] *Ibid.* p.149.

Christian tradition, but in a wider sense essential to the maintenance of any kind of just or harmonious society.

But what exactly is it that feminism has to offer in place of alienation and oppression? It is difficult to answer this without resorting to a kind of forensic analysis of Feminism and its vital qualities, and this in turn is difficult because feminism, as an essentially political practice with its major concerns in the here and now, has a constant current of redefinition and self-critique running through it—and this resistance to final definition can, in itself, be seen as a valuable thing in a culture overloaded with rationalism and the impulse toward scientific scrutiny. There is a large and well-worn catalogue of terms associated with feminism and what it identifies itself with: subjectivity, community, intuition, fertility, holism, flux and so on. There is no doubt that these are necessary aspects of human existence, and few feminists would disavow them as being cardinal "feminist" virtues. The problem is that they are also convenient tags which have been attributed to the essential nature of *women* in the attempt either (by patriarchy) to contain women within a predictable, readily-identifiable framework of gender-specified expectations, or (by some separatist feminists) to make feminism exclusively a "women's group", which equates sexism in general with men in particular, and sets itself up in ideological opposition to them. I would suggest that a feminism which claims the so-called "female" qualities devalued by patriarchal society as redemptive—even essential—within an ailing culture, and yet which avoids rigid gender determinism or political exclusivity, is a feminism which

> offers us hope (perhaps, historically, our last hope) that we can move away from fundamentally life-denying values, principles and policies to life-giving ones....It offers us individually and collectively the possibility of making connections with ourselves, one another, the earth and all that is and can be. It offers us the possibility, thus, of making connections with the rhythms and powers of life.[11]

From a traditional scholarly perspective, these concepts of "life-giving" and "life-denying" principles, of "rhythms and powers", may all sound very portentous, but not easily graspable for the purposes of practical enquiry. It has been said of the New Age that it is more a

---

[11] Haney (1980), p.124.

mood than a movement, and the same could perhaps be said for feminism if feminism were simply an amorphous kind of utopianism, a broad-based impulse toward a "softening" of society whereby nurturing, relational instincts were valued over and above aggressive, competitive ones. But while this impulse is essential to feminism (as it is and has been to a great many other progressive movements), it is feminism-as-political-practice rather than feminism-as-nice-idea which activates perceivable social change. Modern feminism has its roots in the Women's Liberation movement of the 1960's-70's, and while the term "women's liberation" may now be out of fashion, it still at first glance seems as good a name as any for the fundamental historical imperative of feminist politics. But there are some problems with this kind of label. The first, and perhaps the most obvious, is that if you define feminism strictly in terms of women's liberation, it is difficult to avoid the equally strict equation of feminist with victim, thereby subsuming feminism's positive, creative strategies beneath the idea that to be a feminist (perhaps even to be a woman) is, first and foremost, to be in a situation of oppression. Another problem has to do with the integration into contemporary feminist theory of some important and challenging insights concerning subjectivity and power. "Women's liberation" assumes the capacity for voluntary agency on the part of self-determining, autonomous subjects, as well as an understanding of power as something which can be picked up, shrugged off, exploited or resisted more or less at will. Feminism and the subject shall be discussed further in the following chapter, and the theoretical context of a problematics of subjectivity and power in chapter 3: suffice it to say for the time being that there is a movement in feminist discourse away from Enlightenment ideals of self and society, toward the adoption of theoretical perspectives which radically reconfigure just such concepts as "woman" and "liberation". Power, in particular, is put forward by such feminist theorists as Judith Butler as being a good deal more complex than something which we "have" and "use" in the way that we might have or use (or choose not to use) a weapon. Rather than seeking *liberation from* oppressive power—an ideal fraught with practical and theoretical difficulties—feminism should be examining strategies for subversion, displacement and re-

deployment *within* power.[12] An important first step, then, in understanding what feminism is and does, is to examine the power-struc-
tures within which feminism operates.

I have already used the term "patriarchy" a number of times in a
rather vague sense; loose usage to meet the loose understanding that
patriarchy is simply the great social evil against which feminism sets
its face. But a closer look at patriarchy could be helpful; if feminism
embodies a certain resistance to neat systematic analysis partly because of its multifaceted nature, but partly also because this kind of
approach to knowledge is typical of the arid, dissecting rationalism of
the androcentric mind-set, then an examination of that mind-set and
the way it works in our society may reflect something of the nature
and aims of feminism as patriarchy's political Other. It could be said
that, to an extent, patriarchal thought is more amenable to definition
and analysis than its feminist equivalent because it operates in accordance with a concept of reality which upholds rationality, objectivity,
abstract speculation and empiricism as the ideal means of apprehending the true nature of things. In its search for meaning, patriarchal
thought generally inquires, analyses, separates constituent elements,
and arranges those elements in a fixed order, usually a hierarchical
order in which relative value is accorded to each element. Of course,
those who conceive hierarchies generally tend to place their own
values and interests somewhere toward the top, with the concerns of
those who stand in opposition to them toward the bottom, and so the
classic "patriarchal pyramid" is, in its root form, a system of values
according to which the perceived interests of women are subordinated
to those of men.

This, then, is what a feminist critique of society has to deal with; if
patriarchy were simply androcentrism (i.e. a male-centred worldview), then it might be necessary to take no further notice of it than
that afforded by a kind of indulgent mockery, but patriarchy exists in
very real terms as a power structure which directly affects the lives of
those who inhabit it. Paula Cooey's analysis of patriarchy is telling (if
problematic in terms of the kind of theory of power outlined above) in
that it describes the patriarchal structure of society in the familiar lan-

---

[12] Cf. Butler (1990). I am indebted to Niamh Stephenson for critical discussion on
this aspect of feminist politics.

guage of the domination of the many by the few. Cooey sees patriarchy basically as

> the social organization of a culture into systems that are hierarchical
> and male-dominated in terms of power and value. Though slightly more
> fluid than the image of a pyramid suggests, patriarchy, nevertheless, re-
> sembles a pyramid in that an extremely small minority of people hold
> the greatest power over a remaining majority.[13]

This structural imbalance is reflected, in Western society, in the day-
to-day injustices experienced by women in domestic, professional and
religious life. Discrimination and harassment are well-documented
and operate on many levels, from the kind of objectification of
women observable in the language and imagery of advertising
through to the frequency of physical and sexual abuse, and the inade-
quacy of (male-dominated) legal systems in dealing with both perpe-
trators and victims. Women's lack of social power, or at least their
relatively slender means of access to the apparatus of power, can be
attributed in some measure to the way in which patriarchal culture
assigns modes of self-understanding to women which are essentially
male-identified, thus depriving women of any kind of effective autonomy, and confining them within gender-determined social roles. To
quote Paula Cooey again:

> As the word *patriarchy* denotes, the fathers rule the system....within the
> designation of class, ethnicity or creed, a woman's status, power and
> authority, indeed her identity as a woman, derive from her affiliation
> with a man....according to whether he is her father or her husband....The
> substance of her role in society will ordinarily be determined according
> to a division of labour broken down along the lines of sexual difference
> ....the tasks allotted to men will most likely be more highly valued than
> those allotted to women.[14]

Cooey goes on to say that with gender-determined roles come gender-
determined expectations of certain qualities suited to those roles, expectations which reflect "severe dualisms of feeling and reason, body
and mind, nature and culture, and other and self".[15] Women are expected to cultivate characteristics appropriate to their essentially de-

---

[13] Cooey (1990), p.9.
[14] *Ibid.* p.10.
[15] *Ibid.* p.10.

rivative status, traits of "other-directedness" such as passivity, nurture and self-sacrifice. Again, it could be argued that these are valuable qualities at a point in history where our aggressive instincts have a technology at their service which is capable of precipitating disaster on a scale unparalleled in human experience. But in a society whose "norms and values center on male perceptions, interpretations, experience, needs and interests",[16] and where these "male" interests favour detatchment, autonomy and competitiveness as the ideal means to success, a self-sacrificing "other-directedness" renders its agent more vulnerable to exploitation than effective of perceivable change in the social value-system. Thus patriarchy consolidates and maintains its influence: by assigning roles and characteristics to women which are, to a great extent, derivative of or dependent upon a "male" norm, and thereby limiting women's freedom of self-expression (by circumscribing their sense of a "self" to express) and denying them any opportunity to shape or change the practical values of their culture.

The aim of the discussion so far has been to arrive at a broad understanding of sexism, and of the interaction between feminism and patriarchy. In its simplest form, the argument goes like this: sexism is a form of negative discrimination, perhaps the fundamental form of negative discrimination in society because it differentiates according to gender, the difference *par excellence* recognised in all human cultures. Patriarchy is a system of social relations based on sexist principles, a power structure in which the interests of women are determined according to an essentialist idea of the Female, and then devalued and subordinated to the interests of men. Feminism takes many forms, but at the root of all its forms is a commitment to subverting and redeploying power in patriarchal culture, and claiming the right of women to resist and transform exclusively male-identified roles and gender expectations. In what follows, I shall be narrowing the focus of inquiry from society in general to the more specific field of religion (in particular Judaeo-Christian religion); whether or not patriarchal ideology is endemic to it, and the response of feminism to this ideology where it appears.

---

[16] *Ibid.* p.10.

Patriarchal codes and assumptions are evident at most levels of our culture, but religion seems to loom large among them; religious dogma in the West has always had an overwhelming amount to say about sex and gender, and whether its authority is seen as active upon or symptomatic of corresponding attitudes outside the religious sphere, religion and religious issues are never far from any discussion of the roles of women and men in society:

> It is a commonplace that religious values frequently have reflected some of the most basic perceptions, aspirations and values of their own cultures. The importance of this aspect of religion has been matched only by the authority of its tradition in Western thought about the nature of women and men, and by its mediation in helping to shape, legitimise and sanction social attitudes towards the sexes, social expectations of gender-based behaviour, and social rewards and penalties for conformity and deviance.[17]

That religion is a powerful force cannot be denied; exactly what religion acts as a powerful force *for* is more open to question. To assert, as a "religious" person, that religion is an essentially liberating force, a force which acts on behalf of the oppressed in society, is to sail dangerously close to the wind of pure comic irony, especially if one speaks from within the Judaeo-Christian tradition. Critics of that tradition will respond, justifiably enough, by pointing to the militaristic cultural chauvinism of ancient Israel, the ferocity of the Crusades and the Inquisition, the corruption and ostentatious wealth of the modern Church, and any number of other signs which indicate that what Western religion really liberates us from is any hope for establishing a just or egalitarian society. And as far as patriarchal oppression is concerned, it can easily be seen that both Judaism and Christianity are shot through with a clear moral agenda for legitimising the domination of women: from the ambiguous attitudes to women displayed in the Hebrew Bible narratives, through the sexist imagery of the Hebrew prophets and the anxiety and suspicion of women palpable within Rabbinic literature, to the repressive dictates of the Pauline household codes and the virulent misogyny of the early Church Fathers, it is evident that Judaeo-Christian religion both reflects and perpetuates patriarchal ideology. This can hardly be surprising if we

---

[17] Ochshorn (1981), p.x.

consider that the religion developed out of an ancient society which was patriarchal to the core, and while it is perhaps anachronistic to condemn retrospectively a society thousands of years distant from our own on the grounds of a twentieth-century understanding of patriarchy (just as it is anachronistic to assert that Jesus, for example, was a "feminist"), it must nevertheless be wondered whether or not Western religion has outlived its redemptive potential in an age when the struggle of women against patriarchy assumes an increasingly high social profile, and when the divisive, competitive worldview commonly ranged with sexism can be seen as life-threatening on a global scale. I have already indicated that I view domination on the grounds of gender as fundamental to other patterns of domination and subjugation; it follows, then, that a religion which is inherently sexist can provide, at best, only an inadequate agenda for the resistance of any oppressed group within society. And so, more particularly, the possibility of extracting any kind of "liberation theology" from the Judaeo-Christian tradition depends very much upon the extent to which the religion with which that tradition is entwined stands irredeemably in support of patriarchal ideology-in-practice.

I should establish clearly at this point that I do not intend to enter the "is Judaism/Christianity sexist?" debate; not, at least, with any hope of coming up with conclusive answers. To assert confidently that it is not sexist is to fly in the face of four millennia of literature and history which fairly transparently embody sexism in theory and practice. To assert that it *is* sexist, without any hope for redemption, may be defensible at an intellectual level,[18] but seems to deny integrity to the faith and testimony of practising Jewish and Christian feminists who experience growth and fulfilment both as Jews/ Christians and as Jewish/Christian *women.* Any pro or antireligious polemic on my part, therefore, is bound to run into trouble, and so I am more interested in simply accepting that feminism faces a profound challenge from (as well as constituting a profound challenge to) Western religion, and considering ways in which Jewish/Christian feminism might most fruitfully deal with the resulting tensions.

---

[18] Cf. e.g. Daphne Hampson's closely-argued "post-Christian" thesis in *Theology and Feminism* (1990), a critique of Christian theology and the assumptions which lie behind the "historical" aetiology of Christian faith.

The Bible and the Prophetic Tradition

Any examination of Judaeo-Christian religion must sooner or later turn to the bible; I would suggest sooner because it is the bible which is most often cited as ultimately carrying the weight of authority for codes of conduct, morality and social roles. We do not have to look far into the bible to see that its authors and redactors tended to be very much the products of their cultures, cultures in which the interests of women were subordinated to those of men. I have already mentioned the misogynistic tone and imagery running through the prophetic tradition and many of the New Testament epistles; if further proof were needed, we could look to narrative strategies in stories like that of Jephthah's daughter (Judges ch.11) and the Levite's concubine (Judges ch. 19), where the status of women as property to be disposed of—literally—in the interests of the male protagonists is passed over with breathtaking matter-of-factness. And yet women continue to find messages of hope and resistance to patriarchal oppression within the same collection of texts. For example, in among a proliferation of images of the Divine as father, husband, warrior, lord, king, destroyer and judge can be found images of a more compassionate, nurturing and maternal type;[19] they are relatively few in number, but they indicate that there has been a "women's voice" speaking in biblical times, just as contemporary feminism speaks from within patriarchal society today. More generally, a number of feminist theologians and biblical scholars find "prophecies of egalitarianism" in the books of the Hebrew prophets; these prophecies provide hope for the establishment of a just society in which the distribution of power is realigned according the dictates of a bountiful, non-discriminatory God.[20]

Perhaps most significantly, the prophetic tradition as a whole has been seen as providing the key to a creative and holistic interpretation of the bible, as it offers a critique of society which is in keeping with the feminist critical principle and its rejection of hierarchical power abuses. According to Rosemary Ruether, the prophetic tradition, particularly in the books of the later prophets, offers an indictment of the

---

[19] Cf. Exod. 19:4; Deut. 32: 11-12; Isa. 49:15; Hos. 11:4, 13:8; Matt. 23:37.
[20] Cf. Isa. 11:69; Jer. 31:22, 31-34; Joel 2:28-29.

status quo in Israelite society which closely parallels the criticisms brought to bear on patriarchal culture and its power bases. Furthermore,

> this critique of society includes a critique of religion. The spokesperson of God denounces the way in which religion is misused to countenance injustice and turn away the eyes of the pious from the poor. In the words of Amos 5:21, 24: "I hate, I despise your feasts, and I take no delight in your solemn assemblies....But let justice roll down like waters, and righteousness like an ever-flowing stream".[21]

This approach is encouraging, as it indicates that the prophetic tradition (rather like feminism itself) describes an elastic, self-examining process which allows for shifts in interpretation across changing cultural patterns. Could the critique of religion encountered in such books as Isaiah and Amos be stretched to include a critique of the religious legitimation of patriarchal oppression? Stranger things have happened: what now exists in North America under the umbrella of "the black church"—a religious community in which women play a vital, creative role—has developed paradoxically from a slave community which received its Gospel from the hands of its oppressors in the form of a racist, sexist canon specifically geared toward reconciling the slaves to their "God-ordained" role as beasts of burden.[22] The Hebrew prophetic tradition has been cited as the locus of orientation within the bible of black religious consciousness, and this bears witness to the power of that tradition to continue to evolve and transcend its historical moment.[23] But, as I have indicated above, the problem for anyone wishing to use the prophetic tradition in any fundamental way as a means of critiquing patriarchal religion is that much of the prophecy contained therein is couched in relentlessly patriarchal language: God is imaged as either benign or vengeful husband/lover, dispensing mercy or punishment as warranted upon Israel, the faithless wife or harlot.[24] To construe this kind of imagery as being positive for women requires a leap of the interpretative imagination which many, bearing in mind the reality of violence meted out against women by men in

---

[21] Ruether (1985), pp.117-18.

[22] Cf. Gilkes (1989), pp.63-64.

[23] Cf. Cannon (1985), p.35.

[24] Cf. e.g. Jer. 3:12, 50:36-37; Ezek. 16:6-43, 23:1-30; Hos. 2:1-20.

various kinds of relationships and social situations, may find it meaningless or painful to attempt.

It seems, then, that any attempt to locate a critique of patriarchal oppression within the biblical prophetic tradition must inevitably run into the problem of sexist language at its most obstinate. At the same time, however, the prophetic tradition calls for the liberation of *all* oppressed and for an end to all abuses of power and privilege. Does the bible, then, embody a message of redemption which is able to be rescued intact from its linguistic and cultural context?

Text and Context: the Book of Ruth

Phyllis Trible, in an essay which has helped provide the framework for a whole "school" of feminist exegesis, writes of "depatriarchalization" as "a hermeneutic operating within Scripture itself",[25] by means of which just such a rescue operation might be possible. To "depatriarchalize" biblical texts is to read them in the light of a kind of higher theological expectation: "the nature of the God of Israel defies sexism", says Trible optimistically, and so "cultural and grammatical limitations [e.g. the use of sexist language]....need not limit theological understanding".[26] Biblical symbols and stories can be reappropriated and recontextualised to underpin the message of feminism, and the justification for this is implied in the ethos of equality and justice which lies at the root of biblical faith:

> the intentionality of biblical faith, as distinguished from a description of biblical religion, is neither to create nor to perpetuate patriarchy but rather to function as salvation for both women and men....In rejecting Scripture women ironically accept male chauvinistic interpretations and thereby capitulate to the very view they are protesting. But there is another way: to reread (not rewrite) the Bible without the blinders of Israelite men or of Paul, Barth, Bonhoeffer and a host of others. The hermeneutical challenge is to translate biblical faith without sexism.[27]

This approach calls for close reading; the "blinders" of patriarchal religion may, for Trible, amount to no more than "cultural and gram-

---

[25] Trible (1973), p.48.
[26] *Ibid.* p.34.
[27] *Ibid.* p.31.

matical limitations", but they are nevertheless held firmly in place by
centuries of exegetical tradition. If the books of the Hebrew prophets
present rather a formidable hurdle for a non-sexist hermenutics, perhaps the narrative tradition is more amenable to exegesis in keeping
with what we might for the moment agree is "the intentionality of
biblical faith". The book of Ruth seems as good a text as any in which
to look for a "depatriarchalizing" principle; better than most, in fact,
because unlike many or most of the Hebrew Bible narratives, the book
of Ruth is very much a "women's story", and it has been read by
many feminist exegetes as affirmative of women's power to influence
and act upon the workings of patriarchal society.[28] A positive feminist
reading of the story sees Ruth's opening vow of allegiance to Naomi
in 1:16-17 as a completely revolutionary act, the voluntary binding of
one woman to another in a statement of radical faith which mirrors
Abram's seminal act of faith in Genesis 12:15: both characters under-
take a journey to make their home in a strange land, but while Abram
is led to Canaan by a Divine promise of success in his enterprise,
Ruth's sole motive appears to be that of love and sisterhood, with no
apparent expectation of reward. Indeed, in journeying to Bethlehem
with Naomi, the recently-widowed Ruth effectively indicates her lack
of interest in the one avenue of security offered to her by the culture
of the time—that of finding another husband. In her unswerving devotion to Naomi, and in her initiative, as a Moabitess, in forging an
identity for herself within the confines of an alien society, Ruth acts
as an exemplary figure of solidarity and power within patriarchal
culture.[29]

Naomi, on the other hand, appears at first glance to be a good deal
less attractive. Her defeatism and proneness to extravagant lamenta-
tion (1:11-13, 20-21), her seeming obsession with sons and husbands,
and her apparent disregard for Ruth's safety in making her the vulnerable party in an extremely risky plan (3:24) all combine to make
Naomi something other than a model of female grit and sisterhood.
But if she appears in a harsh light, at least it is the light of something
approaching three-dimensional characterisation. Biblical narrators
who condescend to placing a female character anywhere near centre

---

[28] Cf. e.g. Aschkenasy (1986), pp.87-88; Bos (1988), pp.58-64; Brenner (1985),
pp.106-8; Fewell and Gunn (1988); Trible (1978), ch.6.
[29] Cf. Trible (1978), p.173.

stage often display a tedious propensity for presenting her as an arche-
type, or at least as a male-determined stereotype of the Female, to be
praised or judged, and by this means the woman is placed safely outside the realm of immediate, realistic agency within the story. But the
warts-and-all presentation we are given of Naomi comes complete
with the kinds of rough edges and ambiguities that invite psychological inquiry, and these contribute to making her a well-rounded dramatic creation, rather than the all-too-familiar figure of female typology.

This kind of focus on Ruth and Naomi results in Boaz, the male
hero, becoming somewhat marginalised. Although he appears as an
authoritative central character in the story, his status is undermined
(as, by implication, is the patriarchal system within which he operates) by the fact that his role is essentially reactive—everything he
does is in response to the situation that Naomi and Ruth have engi-
neered, and this is borne out explicitly by the "chorus" of women in
4:17, who identify the child born to Ruth as having been born to a
gynocentric lineage: "a son has been born to Naomi", rather than to
the houses of Elimelech or Mahlon, deceased husbands of the female
protagonists.

So close reading reveals a wholehearted affirmation of women as
"paradigms for radicality....women in culture, against culture and
transforming culture".[30] This reading, however, fails to deal with one
element in the story which should be essential to any interpretation;
that is, the role of the narrator. It may be true that a feminist reading
of the book of Ruth like the one briefly delineated above, one which
starts from the theological assumption that "the God of Israel [and, by
implication, the spirit of the Holy Writ of Israel] defies sexism", is
just as defensible as a male-chauvinistic interpretation which rests on
the parallel view that patriarchy is God-ordained. But I would question the assumption that Phyllis Trible's "egalitarian faith" is a clear,
culture-resistant lens through which to view scripture; her very terminology indicates that "biblical faith" comes from the bible, and she
allows that the bible comes from a patriarchal society.[31] More impor-

---

[30]   *Ibid.* p.196.
[31]   Cf. Trible (1973), p.30:

It is superfluous to document patriarchy in Scripture. Yahweh is the God of Abraham,
Isaac and Jacob as well as of Jesus and Paul. The legal codes of Israel treat women pri-

tantly, I do not believe that the "cultural and grammatical limitations"
which Trible finds herself able to sideline can be confined to such issues as androcentric language for (and imagery of) God—not that
even these are to be lightly ignored. The point is that cultural presuppositions operate at the deepest rhetorical level, in the way in which a
story is told, in what is both spoken and left unspoken. A broader perspective on the book of Ruth, one which acknowledges its nature as a
crafted *text*, reveals that the voice which tells the story, which shapes
characters and action by both stressing and suppressing detail, is
clearly the voice of patriarchy.

If, for example, the scene at the threshing floor in 3:6-15 presents
Ruth as claiming a place and an identity for herself within Israelite
culture, it is important to examine the particular language and details
employed by the (presumably male) narrator in relating the events
which take place. The sexual orientation of the episode becomes apparent: Ruth's appearance after dark at the feet of a man whose heart,
we are told, is merry with wine, in addition to the language of "feet"
and "skirts" which characterises Ruth's speech, raises the familiar
spectre of female sexuality as subversive and manipulative, an ethical
commonplace in biblical literature—and one which, in this context,
brings to mind the story in Genesis 19:30-37 of Lot's daughters and
the depraved origins of Ruth's people, the Moabites. This could, in
turn, shed some rather ugly light on the narrative strategy behind the
frequent and pointed identification of Ruth throughout the story as
"the Moabitess". The end of chapter four similarly raises doubts as to
the story's alleged anti-patriarchal bias; hard on the heels of the
women's announcement that " a child has been born to Naomi" comes
the narrator's final word—the child is identified as the descendent of
Perez and the ancestor of David: in short, a son to the house of Judah
and the Davidic line.

There seems to be no way around this contradiction between what
the story is "really about" and the way in which it is told. Trible iso-
lates the closing verses of the book as a kind of coda; it and the generally patriarchal cast of the entire fourth chapter are dismissed as

---

marily as chattels....Considerable evidence indicts the Bible as a document of male su-
premacy.

"alien to the letter and spirit" of the first three chapters,[32] a judgement which I would suggest is fair enough, but which springs from Trible's own desire to render the story palatable to feminist exegetical concerns, rather than from some seed of "depatriarchalizing" polemic within the text itself. Johanna Bos, in her study of Ruth, admits that the actions of Naomi and Ruth ultimately serve the interests of a patriarchal community, but she stresses that

> [o]n a theological level, the well-being of the community is of enormous importance, since its well-being is founded on divine promises....[the house of Judah is] a house which reflects God's choice for Israel and for the creation.[33]

We are uncomfortably close here to the view that patriarchal culture is Divinely prescribed, and the implication that the best we can do is to see it as a kind of cocoon which will shrivel up and fall away as the New Society emerges in God's good time—an idea which may have considerable theological weight behind it, but which can hardly be said to serve the immediate interests of feminism in its day-to-day struggle against sexist thought and patriarchal institutions. Finally, cold water of a more speculative nature is thrown at (if not directly on) the desire to separate text from context by Danna Fewell and David Gunn, who invoke the sordid issue of editorial politics: the view, it is said, that narrative strategy in Ruth serves principally to reflect favourably upon David and the house of Judah

> is especially popular among scholars who wish to date the book of Ruth during the period of Ezra and Nehemiah. The work is, in their view, a polemic against Ezra's and Nehemiah's religious reforms.[34]

It seems, then, that the book of Ruth, being a text which overtly concerns itself with women, might be expected to reveal a biblical attitude to them which satisfies our best expectations of "biblical faith". And a close, detailed analysis of the story does indeed bring positive aspects to light. But the process of interpretation neither begins nor ends there; it is necessarily circular, and while throughout a great deal of biblical literature we find avenues which lead us to symbols for re-

---

[32] Trible (1978), p.193.
[33] Bos (1988), p.38.
[34] Fewell and Gunn (1989), p.59 (footnote to p.53).

demption and transformation of restrictive social structures—Trible's "depatriarchalizing" principle included—our findings are undermined by the patriarchal cast (or militaristic, or racist) of the contexts within which these texts are presented, which are in turn redeemed by the locating of positive symbols of transcendence, and so on. To say that there is a "depatriarchalizing" principle at work within the bible is not to say that the bible can be "depatriarchalized" in any final or conclusive way, as Trible seems to imply when she speaks of the challenge "to *translate* biblical faith without sexism", as though such a translation might be effected as cleanly and sublimely as the "translation", say, of Elijah into heaven. Sexism is endemic to the bible at the narrative, editorial and redactional levels; the dark backdrop, in fact, against which messages for hope and justice for women stand out in such sharp relief.

Text and History: the Search for a Women's Tradition

Is it necessary, then, or even possible to "depatriarchalize" the backdrop, to examine the society of biblical times in search of a "women's tradition" within the patriarchal structure? If we are to attempt any kind of accurate socio-historical reconstruction of the lives of women in early Christian or ancient Israelite times, the bible is at best unreliable as source material; women and their concerns are simply erased from much biblical literature, and in any case, the history that we can glean from biblical texts is fairly obviously concerned with matters other than facticity:

> Israel was acutely conscious about its distinct place in the world, but the biblical self-description does not appear in categories that can easily be translated into facts essential for social scientific analysis....The language is theological; it describes human events in terms of God's actions. Furthermore....the writings reflect later concerns intertwined with original materials.[35]

Thus Carol Meyers on the Hebrew Bible as a historical document, and her words could equally well apply to the New Testament, a collection of texts whose historical details are clearly manipulated to serve

---

[35] Meyers (1988), pp.9-10.

partisan theological interests. Meyers goes on to speak of the potential progress that could be made by means of an interdisciplinary approach to uncovering women's history, one which made use of archaeological and social-scientific expertise in addition to biblical scholarship.[36] There can be no doubt that such an approach would be fruitful, but just how far the benefits would reach is something which should not be overestimated. There is a great deal of discussion in feminist theology and biblical interpretation concerning the possibility of constructing a women's history or tradition from the evidence (as yet still meagre) of archaeological discoveries and ancient texts. I have already quoted Carol Meyers' *Discovering Eve*, a study which claims to reconstruct the everyday life of women in ancient Israel, and the work of Elisabeth Schüssler Fiorenza follows a similar line in the context of the New Testament, as she examines the role of women in the early Christian church.[37] Both authors show that although women are marginalised in biblical literature, the role of women in the cultures from which that literature has emerged was by no means marginal. But there are at least two strong cautions concerning the efficacy of this kind of approach as a means of effectively "depatriarchalizing" the background to biblical texts. The first is that it is not clear exactly how a reconstruction of women's history might further the cause of modern feminists in their struggle against sexism in religion; it may be important to realise how women under patriarchy today share this or that facet of the experience of women under patriarchy in biblical times, but cultures change, the ground shifts, and women today really face a set of problems which differ vastly from those of their foresisters. Daphne Hampson articulates the problem in her critique of Fiorenza:

> even if one considers those women in the modern western world who are less fortunate, they still have, for example, an entirely different legal status than had a first-century woman. The difference in lifestyle between myself (and herself) as white, middle-class women living in the western hemisphere today and that of first-century women is such as to make all comparison meaningless. To be asked to see myself as one in solidarity with first-century women strains my credulity.[38]

---

[36] *Ibid.* pp.11-23.
[37] Cf. Fiorenza (1983) and (1984).
[38] Hampson (1990), p.34.

In addition to this, there is Mary Ann Tolbert's objection that seeking authoritative revelation from history is not only a tactic too commonly used *against* women—as, for example, in the argument that Jesus appointed men as disciples, and therefore only men are fit to be ordained as priests or ministers[39]—but it can also be a manoeuvre which further alienates other marginalised groups whose place in biblical history is impossible to determine, or perhaps even nonexistent:

> While feminist reconstructions have done much to explode the patriar-
> chal myth of women's marginality in early Christianity, the underlying
> assumption that historical participation is a necessary prerequisite for
> full status in the present has not really been challenged. Hence, other
> groups who cannot reconstruct their historical participation (as, for ex-
> ample, certain racial groups, homosexuals, handicapped people, etc.)
> still face disenfranchisement.[40]

But perhaps more importantly, the attempt to solve the problems inherent in biblical texts by going "behind" those texts in search of real life will never be successful while we place our faith in the unquestionable veracity of history. The hermeneutical process in which the positive and the negative, the ideologically acceptable and the unacceptable, exist in a state of continual tension is not caused by some rare virus that plagues only biblical criticism, but is the result of an undecideability which is fundamental to all texts (an important point which will be argued and developed in greater detail in chapters 3 and 4). And history, ultimately, comes to us in the form of a text, complete with all the prejudices of its author. Like the bible, history has a narrative voice, and if it is pristine, unclouded accuracy we are after, a non-reflecting window onto the lives of women in ancient Palestine, will this not be as obscured by twentieth-century Western liberal feminist concerns as it is by the distortions of sexist authorship in any age?

All this is not to say that historical scholarship has no meaning or value for a feminist critique of Western religion. But it must be remembered that the results of such scholarship are generally disseminated as knowledge in the form of written texts, and just as the bible has the (patriarchal) cultural presuppositions of its authors writ large

---

[39] Tolbert (1990), pp.13-14.
[40] *Ibid.* p.14.

all over its claims to history and truth—to say nothing of its calls for justice—so does any "ideological" restructuring of biblical material reflect first and foremost the politics of the architect. And while modern feminist politics may be better and fairer than ancient sexist politics, as a narrative filter neither brings us face to face with what was really going on in the society of biblical times. The point is that whether our search is for a "depatriarchalizing" biblical principle or for a history which (arguably) establishes solidarity between modern and ancient women in patriarchal societies, in either case we are left having to deal with a text and its mediating authorial voice. And so the most immediate concern for a feminist critique of Judaism or Christianity, as for any critique motivated by a "liberation" ethic, is that it should acknowledge its own text-centredness, which means that it should develop a self-conscious hermeneutics which focuses both on biblical literature and on the broader issues involved in how any literature is both produced and received—issues, that is, of how texts "work".

The "Text Itself": Phyllis Trible and the Garden of Eden

The success and influence of Phyllis Trible in the field of feminist biblical interpretation owes much to the comprehensive way in which she deals with the former aspect of this hermeneutical requirement. Her work is almost exclusively text-centred, and she has done a great deal to bring biblical scholarship to the point where it can no longer take for granted its own long-held assumptions about the importance (or lack of importance) of gender issues in exegesis. In *God and the Rhetoric of Sexuality* (1978), Trible identifies her methodology as "rhetorical criticism", according to which operation

> the major clue is the text itself. Thus, I view the text as a literary creation with an interlocking structure of words and motifs. Proper analysis of form yields proper articulation of meaning.[41]

Her approach to a text, then, involves a detailed examination of the words on the page and the way in which they are arranged; in Trible's eyes, the bible is as manifestly "literary" a work as the *Iliad*, the *Od-*

---

[41]   Trible (1978), p.8.

yssey or the *Bhagavad Gita*, and this understanding is essential to any understanding of the bible as Divinely inspired:

> the Bible as literature is the Bible as scripture, regardless of one's attitude towards its authority. And conversely, the Bible as scripture is the Bible as literature, regardless of one's evaluation of its quality.[42]

In *God and the Rhetoric of Sexuality*, Trible sets out her textual *modus operandi*, and then offers rhetorical-critical analyses of three biblical texts: The Garden of Eden story (Genesis 2:4b-3:24), the Song of Songs, and the book of Ruth. Her treatment of Gen. 2:4b-3:24 is worth looking at in some detail here, partly because from a feminist point of view the Garden of Eden story is a crucial piece of biblical literature, having provided the outline for generations of orthodox Christian (and, to a lesser extent, Jewish) doctrine concerning the nature, roles and expectations of women. But also, Trible's analysis of the story provides, in its strengths and limitations, a clear illustration of an exegetical strategy which seems to offer a positive feminist critique of scripture, but which ultimately finds itself limited by some highly questionable assumptions which Trible makes concerning the activities of reading and writing.

Basically, Trible wishes to establish that the Garden of Eden narrative is by no means inherently sexist; that a patriarchal tradition has developed and made normative an interpretation of the story which is based on ideas that "violate the rhetoric of the story", and which "fail to respect the integrity of this work as an interlocking structure of words and motifs with its own intrinsic value and meaning".[43] Her aim is to strip away the layers of culture-specific perspectives from the story and "to contemplate it afresh as a work of art".[44] In doing this, Trible arrives at the conclusion that the notions of male superiority and female inferiority traditionally associated with this story have no essential grounds within "the text itself".

In the following outline of Trible's analysis of Gen. 2:4b-3:24, I have considered only parts of what is a long, detailed and closely-argued thesis, choosing to concentrate on five key points upon which I believe the sexist/non-sexist argument hangs: (a) the order of creation

---

[42]   *Ibid.* p.8.
[43]   *Ibid.* p.73.
[44]   *Ibid.* p.74.

of the man and the woman; (b) the disputed status of the woman as the man's "helper"; (c) the "naming" of the woman by the man; (d) the dialogue between the woman and the serpent; and (e) the significance of the punishments meted out by Yahweh to the human couple. In the first instance, (a), Trible argues against the traditional view that the man holds superior ontological status over the woman because he was created first, and that woman's inferior position in the hierarchy of being stems from her having been created "from" man. Rather, says Trible, the woman can be seen as "elevated in emphasis by the design of the story", as her appearance in the final episode of the drama of creation is perhaps the climax of this part of the narrative, the pinnacle and fulfilment of the creative process rather than some kind of afterthought.[45] In addition to this, the first created earth-creature, ha-'adam, is not "male" but a sexually-undifferentiated being, "neither male nor female but a combination of both".[46] It is only with the creation of woman that sexual differentiation takes place, as now ha-'adam has what he previously lacked: a sexed being to differ *from*. "His sexual identity depends upon hers even as hers depends upon him",[47] and so to all intents and purposes, "male" and "female" as sexual designations are created simultaneously.

We consider next (b), the vexed question of the woman's function—the reason why she was created in the first place. The Hebrew expression used in Gen. 2:18, 20 to denote the kind of companion Yahweh had in mind for ha-'adam is 'ezer k*negdo, translated in RSV as "a helper fit for him", and implying both derivative and inferior status. Trible, however, sees 'ezer as carrying no such connotations; indeed, she cites other passages in the Hebrew Bible where 'ezer is used to describe God, the ineffably superior "helper" of Israel.[48] But the qualifying k*negdo, "corresponding to it", indicates that the relationship is one of identity and equality rather than superiority or inferiority. The woman, then, as 'ezer k*negdo, is "a companion corre-

---

[45] *Ibid.* p.102.
[46] *Ibid.* p.98.
[47] *Ibid.* p.99.
[48] *Ibid.* p.90. Cf. also Exod. 18:4; Deut. 33:7, 26, 29; Ps. 33:20, 115:9-11, 121:2, 124:8, 146:5.

sponding to" *ha-'adam*, "one who alleviates isolation through identity".[49]

It is generally recognised that the act of naming in biblical literature carries particular significance; to name something is to establish authority or at least ontological precedence over it, and a reading of Gen. 2:23 in line with patriarchal exegetical tradition suggests that just as *ha-'adam* named the animals and thus asserted dominion over them, so the man's "naming" of the woman implies his authority over her. But Trible points out that the standard Hebrew naming-formula involves the use of both the verb "call" (*qara'*) and the noun "name" (*shem*), to form the formulaic phrase "to call the name" and to connote the existence of some kind of hierarchical relationship.[50] The Hebrew of Gen. 2:23, however, in which *ha-'adam* "names" the woman *'ishshah*, employs the verb *qara'* but not the noun *shem*, and so according to Trible, *ha-'adam*'s act is simply one of recognition:

> The earth-creature exclaims, "This shall be called *'issa*". The noun *name* is strikingly absent from the poetry. Hence, in calling the woman, the man is not establishing power over her, but rejoicing in their mutuality.[51]

Turning to (d), the dialogue at the beginning of Genesis 3 between the woman and the serpent: it has been affirmed with depressing regularity and fervour that the serpent, as the incarnation of evil-in-creation, chooses to tempt the woman because it recognises that she is spiritually and intellectually inferior to the man, more vulnerable to subtle argument and likelier to succumb to a temptation which appeals to the base instincts of appetite—and sure enough, events prove that the serpent is a perceptive judge of female nature. Trible recognises that the serpent is used in the story as an agent of discord and a threat to "the harmony of life" in the Garden,[52] but she sees the woman's performance in the drama as anything but shameful or weak. The serpent addresses her in plural verb forms, implicitly conferring upon her the honour of "spokesperson for the human couple....equal with the man

---

[49] *Ibid.* p.90.
[50] *Ibid.* p.99.
[51] *Ibid.* p.100.
[52] *Ibid.* p.108.

in creation".[53] The woman's statement that Yahweh forbade not only
the eating but the *touching* of the fruit involves an embellishment
which is similar in intention and style to the Rabbinic activity of
"building a fence around the Torah", or putting imaginative commentary to the service of protecting the essence of a Divine decree.
"Theologian, ethicist, hermeneut, Rabbi, [the woman] speaks with
clarity and authority",[54] and in eating the fruit, she makes a reasoned
and independent decision in the full and complete realisation that such
an act will be "sapientially transforming". The man, by contrast,
maintains a deep and unimpressive silence throughout all this. Present, but no doubt only dimly aware that nothing less than the dawn of
civilisation is being initiated before his very eyes, he takes his cue un-
questioningly from his more dynamic partner:

> He does not theologize; he does not contemplate; and he does not envi-
> sion the full possibilities of the occasion. Instead, his one act is belly-
> oriented, and it is an act of acquiescence, not of initiative. If the woman
> is intelligent, sensitive and ingenious, the man is passive, brutish and in-
> ept.[55]

Finally, we come to (e), the close of the drama (Gen 3:8-24), where
the traditional understanding of events is that the outraged Deity
punishes his wayward humans in a manner which determines their
subsequent fortunes in the world as we know it: the man, because he
has listened to the advice of the woman (Heb. *qol 'ishthekha*, "the
voice of *your* woman" says Yahweh, forgetting in his anger his
egalitarian principles), is doomed to eke out a meagre living in the
sweat of his brow from a hostile earth, and finally to return to the dust
out of which he was fashioned. As for the woman, she has to endure
labour pains (or unspecified problems in addition to bearing children,
depending on the favoured translation of *'ishshbonekh w^eheronekh*),
and a life of servitude to a husband she nevertheless desires; the role
of women as tied to men, both sexually/emotionally and according to
the dictates of female obligation is thus seen as Divinely ordained.
Trible, however, while agreeing that in this "decree" we find the
origins of patriarchal society, sees it more as a premonitory statement

---

[53] *Ibid.* pp.108-9.
[54] *Ibid.* p.110.
[55] *Ibid.* p.113.

of fact by Yahweh than the deliberate instigation of a repressive social structure. Disobedience has resulted in hierarchy where once there was mutuality, but the initiative in this was taken by the human couple, not the Deity, so the male/female tension is the consequence of a human event, not the fulfilment of a Divine oracle:

> His [i.e. the man's] supremacy is neither a divine right nor a male pre-rogative. Her subordination is neither a divine decree nor the female destiny. Both their positions result from shared disobedience. God de-scribes this consequence but does not prescribe it as a judgement.[56]

This brief summary of the key points of Phyllis Trible's argument should suffice to show that she has interpreted the Garden of Eden story in a way which seriously challenges any traditional patriarchal reading, and which indicates that such a reading is by no means given at the rhetorical or linguistic level. But whether or not her own read-ing is finally "correct", or closer to the core of the text than a more sexist interpretation is maybe not so clear. She has been convincingly refuted at the level of their own "rhetorical criticism": David Clines, for example, has countered that *'ezer* does in fact imply hierarchy, as a helper is by definition someone who operates according to someone else's previously-established agenda,[57] and so the implication is that the woman, as *'ezer*, is created from the outset as a secondary, other-directed being. Anne Gardner throws a similarly sceptical light on the meaning of *kᵉnegdo*, which, she argues,

> simply denotes a complementary creature, one of the same species, and says nothing about the balance of the relationship between the male and the female.[58]

Gardner also considers the implications of the woman's ontological predicament, pointing out that if *ha-'adam* is linguistically related to *ha-'adamah*, and if the earth-creature is created "to till and to keep" the earth (Gen. 2:15), then the linguistic relationship between *'ish* and *'ishshah* could mirror a correspondingly hierarchical relationship of primacy and servitude between the first and second created humans.[59]

---

[56] *Ibid.* p.128.
[57] Clines (1990), pp.30-32.
[58] Gardner (1990), pp.5-6.
[59] *Ibid.* p.7. Trible's comment on the naming of *'ishshah* by *'ish* is that

I would similarly point out that this structure is mirrored again in the
distribution of punishments, as the man's punishment relates back to
the earth from which he was taken, and the woman's punishment relates to the man: for all Trible's arguments that the punishments are
descriptive and not prescriptive, the fact that they hark back struc-
turally to the mythical creation of the species as well as forward into
history suggests that something other than human agency is at work in
the institution of gender-determined hierarchy. Still operating at the
rhetorical level, but from a slightly different perspective, Susan Lanser has wondered pertinently why, if Trible is correct in arguing that
the man and the woman share equal responsibility for their disobedience, "male dominance should be the particular consequence" for this
act.[60] Moreover, Lanser charges Trible with carrying out a too-
rigorously-formal analysis which ignores the "inferential" structure of
the text: for example, a simple cause-and-effect view of the punishments, one that sees the humans' transgression as a historical act with
historical consequences which God merely describes from a position
of detatched observation, is a view which ignores the fact that from
the moment the tree of knowledge is mentioned in the story, the prohibition delivered and death threatened, a palpable weight of dramatic
tension hangs about the narrative, creating

> an over-determined context in which God is *expected* to deliver punish-
> ment long before he does so, and the pronouncements of 3:14-19 fulfil
> this expectation even if their surface form allows other possibilities.[61]

These counter-interpretations to the kind of exegesis offered by Trible
rely themselves on close rhetorical-critical reading; a brief look at the
Garden of Eden story in its wider context both as part of the canonical
corpus of the Hebrew Bible and as an ancient Near Eastern mythological text should further problematise claims to locating any anti-

---

the phrase joins *'is* and *'issa* to produce a pun, not to give information about the creative
process (nor about philology) [1978, p.101],

but she fails to recognise here that this pun involves a "creative process" in language
whereby a secondary term is derived from a primary one, and she does not take issue
with the highly significant question of *why* such a pun should be made by the author
at this point.

[60] Lanser (1988), p.75.
[61] *Ibid.* p.75.

patriarchal rhetoric which is notionally "intrinsic" to the story. George
Ramsey has taken issue with Trible on the question of naming, and
while he too wishes to establish that the utterance of the word
'ishshah at Gen. 2:23 does not constitute an act of domination, he re-
futes the suggestion (central to Trible's argument) that the Hebrew
naming-formula is limited to the use of the verb *qara'* in conjunction
with the noun *shem*. Ramsey cites a number of biblical passages in
which the act of naming is performed,[62] and he finds that in addition to
qara'....shem, a formula is often employed which makes use of *qara'*
together with the inseparable pronoun represented by *lamedh*. The
latter formula is used in Gen. 2:23, and according to Ramsey, it is
more a variation on a theme than a significant break with rhetorical
tradition:

> Rather then there being a "radical" difference between Gen. 2:23 on the
> one hand and 2:19-20 [the naming of the animals] and 3:20 [the naming
> of the woman "Eve"] on the other....what we discover is that 2:23 sim-
> ply uses one variation (*qara'* with *lamed* plus the pronoun *zo't*) to ex-
> press the act of naming, whereas 2:19-20 and 3:20 use another variation
> (*qara'* plus *sem*).[63]

Background knowledge of a different sort qualifies Trible's positive
portrayal of the relationship between the woman and the serpent.
Anne Gardner's article, quoted above, examines Genesis 2:4b-3:24 in
the light of parallel Mesopotamian mythology, and she criticises Trible for ignoring "the rich mythological background upon which the
Yahwist writer of Genesis 2:4b-3 draws".[64] This mythological background includes, among other things, the symbols, legends and rituals
of Near Eastern goddess cults, almost all traces of which have been
excised (if indeed they were ever there in the first place) except for
the occasional piece of strident polemic directed against heathenish
Canaanite religious practices. Gardner, however, identifies a kind of
literary subconscious within the Garden of Eden story, which places
the story firmly within its cultural/mythological context, and where
sinister shadows of anti-goddess ideology lurk sharklike beneath the
surface of the text. The serpent, for example, is a widely-recognised

---

[62] Ramsey (1988), p.27.
[63] *Ibid.* p.29.
[64] Gardner (1990), p.3.

sexual emblem featuring prominently in the symbolic structure of goddess-cults, which are "intimately connected with sexuality and fertility".[65] Sexual experience is linked to wisdom in myths such as the Gilgamesh epic, where the savage Enkidu gains wisdom, "broader understanding" and godlike status through intercourse with a Temple prostitute.[66] The serpent and the acquisition of knowledge are of course key elements in the Genesis text, and if the formal mythological serpent-goddess-sexuality-knowledge chain of association appears to be broken in Eden by the tree as the source of knowledge, this too can be accommodated within the symbolic tradition of goddess religion:

> Snakes are often pictured with the goddess, sometimes standing upright beside her, with the deity herself represented beside a fruit-bearing tree.[67]

This associative structure enables us to read the Garden of Eden story as redolent with Israelite patriarchal/monotheistic politics: Yahweh warns his children away from fertility cults (as symbolised by the fruit-bearing tree); disobedience results in a kind of knowledge which is linked to nakedness and shame (a kind of guilty sexuality is apparent here); and Yahweh's subsequent displeasure is the anger of the jealous God of Exod. 20:5, whose creatures have been seduced by the representative of a rival Deity. The gender of this rival Deity can be inferred by the fact that the serpent (itself traditionally associated with goddess cults) chooses to speak with the woman, in the realisation that she will be particularly attracted to the kind of knowledge it has to offer. And the punishment meted out to the woman places her, significantly enough, "firmly under the control of her husband",[68] who will presumably ensure that her cultic activities remain circumscribed within the Law of the God of the Patriarchs of Israel.

The foregoing outline of readings of Gen. 2:4b-3:24 which contradict, in some way or other, that of Phyllis Trible is not meant simply as a bombardment of arguments intended to knock Trible down a few rungs on the ladder of acceptable biblical hermeneutics. Rather, I

---

[65] *Ibid.* p.12.
[66] *Ibid.* pp.12-13.
[67] *Ibid.* p.13.
[68] *Ibid.* pp.14-15.

hope to have shown that Trible's is just one of a whole chorus of voices and counter-voices all clamouring to be heard and understood. It is easy enough for me to point out what I see as gaps in Trible's interpretation and to find other readings which have corresponding strengths; further study would no doubt in turn show that the work of Clines, Lanser, Ramsey, Gardner and any number of others—myself included—embodies gaps and inconsistencies which could be made coherent by using Trible as a reference. What would be difficult (I would say impossible) would be to establish incontrovertibly that any one interpretation was complete or final, that one interpretative voice spoke the "truth" about the Genesis story in opposition to a host of false hermeneutical prophets. There is an important *caveat* here for feminist hermeneutics, where the strong political imperative at work in interpretation can overly polarise the position of the interpreter: it is, I believe, as mistaken to make triumphant, comprehensively pro-feminist statements out of texts (especially in biblical literature) as it is to read the same texts as wholeheartedly pro-patriarchy, as Danna Nolan Fewell has commented:

> any reading that produces a text with a complete thematic unity....is a misreading. We are called upon constantly to reread. What this means in feminist literary criticism is this: we cannot naively accept positive feminist texts as unmediated words of liberation, neither can we reject patriarchal texts as unredeemable words of subjugation.[69]

It is possible that Trible does not seek explicitly to establish Gen. 2:4b-3:24 as a text with "a complete thematic unity"; it could be that she is simply working through some of the redemptive possibilities suggested by what she sees as the "depatriarchalizing" principle within it. But while Trible on one hand appears to eschew dogmatic ideology, claiming with an easygoing flexibility to see the bible as

> a pilgrim wandering through history to merge past and present ....composed of diverse traditions that span centuries, [embracing] claims and counterclaims in witness to the complexities and ambiguities of existence,[70]

---

[69] Fewell (1987), p.82.
[70] Trible (1978), p.1.

she displays, on the other hand, a devotion to the semantic integrity of "the words on the page" of scripture which has, in fact, very little to do with past, present, diverse traditions, claims or counterclaims. Her explication of the literary assumptions behind her methodology bears this out:

> I view the text as a literary creation with an interlocking structure of words and motifs. Proper analysis of form yields proper articulation of meaning....A literary approach to hermeneutics concentrates primarily on the text rather than on *extrinsic factors* such as historical background, archaeological data, compositional history, authorial intention, socio-logical setting, or theological motivation and result....the stress falls upon interpreting *the literature in terms of itself*,[71]

and her avowed intention concerning Genesis 2:4b-3:24 is

> to respect the integrity of this work as an interlocking structure of words and motifs with its own intrinsic value and meaning.[72]

There are two main problems here: the first is that if you consign history, archaeology, authorship, sociology and so on to the critical Hades of "extrinsic factors", then you are left with rather a blank page, and if Trible's own reading of the Garden of Eden story runs to some seventy very full pages, surely this has everything to do with her own social background, her theological motivation, and her intentions as an author. To claim that your own politics are inherent in "the text itself" is precisely what many feminist critics have denounced as a dubious interpretative manoeuvre; it has always been an important strategy of apologists for patriarchal religion to read their own self-serving ideology into the bible and claim that its authority is self-evident, intrinsic to scripture and therefore resistant to subjective reappraisal or the challenge of alternatives. In saying that her reading of scripture is final and autonomous (which she unavoidably does when she claims to have tapped into scripture's "intrinsic value and meaning"), Phyllis Trible sets up a monolithic interpretation which rests on the false assumption that her own participation in the process is "scientific" and

---

[71] *Ibid.* pp.8-9 (my italics).
[72] *Ibid.* p.73.

purely objective, and which owes much to the dualistic logic of proper/improper "articulation of meaning". The other objection is that feminist theology is something which has grown out of a primarily historical struggle, and which works to remedy a social disease; it is a politically explicit practice. But if the literature with which it deals is somehow sealed off from history and depoliticised to become "the text in terms of itself", it can ultimately have only a limited part to play in the process of continued historical change which does, after all, provide the arena for all progressive theologies, whether feminist, liberationist or environmentalist.

So rhetorical criticism, as employed by Phyllis Trible and the many biblical scholars who follow in the same exegetical vein, is essentially a static activity which attempts to establish the text as a kind of counter-myth. The familiar patriarchal creation myth presents the eating of the fruit as the archetypal Sin, with the serpent and Eve as its archetypal agents. In this light, "fallen" society as we know it is steeped in the rituals which keep the myth alive: our moral transgressions re-enact the exemplary Sin, and when women exercise guile, lack of control and any number of other crimes to which they are said to be naturally inclined, they are then most clearly epiphanies of Eve and her exemplary manifestation of dangerous female nature back in the time of sacred Beginnings. Thus it becomes a "sacred" or scriptural injunction to mistrust and try to control women. Phyllis Trible certainly redresses the balance, but in a manner which nevertheless conforms to patriarchal critical practice, in that she too calls timeless truth, or what the text "really means", into the service of fixing and furthering her own interests; interests which have a historical and not a mythological ancestry, and which could hardly have been further from the minds of the people who put the story together—their motives seem to have been more along the lines of carrying out a Yahwist salvage-and-demolition job on a rival mythology than of producing a feminist classic. So Phyllis Trible locates her heart's desire at the heart of the text, and like so many other exegetes mistakes her own hermeneutical politics for the "intrinsic value and meaning" of scripture. There can be no doubt that it is a timely comeuppance for patriarchal religion to have its own creation myth transformed into the story of a courageous heroine and her effete male sidekick. But this too is a chauvinism of sorts, and the assumptions which lie behind it pose problems for feminist hermeneutics, or for any hermeneutics which seriously espouses a programme of social equality and reform.

What feminist theology and biblical interpretation must be based on, then, is a theory which does not seek to demarcate so confidently between the "intrinsic meaning" of scripture and its alleged distortions, between what is orthodox and heterodox according to feminist principles, and so which resists inflexibility and closure in interpretation. The following two chapters will see the attempt to outline the mechanics of such a theory; first by considering two kinds of critical positions commonly taken up by feminist theorists and assessing their strengths and weaknesses, and then, in chapter 3, by examining the deconstructive strategies of Jacques Derrida and looking at the viability of deconstruction as an effective feminist exegetical framework.

CHAPTER TWO

THE CONCEPT OF "WOMAN" IN INTERPRETATION

TO STEP OUTSIDE OF PATRIARCHAL THOUGHT MEANS: Being sceptical toward every known system of thought; being critical of all assumptions, ordering values and definitions.[1]

Gerda Lerner's rigorous formula for non-patriarchal thinking carries the daunting implication that feminist theory and practice demand nothing less than a kind of cultural revolution—to refuse to take for granted the governing "assumptions, ordering values and definitions" of patriarchal society is, for women in Western culture at least, to think and act in a spirit of radical criticism which may lead to a complete overhaul of our inherited metaphysical/philosophical tradition. And indeed this dramatic prospect is not unlikely: if, as Lerner implies, "every known system of thought" is in some way patriarchal, then feminist criticism must inevitably venture into the unknown, or at least the unfamiliar, to disturb and bring us uncomfortably face-to-face with some of our most cherished and deeply-held (mis-)apprehensions concerning ourselves and our society. In what follows, I am working on the assumption that Lerner's premise is valid—that our society *is* a patriarchal one, although perhaps not irredeemably so—and that the first task of any feminist practice is to dismantle or harass patriarchal values wherever they operate. In the previous chapter I offered a brief description of patriarchy more or less by way of introduction; what I propose to do in the following discussion is to look in closer detail at the dominant mechanisms at work in patriarchal thought, to consider the potential for a feminist response or alternative to a patriarchal worldview, and finally to translate the argument into biblical-critical terms, outlining the necessary criteria for an effective feminist biblical hermeneutics.

---

[1] Lerner (1986), p.228.

Patriarchal Dualism

It is difficult to trace patriarchy back to any point of origin, either historical or psychological. Gerda Lerner's *The Creation of Patriarchy* is less of a Genesis-story than its title suggests, as its first two chapters offer no more than a thorough but speculative overview of various theories of patriarchal origins, before commencing its historical inquiry roughly around the time of the emergence of archaic urbanised states. Similarly, mythological or religious ontologies of patriarchy are fascinating but ultimately frustrating for anybody looking for hard evidence of a pre-patriarchal society or culture.[2] It can be argued, however, that there are certain salient features of patriarchy in Western society which can be criticised regardless of origins. Perhaps the most important and pervasive of these is dualism, or the division of reality into conceptual pairs of opposites. Dualistic thought has a long and complex philosophical history,[3] but in all its manifestations it stakes out the nature and limits of reality by placing male and female, spirit and flesh, reason and instinct, culture and nature, self and other all at corresponding conceptual poles, and sees the relationship between the elements in each pair as discrete, a relationship of radical difference and opposition. While there can be no doubt that male, female, civilisation, nature and so on "exist", and that ranging them in pairs can facilitate one way of understanding how each relates to the other, critics of dualism point out that such binary oppositions lead to hierarchical patterns of thought and behaviour which can also be exploitative. Certainly in patriarchal thought, the two terms in any pair of opposites are "regulated by the law of contrariety",[4] with all the connotations of disagreement that "contrariety" implies: rather than being accorded equal value, the terms are divided with one being seen as somehow more worthy or desirable than the other. Male, culture, rationality, logic, transcendence and so on all become identified with each other

---

[2] Cf. Baring and Cashford (1991), especially pp.660-62 on the process by which Goddess-myth changes to God-myth.

[3] A history well-documented from the perspective of gender in Lloyd (1984).

[4] Grosz (1989), "Difference" p.xvii.

by virtue of the fact that they all occupy the "positive" side of the theoretical boundary, while female, nature, emotion, intuition and carnality are all seen as interrelated "negative" concepts.

Criticism of this kind of hierarchical worldview ranges beyond exclusively feminist issues: the validity of the subject/object dichotomy, for example, has been thrown into question by modern particle physics and its understanding that the conductor of an experiment is not a purely independent observer, but an active participant whose input directly influences the experiment's results. In the world being mapped out by "the new physics", subject and object are intimately related, and the faculty of pure rational detatchment on the part of the former is made problematic. Gender issues of some kind, however, never seem to be far from the centre of any examination of dualistic thought. The Greek philosophical foundations of Western metaphysics, for example, provide the traditional rationale both for dualistic hierarchy and for misogyny, as the Platonic/Aristotelian discussions of form and matter demonstrate.[5] The dualistic elevation of culture over nature (which has led to mass industrialisation, the exploitation of natural resources and many current global ecological crises) also has its suggestive parallels with patriarchal domination: nature-as-woman (mysterious, enigmatic, dangerous and yet passive), subjected to the penetrating scrutiny of rational empiricism, finds herself analysed, quantified, manipulated, and yet feared by the men of science who seek to control her.[6] Similarly, the oppression of such groups as Jews and blacks has, in the past, been upheld by the belief that these people are "like women....more carnal and irrational than the dominant men".[7] The tendency of a sexual politics to emerge, either explicitly or symbolically, wherever a dualistic worldview takes concrete, institutionalised form, indicates both that dualism and patriarchy are enmeshed at a fundamental level, and that the most effective and far-reaching critique of dualism is likely to be articulated in feminist terms.

A recurrent feature of dualistic constructs, and one which principally accounts for their hierarchical organisation, is the tendency for only one term in any pair of opposites to be seen as positive, or pos-

---

[5] Cf. Cantarella (1987), chs. 2 and 4; Lloyd: *op. cit.* pp.2-9.

[6] Cf. Merchant (1982); Ruether (1975) ch.8, (1979).

[7] Christ and Plaskow (1979), p.5.

sessing its own identity, while the other term is seen as derivative, taking its identity from its opposite. Elizabeth Grosz outlines the pattern as follows:

> Dichotomous structures take the form of A and not-A relations, in which one term is positively defined and the other is defined only as the negative of the first....Within this structure, one term (A) has a positive status and an existence independent of the other; the other term [not-A] is purely negatively defined, and has no contours of its own; its limiting boundaries are those which define the positive term.[8]

In patriarchal terms, this means that "woman" is a radically negative concept. The male is seen as independent and carries not only the privilege of self-definition, but also the power of defining his "other", and so the clearest definition of woman on offer in patriarchal discourse is that she is "non-man"—if the male is active, rational, spiritual, logical and autonomous, the female is by definition passive, irrational, carnal, illogical and heteronomous, or subject to laws imposed from outside her sphere of influence:

> The construction of such categories as and through opposition expresses and reveals the philosopher's desire for control and domination. Once these oppositions are seen as fictive, asymmetric, and conditions of possibility for the philosopher's story, then a premise that underlies all variants of the metaphysics of presence can be revealed: to be other, to different than the defining one, is to be inferior and to have no independent character or worth of one's own; for example, "woman" is defined as a deficient man in discourses from Aristotle through Freud. The superior member of the pair maintains his innocence.[9]

Responses to this within feminist discourse are not unanimous; generally, in fact, one of two contrary positions is adopted. Both positions have been considered at some length in an article by Linda Alcoff appropriately subtitled "The Identity Crisis in Feminist Theory" (*Signs* 13:3, 1988), in which the vexed concept of woman is discussed. Alcoff's stated concern is not with patriarchal dualism, but it seems clear to me that to consider the definition of woman is inevitably to take issue at some point with patriarchal dualism, given that

---

[8] Grosz: *op. cit.* "Dichotomy" p.xvi.
[9] Flax (1992), p.453.

the dominant social discourses within which the definition of woman is an issue (medicine, psychology, anthropology, religion) are, in the main, both male-dominated and based on the kind of hierarchical subject/object epistemology described above. Alcoff states that

> [m]an has said that woman can be defined, delineated, captured—understood, explained, and diagnosed—to a level of determination never accorded to man himself, who is conceived as a rational animal with free will.[10]

For this reason I believe that the two approaches to an understanding of the concept of woman discussed by Alcoff are also two key positions from which to criticise patriarchal dualism and the sexist ideologies which it fosters.

Cultural Feminism and the Gendered Subject

The first position or type of feminism Alcoff discusses is "cultural" feminism, described as

> the ideology of a female nature or female essence reappropriated by feminists themselves in an effort to re-validate female attributes.[11]

In cultural feminist theory, a dualistic structure is maintained but the hierarchy is reversed: what was before called passivity is now seen as a tranquil capacity for peaceful influence; irrationality becomes a sensitive, intuitive awareness unbounded by the artificial constraints of logic; rank carnality becomes a powerful sexuality, and women's close ties with wild, untamed nature are affirmed and celebrated; powerlessness becomes the will to nurture, and to foster a non-competitive, non-hierarchical understanding of authority. The gender-determined identification of femaleness with some qualities and maleness with others goes essentially unchallenged, and the oppressive machinations of patriarchy are seen as stemming not from the perpetuation of dualism or biological determinism, but from men's usurping of power that belongs specifically to women—power

---

[10] Alcoff (1988), p.406.
[11] *Ibid.* p.408.

which, residing in the female nature, is only half-glimpsed and half-understood (but wholly feared) by men.[12] Alcoff chooses the term "cultural" feminism because of the view, held by such writers as Mary Daly and Adrienne Rich, that since society as it exists is irredeemably infected with sexism and misogyny, it must be up to women to redefine and re-evaluate themselves outside the boundaries of patriarchal culture, and so to develop a women's counterculture whose language and values reflect and celebrate female nature.[13]

There can be no doubt that sexism is endemic to all levels of Western society, and that aspects of the alternative culture offered by cultural feminism are invaluable for individuals who, having suffered the various forms of alienation, humiliation and violence which sexism perpetuates, need to find healing and a sense of self outside the debilitating environs of patriarchy. For some, a journey toward self-discovery cannot be undertaken without moving into new territory which is exclusively women's space. But cultural feminism as a totalising strategy, advocated as *the* answer to patriarchy, presents problems. While accepting that traditional sources of knowledge concerning women are contaminated with sexism, and that patriarchy both devalues and seeks to control women's sexuality, Alcoff nevertheless treats the cultural feminist premise that there exists a "female essence" with suspicion. Statements such as Daly's assertion that "female energy is essentially biophilic",[14] and Rich's

---

[12] *Ibid.* pp.408-10.

[13] *Ibid.* pp.410-11. At this point it might be asked why Alcoff does not use the more familiar term "radical feminism", an appellation commonly associated with the work of such feminists as Daly and Rich (and indeed freely used by Daly herself). Alcoff's statement of the difference between cultural and radical feminism is puzzling:

> there is a tendency within many radical feminist works toward setting up an ahistorical and essentialist conception of female nature, but this tendency is developed and consolidated by cultural feminists, thus rendering their work significantly different from radical feminism [p.411].

It is unclear to me how the "developed and consolidated" radical feminism that is cultural feminism is "significantly different" from its radical feminist antecedents, particularly as Alcoff goes on to criticise cultural feminism for holding the same "essentialist conception of female nature"—cf. p.411.

[14] Daly (1978), p.355.

belief in a body-oriented "female consciousness"[15] indicate that for these and other cultural feminist writers,

> feminist theory, the explanation of sexism, and the justification of feminist demands can all be grounded securely and unambiguously on the concept of the essential female.[16]

But to outline the programme for women's resistance to patriarchy on the basis of an innate femaleness—and, by implication, to equate patriarchy with an innate maleness—rests on a universalising outlook which ignores variety in women's lives and experience, and which sidelines such phenomena as, for example, white middle-class women who contribute to the oppression of their poorer sisters, or men who reject male stereotyping and suffer under patriarchal expectations of what it is to be a man:

> white women cannot be all good or bad; neither can men from oppressed groups.[17]

Alcoff also criticises cultural feminism for being overly culture-specific: the qualities claimed by Anglo-American feminists as inherently female may not necessarily be seen as such by women in other cultures, and so cultural feminism takes insufficient account of the fact that gender divisions occur according to different criteria in different societies[18]—in theorising Woman and supporting its arguments with our own Western academic biological or psychological explanations, cultural feminism too often becomes a forum in which Anglo-American or Western European women speak for all women everywhere. This is a persistent problem in feminist discourse, and one which surfaces as soon as the impulse to proselytise overcomes the respect for difference:

> we cannot separate *worldwide* feminism from a certain fundamental europeanization of world culture.[19]

But perhaps most importantly, Alcoff points out that cultural feminism's insistence on the importance of female nature to feminist

---

[15] Rich (1979), p.18.
[16] Alcoff: *op. cit.* p.408.
[17] *Ibid.* p.412.
[18] *Ibid.* p.413.
[19] Derrida (1982a), p.69 (my italics).

theory and practice is only a shade removed from the establishment of dogmatic criteria for inclusion in the ranks of the "truly" feminist: if liberated women can only exist as such in a gynocentric universe, then those who choose to live elsewhere are not only deluded and still oppressed, but somehow also denying their femaleness, and so (to quote Elisabeth Schüssler Fiorenza), sisterhood risks coming to be understood "not as the bonding of the oppressed but as the gathering of the ideologically 'pure'".[20] Cultural feminism, in positing an essential female mode of being which is tied to gender, gives rise to "unrealistic expectations about 'normal' female behaviour"[21]—and in this prescriptive tendency, of course, it mirrors patriarchy. Nobody will argue that peacefulness, identification with nature, intuition, selflessness and other traditionally woman-associated attributes are crucial to any envisioning of a more holistic, egalitarian society, but

> to the extent that [cultural feminism] reinforces essentialist explanations of these attributes, it is in danger of solidifying an important bulwark for sexist oppression: the belief in an innate "womanhood" to which we must all adhere lest we be deemed either inferior or not "true" women.[22]

The main problem with cultural feminism with regard to patriarchal dualism, then, is not that it reasserts the value of "feminine" qualities, but that it rigidly equates the feminine (a social construct) with the female (a biological entity). For cultural feminism, biology is—ideally—destiny, and the dualistic view of gender which upholds patriarchal views of women is inverted but not in any other way substantially challenged: male and female still exist at opposite poles, and the relationship between them is one of antagonism. In other words, patriarchal dualism is rejected because it is patriarchal, but not because it is dualism.

Poststructuralist Feminism and Relativism

A very different response to patriarchy, and one which also chal-

---

[20] Fiorenza (1983), p.26.
[21] Alcoff: *op. cit.* p.413.
[22] *Ibid.* p.414.

lenges cultural feminism, is that which deconstructs the opposition of male and female, and relativises sexual identity, taking to its logical conclusion Simone de Beauvoir's famous observation that

> [o]ne is not born, but rather becomes, a woman....it is civilization as a whole that produces this creature....which is described as feminine.[23]

This approach is referred to by Linda Alcoff as "poststructuralist" feminism, and it relies on a strategy whereby "gender loses its position of significance"[24] in feminist discourse. The term "poststructuralist" refers to the use made by this type of feminism of the work of (among others) Jacques Lacan, Jacques Derrida and Michel Foucault, thinkers often labelled "poststructuralist" simply because of their philosophical roots in structuralist linguistics and anthropology, but who might also (according to Alcoff) be termed "post-humanist" or "post-essentialist". Perhaps the most widely-recognised premise of poststructuralist thought is

> that the self-contained, authentic subject conceived by humanism to be discoverable below a veneer of cultural and ideological overlay is in reality a construct of that very humanist discourse. The subject is not a locus of authorial intentions or natural attributes or even a privileged, separate consciousness. Lacan uses psychoanalysis, Derrida uses grammar and Foucault uses the history of discourses all to attack and "deconstruct" our concept of the subject as having an essential identity and an authentic core that has been repressed by society.[25]

The problem for cultural feminists here is obvious: poststructuralism holds that the female "essence" or subject valorised by Daly, Rich and others is not only *not* anchored in the unassailable fact of biological gender, but is actually a creation of cultural feminist discourse, having no independent existence of its own. Just as classical humanism speaks of a unique selfhood at the heart of the individual which constitutes who that person *is*, so cultural feminism presupposes an essential "womanhood" at the heart of the female individual which is definitive and fixed. Poststructuralism, on the other

---

[23] de Beauvior (1972), p.273.
[24] Alcoff: *op.cit.* p.407.
[25] *Ibid.* p.415.

hand, is committed to the concept of the subject as the site of conflict and change, and of subjective experience as being determined by social discourses and practices, rather than as originating in the rational, self-aware "I". And so for poststructuralist feminism, Woman or the female subject takes its meaning from the discursive context in which it is located.

Discursive contexts are many and varied, as are the modes of experience available within them. The discourse of traditional conservative Catholicism, for example, having its own political interests and putting forward its own particular arguments for the organisation of society, offers a limited range of subject positions for women to assume: virgin, nun or mystic; wife or mother. In another discursive context, created by the shared assumptions and commercial interests of a particular wing of the magazine industry, Woman is career-oriented, business-suited, expensively groomed and (hetero-) sexually confident. Within separatist feminist discourse, traditional religion and the family are seen as the key instruments of patriarchal oppression, monogamous sexuality as a masochistic enslavement to male desire, and so Woman is earth-centred, creative, women-identified, sexually diffuse. These discourses offer different subject positions or identities to the individual, and the relationship between them is unstable and contentious, as Chris Weedon comments:

> Discourses represent political interests and in consequence are constantly vying for status and power. The site of this battle for power is the subjectivity of the individual.[26]

The theory of discourse and power has been most fully articulated by Foucault, whose belief it is that meaning, experience and subjectivity are inseparable from the workings of social discourses, and that the constant struggle for dominance between discourses results in perceived fragmentations and contradictions within the self, and in the inability to make final sense of experience. Foucault's cultural diagnosis is that "the least glimmer of truth is conditioned by politics",[27] and he wonders whether in fact we might be "totally imprinted by history".[28] Similarly, Derrida has posited that

---

[26] Weedon (1989), p.41. Cf. also Foucault (1970).
[27] Foucault (1979), p.5.
[28] Foucault (1984), p.83.

subjectivity is constituted by the play of textuality (Derrida's "text" is in some, but only some, respects cognate with Foucault's "discourse") and Lacan also sees the subject as "socially, linguistically and libidinally *constructed*".[29] Further discussion of Lacan and Foucault lies outside the scope of this study, and of Derrida a great deal more will be said later: for the moment, it should be clear enough that poststructuralist feminist theories of subjectivity have uncomfortable implications for any discourses, feminist or patriarchal, concerned with questions of women's definitive selfhood and experience.

The poststructuralist emphasis on social discourse and practice, on the *production* of subjectivity, offers an excellent perspective from which to analyse and challenge a key premise of patriarchal oppression. Once the concept of predetermined gender identity is seen as the product rather than the ground or authorisation of discourses concerning women, the idea that women should conform "naturally" to a certain set of cultural criteria is effectively done away with. Women can, at least in theory, become free to explore a variety of subject positions, unencumbered with any social expectations pertaining to their biological sex. Of course, female anatomy and the roles associated with it (such as motherhood) cannot be relativised out of existence, but neither can the significance of anatomy or biological nature be any longer fixed. The problem, however, lies in making the shift from theory to practice: if "woman", or the female subject, is no longer definable in terms of specific gender, and if "women's experience" is as indeterminate as the subjectivity which underlies it, then how and where is a feminist politics to be grounded? Linda Alcoff's principal objection to poststructuralist feminism is centred around this question, and it is with some anxiety that she quotes Derrida:

> Perhaps...."woman" is not a determinable identity....Perhaps woman —a non-identity, non-figure, a simulacrum—is distance's very chasm, the outdistancing of distance, the interval's cadence, distance itself.[30]

Julia Kristeva, a theorist whose work owes much to Derrida and Lacan, is cited as having a similar outlook:

---

[29] Grosz (1989), p.24.
[30] Derrida (1979a), p.49 (quoted in Alcoff: *op. cit.* p.417).

A woman cannot be; it [*sic*] is something which does not even belong in the order of being. It follows that a feminist practice can only be negative, at odds with what already exists, so that we may say "that's not it", and "that's still not it".[31]

A welter of troublesome concerns arises here. Derrida and Kristeva do not, I believe, seek somehow to erase the female; the realm of identity" or "the order of being" to which woman is said not to belong is that constituted by the oppositional discourse of patriarchy, governed as it is by the dualistic split between male and female, and so woman, defined as "non-man", indeed has no being or identity of her own here. But where, then, does she exist? It seems that the price paid for freedom from gender expectations is a kind of terminable invisibility, which might be agreeable enough if not for the fact that women are, now and for the foreseeable future, very much in need of a visible presence and an audible voice within patriarchal culture, a recognised position from which to challenge, fight and offer alternatives to oppression. Alcoff succinctly states the case:

If gender is simply a social construct, the need and even the possibility of a feminist politics becomes immediately problematic. What can we demand in the name of women if "women" do not exist and demands in their name simply reinforce the myth that they do? How can we speak out against sexism as detrimental to the interests of women if the category is a fiction? How can we demand legal abortions, adequate child care, or wages based on comparable worth without invoking a concept of "woman"?[32]

Identity Politics

One solution is to develop a theory of subjectivity which steers feminist political practice between the essentialism or "manichean ontology"[33] of cultural feminism and the all-pervasive relativism of poststructuralism's more extreme advocates. It is a solution implied in Chris Weedon's comment on discourse and power; the idea that

---

[31] Kristeva (1981), p.137 (quoted in Alcoff: *ibid.* p.418).

[32] Alcoff: *ibid.* p.420.

[33] *Ibid.* p.412.

the battle for status and influence between social discourses, a battle whose conflicts and tensions constitute the unstable, shifting nature of the subject, is "a battle in which the individual is an *active but not sovereign* protagonist".[34] This leaves room both for the recognition that our identity is to a large extent constructed for us, and for the possibility of that identity nevertheless being used as a point of departure for political action. Alcoff calls this "identity politics", and cites by way of example "assimilated Jews who have chosen to become Jewish-identified as a political tactic against anti-Semitism", and women who choose to claim their identity as women in order to speak out against sexism and misogyny.[35]

One advantage of identity politics in feminist theory is that it avoids the necessity of a dualistic commitment *either* to cultural feminism *or* to what Alcoff sees as hardline poststructuralism: "femaleness" or women's experience becomes non-essentialised and dependent on its historical context, while at the same time the impulse to erase or deny the relevance of women's experience is checked by the grounding of that experience in shared understandings and practices which, while relative to their social location, nevertheless provide a consensual platform for an identifiably feminist politics. The efficacy of identity politics is apparent in such areas as the struggle for fairer legislation concerning rape and sexual violence. The patriarchal prejudices rife within Western legal systems are never more visible than in rape cases; in an overwhelming num-

---

[34] Weedon (1989), p.41 (my italics).

[35] Alcoff: *op. cit.* p.432. I should note that Alcoff's (and subsequently my) use of the term "identity politics" is potentially confusing, as the same term can be found elsewhere to carry precisely the opposite sense of what is intended here. Judith Butler, for example, has written that

> [t]he foundationalist reasoning of identity politics tends to assume that an identity must first be in place in order for political interests to be elaborated and, subsequently, political action to be taken [1990, p.142].

"Identity politics" for Butler appears to denote a politics grounded in the notion of a pre-discursive subject, which for *feminist* politics means something closely akin to Alcoff's "cultural feminism": politics, that is, governed by "identity". For Alcoff, however, identity politics involves—as we shall see—the radical politicisation of the subject, the idea that one's identity is constructed through one's political action, rather than the other way around: "identity" governed by politics.

[36] Marcus (1992), pp.398-99.

ber of instances, the woman involved suffers under the assumption that she is, simply by virtue of her femaleness, to some extent sexually available, and so the responsibility falls upon her to prove that she neither invited, consented to nor enjoyed the attentions of her assailant (the myth of sexual availability and provocation on the part of the woman is further underlined by tabloid press reports which, while calling in aggrieved tones for harsher police action and criminal penalties, still seldom fail to describe the rape victim as "young" or "pretty"). But a feminist response to this situation need say neither that the rapist is nothing other than a male showing his true colours, nor (on the other hand) that the experience of sexual violence is only relatively outrageous or traumatic by social convention. Similarly, the sexual vulnerability of women in Western society has been endlessly documented, and the experience of some kind of sexual exploitation is common to most if not all women, yet this is not necessarily due to any kind of innate male aggression, or sexual magnetism essential to the female nature: rather, the situation is the result of a complex pattern of social assumptions and practices. Sharon Marcus has argued that the discourse surrounding sexual violence (what she calls "the rape script") is itself actually determinative of the female subject to a degree which needs to be challenged:

> The rape script describes female bodies as vulnerable, violable, penetrable, and wounded; metaphors of rape as trespass and invasion retain this definition intact. The psychological corollary of this property metaphor characterizes female sexuality as inner space, rape as the invasion of this inner space, and antirape politics as a means to safeguard this inner space from contact with anything external to it. The entire female body comes to be symbolized by the vagina, itself conceived of as a delicate, perhaps inevitably damaged and pained inner space....We do not need to defend our "real" bodies from invasion but to rework this elaboration of our bodies altogether. The most deep-rooted upheaval of rape culture would revise the idea of female sexuality as an object, as property, and as an inner space.[36]

This radical reformulation or displacement of female subjectivity—involving the political action of women who, while choosing to

---

[37] Alcoff: *op. cit.* p.433.

speak from their experience of the reality of sexual violence, still refuse to be seen as victims or as sexually passive by (female) nature—is one example of identity politics in practice: the adoption of
subject positions (albeit not completely freely; the availability of
choices is no less culturally-determined than the subject itself)
which enables the individual

> [to] say at one and the same time that gender is not natural, biological,
> universal, ahistorical, or essential and yet still claim that gender is
> relevant because we are taking gender as a position from which to act
> politically.[37]

Sexist ontologies of woman, based on gender-specific male/female
dualism, are thus undermined, just as the dualistic opposition that
exists between woman-as-biological-fact and woman-as-cultural-
fiction is deconstructed, with each relying on the other for its
meaning. The significance of gender, or what it means to be a
woman, becomes fluid and dependent on the force of discursive influence, while the play of discourse is constrained, and the meaning
of gender provisionally held in place, by the limited range of subject
positions available to the individual at any one time. One very desirable result of this kind of formulation is that the subject, or the
"essence" of the Female, is no longer the exclusive province of theory, but something inseparable from what one *does* in day-to-day
life:

> my argument is that there need not be a "doer behind the deed", but
> that the "doer" is variably constructed in and through the deed.[38]

What remains now is to begin to translate this rather lengthy theoretical outline into the language of feminist biblical hermeneutics.
For the rest of this chapter I will look at patriarchal dualism and essentialism in interpretation; poststructuralism will be considered in
greater detail in the following chapter, where I will discuss the relevance of deconstructive biblical criticism to feminist exegesis.

Criticism in Search of "Truth"

The historical struggle for authority in biblical interpretation has

---

[38] Butler (1990), p.142.

[39] Cf. the *Cratylus* in Fowler (1926), pp.11-91.

most often been carried out with competing exegetical voices claiming to have divined the authentic, God-breathed meaning of scripture, and until fairly recently those voices have spoken also in the interests of patriarchy. The bible is, for the most part, a collection of texts which largely reflect the values of patriarchal cultures; church and synagogue are, traditionally, patriarchal institutions; the canonical works of both Jewish and Christian exegetes are regularly punctuated with prescriptions aimed at subordinating women to male authority in political and liturgical practice; it should therefore come as no great surprise to find that the dominant values and assumptions behind traditional biblical hermeneutics are often the same values and assumptions which uphold patriarchy. It should be noted at this point that I will later put forward Rabbinic midrash as a mode of interpretation which has, in many respects, its theological and methodological uses for feminist hermeneutics; in the critical discussion which follows here, I will therefore be speaking mainly of exegesis in the Christian tradition.

The differences between the Jewish and the Christian traditions are many and profound; few would dispute that the differences exist, but any attempt to ground them in a philosophical bifurcation of Hebrew and Greek thought results in sharp controversy. This controversy will be examined in greater detail in chapter 4; for the purposes of the present argument I am accepting simply that Christianity has inherited, to a large extent, the Greek metaphysical tradition concerning matters of language, truth and interpretation. From the early Gnostics to the moral theologians of the twentieth century, the Platonic/Aristotelian concept of truth or ultimate Meaning as residing in a realm beyond language or sensual apprehension has greatly influenced Christian scriptural hermeneutics. Plato posits the existence of an unchanging realm of Ideas, immutable forms which exist beyond the contingencies of language and the senses, for which language in particular provides only a roughly imitative approximation;[39] this is an idea reproduced in the Pauline concept of a transcendent God in whom absolute truth rests, but who in this life can

---

[40] Lloyd (1984), p.9. Cf. also Aristotle: *Categories — de Interpretatione* trans. J. Ackrill (1963); Handelman (1982), pp.3-15; Boman (1960), ch.1.

only be apprehended as "through a glass darkly", and also more significantly in Paul's warning that in matters of exegesis, truth lies *behind* the text (" the written code kills, but the Spirit gives life"—2 Cor. 3:6). Aristotle differs from Plato in that he sees the *ousia* or primary essence of a thing as residing within the thing rather than in an eternal realm of Forms, but he nevertheless sees this essence as being abstracted from its material properties, knowable only by means of a movement beyond language and the senses; the paradigm of knowledge remains "the contemplation by a rational mind of something inherently mind-like, freed of matter".[40]

Biblical interpretation carried out on the basis of this understanding of language and truth has only too easily served the interests of hierarchical authority in general and of patriarchy in particular. The idea that there is a sphere beyond linguistic exchange where things simply *exist* in a purely pre-verbal state means that the philosophical ideal is to conceptualise, to think in the abstract and not to get bogged down in the distracting particularities of words. The familiar virtues of rationality, logic and abstract thought become valorised, and inevitably the male is held to better-equipped than the more emotional female for transcending the mundane order, penetrating the veils of illusion, apprehending the higher Truth and disseminating it as unimpeachable orthodoxy. According to this kind of exegetical practice, language needs to be disciplined, to be made as stable as possible so that it mirrors as faithfully as possible the immutable realm of pure Meaning: for Aristotle, the ideal speech act is one which has one meaning and one meaning only; while similarly in Plato's dialogues we can see that self-contradiction, or inconsistency in meaning, is the cardinal rhetorical sin. This results in interpretation which is essentially monolithic and hierarchical, as well as patriarchal: an authentic reading of scripture is ideally unambiguous in addition to being disinterested and apolitical; it is that which seems most closely to approach the numinous, univocal reality behind the text, and so it must be fixed and reproduced as orthodox exegesis over against other readings which compete for the same

---

[41] Studies of exegesis as political practice exist to cover most if not all aspects of Church history: of particular relevance to feminist issues are Cannon (1989) on racism; Fuchs (1985) on narrative; Kristeva (1986) and Warner (1985) on Mariology; Ranke-Heinemann (1990) on sexuality.

status. Claims of disinterestedness, however, run into significant problems when the "authentic" becomes the authoritative, and the forces of power come into play—even a brief glance at the shortest chapter in Christian church history will reveal that wherever issues of orthodoxy and heterodoxy arise, and ecclesiastical or state power is brought in to settle them, what in fact becomes clearly visible is the inextricability of politics and faith, of discourse and truth.[41] But doctrinal readings of scripture, including those which seek legitimation for the patriarchal domination of women, continue to be predicated upon the denial or marginalisation of politics in exegesis: biblical revelation is said to take place when the plane of language and social discourse is transcended—a possibility more open to men than to women by virtue of their superior rational faculties.

At the end of the previous chapter, I indicated that feminist biblical hermeneutics should be wary of strict demarcation between what is intrinsic or "essential" to scripture and what is not, and I hope now to have demonstrated at a more general level that essentialism both in theory and in textual-critical practice relies on a dualistic philosophy which conceals its own mechanisms and is too neatly congruent with the workings of sexist ideology. Indeed, any preoccupation with correct or authentic meaning in interpretation has its explicitly patriarchal overtones, as Jonathan Culler has argued:

> if one tried to imagine the literary criticism of a patriarchal culture, one might predict several likely concerns: (1) that the role of the author would be conceived as a paternal one....(2) that much would be invested in paternal authors....(3) that there would be great concern about which meanings were legitimate and which illegitimate (since the paternal author's role in the generation of meanings can only be inferred); and that criticism would expend great efforts to develop principles for, on the one hand, determining which meanings were truly the author's own progeny, and on the other hand, controlling intercourse with texts so as to prevent the proliferation of illegitimate interpretations.[42]

This anxiety is compounded in biblical interpretation, where the author of the text's meaning is often held to be God—"legitimate"

---

[42] Culler (1987), pp.60-61. Cf. also Elizabeth Castelli's comments on the religious and sexual connotations of "faithfulness" in translation and interpretation (1990).

meaning becomes even more jealously guarded, as well as constituting the object of a critical but never fully satisfied desire which
dooms the exegete to the multiplication of interpretations and re-in-
terpretation's in the search for a final, stable one.

Culler's implicit metaphor of the text as the passive yet wanton
bearer of meanings, meanings which must variously be accepted or
rejected as legitimate or illegitimate according to their paternity, is
neither accidental nor insignificant: essentialist interpretation, dependent as it is on dualistic, oppositional logic, evinces a sexual
politics which renders the text "female" in the worst of ways. In
biblical interpretation, essentialism generally takes two forms: one is
that of scripture as mysterious and unapproachable, possessing an
enigmatic soul which is yielded up to the apprehension of the reader
only by means of inspiration or a kind of mystical communion. This
approach stems from an understanding of the biblical text as absolutely sacred, a divine Code whose deciphering is dependent upon
special revelation. The other commonly-encountered mode of essentialist exegesis is that which has been criticised in the previous
chapter: the search for "proper articulation of meaning" predicated
on the idea of the text as an object, as Phyllis Trible's "interlocking
structure of words and motifs" with an "intrinsic value and meaning" accessible to the interpreter with the right hermeneutical tools
and skills. Text-as-radically-Other, to be approached with holy
dread or at least with reverent caution; or text-as-recognisably-other,
still fascinating but accessible by means of rational, analytical inquiry into its nature: seen in this light, the essentialist approach
should flash a clear warning to anyone familiar with the workings of
patriarchal social anthropology. Exegesis in pursuit of authentic
meaning acts upon the text in much the same way as that in which
patriarchal institutions, from science to religion, have traditionally
acted upon women: the Female has been fetishised and deemed to be
worthy of a kind of mystified awe, while at the same time women
have been studied, scrutinised, analysed, categorised, weighed and
measured across a range of discourses, all in the search for their
"nature". And just as women, in conforming to the social expectations laid down for them by the results of such inquiry, take their
place in the natural order of things and earn the respect intrinsically
due to their sex, so an essentialist view of the bible sees "correct"

hermeneutical assumptions and techniques as the means of preserving the God-ordained veracity and sanctity of the text.

I do not wish to labour the parallel between woman and text; the point is that feminist biblical criticism should regard essentialist approaches to meaning of any kind with particular suspicion, recognising that essentialist arguments have been employed not only by religious institutions in fixing biblical meaning, not only by patriarchal institutions in formulating restrictive gender-deterministic models for women, but also as a means of justifying institutionalised domination in too many historical instances—the witch, the Jew, the black, the poor, the unemployed: all have been systematically stereotyped at some point in the attempt by those who wield hostile power over them to explain, justify and legitimise their oppression.

The main criticism of biblical hermeneutics in pursuit of intrinsic or essential meaning, then, corresponds to the criticism offered earlier of cultural feminism: in both cases, the methodology looks too much like patriarchy, and the result looks too much like fixed ideology, leaving no room for historical or cultural change or alternatives. While feminist biblical hermeneutics must make the bible somehow meaningful and positive to women by operating according to a recognisably feminist agenda, it must also remain open to diversity across and within cultures. Similarly, feminist interpretation of scripture must speak to and from women's experience, but we have already seen that to ask, as we must, "*which* women's experience?" hardly delimits the field of inquiry: poststructuralist theories of subjectivity argue that experience is not tied to gender or to any other putative ground of individuation, but rather constituted in a complex web of discourses and varied subject positions. To make the bible relevant to the struggle against patriarchal oppression, feminist exegesis must accommodate as many varieties of women's experience as there are cultures, religions, classes, families, individuals; but at the same time, it must avoid the kind of extreme historical determinism that relativises immediate political issues out of focus. A hermeneutics which, in keeping with the suggested criteria for feminist theory outlined above, is politically explicit, resistant to essentialism or ideology, and open to pluralism in interpretation; which operates according to the idea of meaning as a process rather than an ahistorical entity, and yet which avoids marginalising either

the role of concrete religious faith or the attendant need to make
some kind of practical sense out of existence. The preceding discussion could perhaps be criticised for taking place largely in the
realm of the abstract, with reference to Platonic ideals of pure
feminist Forms; in what follows, I will attempt correctively to narrow the focus and evaluate the potential for feminist biblical interpretation in the context of existing literary-critical practice.

CHAPTER THREE

DECONSTRUCTION AND FEMINISM

It is interesting to see that increasingly in biblical studies, the gap
between studying the bible as the Word of God and studying it as
literature is narrowing. The argument seems to be gaining currency
that the status of the bible as Sacred Literature is not necessarily debased by placing equal importance on its small-"l"-literary characteristics, or at least that to defend the bible against the creeping tide
of secular (post)modernism in literary studies, one must be able to
argue with the heretics on their own terms. Hence the emergence of
lively discussion in most modern journals of biblical criticism which
deals both sympathetically and antagonistically with neo-histori-
cism, Marxism, structuralism, semiotics, reader-response criticism,
speech act theory, deconstruction, and so on. One by-product of all
this can be a sense of "vertigo in the face of....endless theoretical
proposals";[1] the exegete could perhaps do with a little more freedom
from choice, and indeed a rearguard offensive against pluralism in
interpretation is constantly being waged by those who say that some
hermeneutical modes are by nature antithetical to biblical criticism.
This is a revealing and significant assertion which will be considered further on; for the time being I wish simply to indicate that
feminist interpretation of the bible currently has at its disposal a
broad range and variety of critical methodologies, reading strategies
which were barely accessible twenty or even ten years ago outside
the discursive boundaries of literary and linguistic studies. Feminist
biblical hermeneutics, then, could be said to be coming into its own
at a time when the language of modern literary theory is being increasingly accepted as legal tender in the field of biblical scholarship.

---

[1] Jobling (1990), p.82.

This statement presupposes, of course, that feminist interpretation of the bible should want to have anything to do with modern literary theory, an assumption which is by no means uncontested. The role of theory in feminism generally is a contentious issue. Theory appears, after all, to offer a means of universalising experience, of going in deep below the surface of particular phenomena to discover what is "really" going on, and in this respect theory constantly courts the kind of essentialism which, I have argued in the previous chapter, poses serious problems for feminism. How can feminist theory resist the tendency to establish one universal category of Woman? A common response to this question by feminist theorists is to invoke difference:

> "Differences" has become a given of academic feminisms; feminism has been modified and pluralized. No longer one, feminisms are marked by nation and race....by class, ethnicity, sexuality: black feminism, latina feminism, lesbian feminism, middle-class "mainstream" feminism, and so on. It would seem that dealing with the fact of differences is *the* project of women's studies today.[2]

The question still remains, however, as to how the project of women's studies should incorporate "the fact of differences". To interrupt the idealising tendencies of feminist theory by invoking difference as a *fact* should not, in itself, constitute a solution: indeed, as soon as "the fact of difference" becomes a solution for theory rather than a problem, we have a new problem, or rather a new version of the old problem—that of difference enshrined as Difference and sanctified as icon of the eternal Female:

> "Differences" has passed into the realm of the slogan which makes it even harder to think, of course, since slogans are by their very nature self-evident: you are either for or against differences, for or against diversity....What is foreclosed is the possibility of thinking differently about differences, yet that is precisely what is to be done. Otherwise differences will remain as evident as self-identity once was, and just as women's studies once saw woman everywhere, the academy will recognise differences everywhere, cheerfully acknowledging that since everyone is different, everyone is the same.[3]

---

[2] Crosby (1992), p.131.
[3] *Ibid.* pp.139-40.

A theory, then, which pays full respect to difference (as any gender-based theory, or any political theory at all, must do) has to ensure that this acknowledgement is of a restless, interruptive nature; the acknowledgement of difference not as some pearl of sacred significance, but rather as the obnoxious piece of grit and the activity of making-signified with which it is itself identified. "Difference is not a thing to be argued, but a process always underway".[4] The approach to theory which this necessitates is of a different order to that which underlies empiricist or historicist projects; it is an approach which sees difference as something operating not just between determinations of truth but within them as well. If the fundamental imperative of radical political thought is to interrogate the means by which knowledge is produced, then indispensable to this interrogation is the notion that difference is always at work, subverting all determinate structures of thought and ensuring that knowledge, in its complex cultural/historical context, always differs *from itself.*

The greater part of this chapter, then, shall be devoted to arguing generally that feminism can benefit greatly from a radical theory of difference, and in particular that feminist biblical interpretation can benefit from a literary-critical alliance with such a theory. By way of examining the means of forging this kind of alliance, I wish to turn first to deconstructive criticism and the work of Jacques Derrida, in order to evaluate the efficacy of his insights for feminist biblical hermeneutics.

Structuralism and Deconstruction

It is extremely difficult, for reasons which will shortly become clear, to establish exactly what deconstruction "is"; one of the most pressing questions asked by Derrida is whether or not anything, including deconstruction, can be said to partake unproblematically of what our dominant Western philosophical tradition has identified as Being. For the time being, and for the sake of convenience, we will label deconstruction as a practice (or set of practices), one which has its roots as *literary-critical* practice in the structuralist linguistics of Ferdinand de Saussure. The *Course in General Linguistics*, a recon-

---

[4] *Ibid.* p.140.

struction of Saussure's lectures at the University of Geneva pieced together by some of his students after his death, was first published in 1915, and in this text was developed explicitly for the first time the structuralist axiom that language is a self-contained sign-system which has, essentially, little to do with anything beyond itself, including what we might romantically call meaning. Saussure's most important argument in the *Course* was that the linguistic sign is basically arbitrary, having no essential link with the thing it is supposed to represent. At the phonemic level, it can be seen that the word "mouse", for example, is not somehow ontologically connected to what it signifies, but rather takes its meaning from its place in the language chain, and is recognised by virtue of its difference from other signifiers. "Mouse" is not meaningful because it materially conjures up, in and of itself, one of the smaller species of the genus *Mus* of rodents, but because it *is not* "house", "louse", or "moose". This is the fundamental principle informing all structuralist and poststructuralist linguistics: it can be identified in Chris Weedon's argument, for example, that the relationship between the word "whore" and a woman who exchanges sex for money, is basically arbitrary; the English language might well have used any other word to signify such an individual, and indeed other languages do. There is "no natural connection" between the signifier and the concept which it signifies, and the meaning of words is "not intrinsic but relational"; "whore" derives its meaning through its difference from "other signifiers of womanhood such as 'virgin' or 'mother'".[5]

This key structuralist concept of language as a system which refers to nothing beyond itself explains why we understand our own language when spoken with a heavy foreign accent, as the context, the relationship between the word and other words, provides the meaning—it is only in recognising the pattern of an utterance that we approach an understanding of it. Signifier and signified can never share a common identity, having as they do only a conventional or arbitrary connection to each other, and it is this understanding which informs Saussure's much-quoted dictum that "in language, there are only differences *without positive terms*".[6] In the chain of signifiers that is language,

---

[5] Weedon (1987), p.23.
[6] Saussure (1960), p.120.

each [signifier] means what it does....through its difference from all the concrete "signifiers" around it. The identity of each sign is determined by its distinction from all the other signs—an identity which can never be separated from the system which the signs together constitute.[7]

This basic article of structuralist faith (or scepticism) is crucial also to deconstruction, and it implies that as far as final or "true" meaning is concerned, language is a radically unstable phenomenon. Both Derrida and Saussure would, like most people, acknowledge that if you go to a dictionary in search of the meaning of the word "mouse", what you find is neither a concrete signified (a mouse pressed between the pages of the book at "M"), nor an ideal Form or essence which the word represents (the *ousia* of mouse), but simply more words, whose meanings are defined by more words again, and so on *ad infinitum*—or indeed *ad nauseam* if you are an existentialist. Signifiers lead only to other signifiers, and the same applies to larger patterns of signification such as codes, idioms and texts: of making many books there can be no end, because ultimate or final meaning is always deferred. This has profound implications for knowledge of all kinds, particularly for those forms of knowledge such as philosophy and theology which have long been committed both to reading and writing, and to at least some kind of concept of truth. If a signifier (which, usually understood as a single word, can also be a more complex verbal unit such as a phrase, a paragraph, a page, a chapter, and so on) is by nature unstable and refers to nothing outside a web of other equally unstable signifiers, then the activity of reading, by means of which it is often assumed we can apprehend the meaning "behind" a text, is an endeavour which in fact

cannot legitimately transgress the text toward something other than it ....or toward a signified outside the text whose content could take place, could have taken place outside of language, that is to say, in the sense that we give here to that word, outside of writing in general.[8]

Derrida's somewhat opaque pronouncement can be taken here to mean that if there exists any pure, objective truth, any

---

[7] Wolosky (1982), pp.288-89.
[8] Derrida (1976), p.158.

"transcendental signified", it is not to be apprehended through language. Whether speaking or writing, listening or reading, we cannot "transgress the text" either to convey or to receive stable meaning which exists outside the differential play of signifiers.

Logocentrism, Speech and Writing

This is the ground on which deconstruction poses its most ominous threat to the dominant Western philosophical tradition, a tradition rooted in classical Greek metaphysics and dependent very much upon the Platonic/Aristotelian concepts of language and truth outlined in the previous chapter. The concept of objective, stable truth (*ousia, logos*, reality, Being) as something toward which language points, and to which rigorous reason and logic provide access, is a concept which can be traced through the canonical texts of Western philosophy: from the works of Plato and Aristotle, on to Descartes, Rousseau, Kant, Hegel and beyond, the dominant assumption has been that

> Being can be known and experienced in its immediacy; language transfers meaning neutrally without interfering in the underlying thoughts it "expresses"; knowledge undistortedly reflects reality in truthful representations. These beliefs retain the concept as a pure idea, existing independent of particular languages or forms of expression.[9]

Derrida has said that the belief in unmediated Meaning which haunts Western philosophy, along with "all the names related to fundamentals, to principles, or to the center" and the search for an Archimedean point of knowledge, have "always designated *an invariable presence*",[10] and Derrida accordingly coins the roughly-interchangeable terms "metaphysics of presence" and "logocentrism" to denote this assumption of transcendent and unassailable truth. It is this reliance on the metaphysics of presence, this logocentric commitment to the existence of a unified conceptual order toward which philosophy points the way, that has resulted in a certain

---

[9] Grosz (1989), p.28. Cf. also Derrida: "Tympan" in Kamuf (1982), pp.146-68.
[10] Derrida (1978), p.279 (my italics).

self-privileging of philosophical thought. In her discussion of Derrida, Elizabeth Grosz writes that philosophy, as the study of knowledge itself, has strong vested interests in presenting itself as foundational and non-contingent:

> Philosophy cannot acknowledge its *constitutive* dependence on language, on textuality, on the ambiguity and openness of all discourse....It cannot acknowledge its own (textual) corporeality. It conceives of itself as fundamentally *translatable*, capable of being expressed, ideally, in logical symbols to avoid any imprecisions or ambiguity, a language honed and purified of all its materiality, resistant to intention.[11]

It should be noted, of course, that to speak of philosophy in this way is to gloss over the ideas of a great many thinkers in the Western tradition—Nietzsche, for example—for whom truth and the transparency of language have been by no means given or self-evident. Still, I am arguing that any philosophical discourse which does stem from logocentric assumptions faces a substantial challenge from Derrida's appropriation of the structuralist view of language as differential and indeterminate: if words refer only to other words, even at the most basic level of recognition, then the attempt to anchor concepts of transcendent truth and meaning in philosophical argument (or indeed in any kind of argument) is, from the outset, greatly at odds with itself.

Derrida sees logocentric thought as depending very much upon a philosophical commitment to binary oppositions. In its attempt to deal with stable, fundamental principles, logocentrism posits stable norms or essences and discusses them in relation to deviations or "subdeterminations".[12] The tendency then to dichotomise the (dominant) ideal and the (dependent) derivation in a hierarchical positive/ negative structure constitutes for Derrida the classic metaphysical manoeuvre:

> the enterprise of returning "strategically", ideally, to an origin or to a "priority" held to be simple, intact, normal, pure, standard, self-identical, in order *then* to think in terms of derivation, complication, deterioration, accident, etc....conceiving good to be before evil, the

---

[11] Grosz (1989), p.28.
[12] Derrida (1976), p.12.

positive before the negative, the pure before the impure, the simple before the complex, the essential before the accidental....[t]his is not just *one* metaphysical gesture among others; it is the metaphysical exigency, that which has been the most constant, most profound and most potent.[13]

One might well add male-before-female to the list and consider that patriarchy, with its strategic return to a male norm, is clearly another manifestation of the metaphysics of presence. It is on the grounds of this question of dualism that deconstruction parts company with structuralism, as the latter is held by Derrida to be governed to a great extent by the logic of binary opposition, in spite of the valuable insights into language which it offers.

Derrida locates, for example, in the work both of Saussure and of other structuralists such as Roland Barthes, a privileging of speech over writing as the paradigmatic linguistic act.[14] The idea of writing as secondary, as the representation or imitation of speech (made explicit in Saussure's statement that "spoken forms alone constitute the object" of linguistic analysis[15]) is an idea which links structuralist linguistics to Western metaphysics at a crucial point. Speech, according to the Platonic concept of the relationship between language and meaning, is closer to pure, unmediated Meaning than writing: in any speech act, speaker and utterance occupy the same place at the same time, and so the listener has access to sound and sense simultaneously. If the meaning is unclear, its author (the speaker) can be questioned or engaged in some kind of expository dialogue, and so meaning is closer to being "present" than in the case of writing. Writing is seen as derivative and even treacherous: practised in the absence of a reader, and read in the absence of its author, its original context is often difficult to determine, and a difficult written text remains obstinate and inscrutable in the face of any attempt to make it clarify its "correct" sense. Writing, therefore, is held by Saussure to inhabit the "promiscuous public realm"[16] of interpretation, where signification is never certain or fixed, while speech involves a use of

---

[13] Derrida (1988), p.93. Cf. also Culler (1987), pp.92-93.

[14] Cf. Derrida (1976), ch. 2 "Linguistics and Grammatology"; also Norris (1982), pp.24-32.

[15] Saussure (1960), p.24.

[16] Norris (1982), p.28.

language which is more intimate, more immediate, and closer to the meaning behind words, by virtue of its close proximity to the speaker or producer of meaning.

Derrida's response to this seems at first absurd: he posits the primacy of the inscribed or written sign, and indicates that speech is actually a form of writing. But this is not done in such a way as to preserve the dichotomous opposition between writing and speech (i.e. by elevating writing over speech and maintaining that there is a qualitative difference between the two); rather, Derrida stretches the sense of "writing" to make it a designation which covers all linguistic practice *including* speech.[17] There are certain qualities or characteristics of writing which have conventionally been stressed in the attempt to attribute secondarity or derivation to the written word. They have to do with "absence and misunderstanding":[18] the written word, it is argued, can function—usually does function—in the absence of any putative guarantor of meaning (i.e. its author); it can be reproduced infinitely and read without any knowledge of its author at all; it is not bound to the context of its inscription, and so is open to widely varying interpretations which deviate from its "original" sense—in all this, writing is a slippery phenomenon. But Derrida, while not denying the legitimacy of these accusations, questions whether speech is any more capable than writing of transparently yielding up its meaning. The deconstructive view of all language, spoken or written, as a system of signifiers which relate differentially to each other, and never to any fixed Presence beyond the system, implies that the things which make writing seem a debased form of speech are actually just as applicable to speech itself. Speech is, in fact, infinitely reproduceable by word-of-mouth, and so it can function in the absence of both an original speaker and a context, and the speaker as the "author" of his or her own utterance has no absolute or final control over the utterance's meaning, even in dialogue with an interlocutor.[19] It is only according to the logocentric view of language as a window onto unmediated truth that the "writtenness" or textuality of speech is denied or ignored:

---

[17] Cf. Derrida: "Signature Event Context" in (1988), pp.7-21.
[18] Culler (1987), p.103.
[19] Cf. Mackey (1983), pp.259-61.

logocentrism....has always placed in parenthesis, *suspended*, and suppressed for essential reasons, all free reflection on the origin and
status of writing,[20]

but the metaphysical (if not the historical) priority of speech over
writing is profoundly disrupted when language itself comes to be
seen as "inscribed" or secondary, as always-already divorced from
any stable referent:

> The thesis of the *arbitrariness* of the sign....must forbid a radical dis-
> tinction between the linguistic and the graphic sign....If "writing"
> signifies inscription and especially the durable institution of a sign....
> [then] writing in general covers the entire field of linguistic signs.[21]

"Trace", Différance and Textuality

The dualistic positioning of speech and writing at hierarchical odds
with each other is thus countered by showing how the distinction
between them is essentially a false one. In general, it could be said
that if the "metaphysical exigency" is to perpetuate conceptual di-
chotomies, then the questioning of all binary oppositions is deconstruction's corresponding primary impulse, and Derrida comes up
with a range of terms and manoeuvres which serve this purpose.
Probably the best-known of these are "trace" and *différance*, neolo-
gisms (or, more accurately, neographisms) employed to deconstruct
the fundamental metaphysical opposition of presence/absence by
indicating the simultaneous condition of both. It is difficult to try to
explain exactly what either "trace" or *différance* is, as by definition
neither belongs fully to the realm of presence or "is"-ness. They are
examples of a number of terms which Derrida is constantly at pains
to point out are in fact "nonterms, nonconcepts, nonrealms, non-
principles—were they otherwise....they would become newly
masked ontological terms for full presence".[22] Where dualism posits
the existence of stable or present Concepts and sets each in opposition to its derived Other (cf. notes 8 and 9 to the previous chapter),

---

[20] Derrida (1976), p.43.

[21] *Ibid.* p.44.

[22] Lentricchia (1980), p.172.

"trace" and *différance* occupy the space between the two, with a foot, as it were, in each camp, and thus they have been described as "hinge" terms, existing

> beyond the binary pair, confounding binary logic by participating in both terms....They signal the "origin" of these metaphysical [i.e. dualistic] terms and reveal a kind of space of free play not captured in the web of binary categories.[23]

"Trace", for example, is what disrupts the possibility of anything being fully present or possessing a complete identity in and of itself. It suggests that identity is, paradoxically, fundamentally bound to what it is not. To take for example the male/female opposition: as a male, I do unarguably possess biological characteristics which culturally determine my gender. But that gender is not self-identical: equally essential to the attribution of my biological traits to maleness is the fact that they are *not* those traits which culturally determine femaleness. In other words, my maleness is determined by, as much as anything else, the *absence* of those characteristics which would mark me as female. Or, to put it still another way: if there were no such thing as female gender, then the concept of male gender would be meaningless. The "trace" of Other in defining Self is the necessary condition of selfhood, just as the "trace" of Self is essential to the recognition of the Other as such. Male and female, black and white, identity and difference, good and evil, life and death, being and nothingness—the "trace" of each term in its binary opposite means that rather than being radically opposed, each is in fact bound up in the other's identity at the deepest level:

> The structure of the sign is determined by the trace or track of that other which is forever absent....[trace] is the mark of the absence of a presence, an always already absent present, of the lack at the origin that is the condition of thought and experience.[24]

---

[23] Grosz (1989), pp.30-31.

[24] Gayatri Chakravorty Spivak, in the preface to Derrida (1976), p.xvii. Cf. also Raschke (1982):

> The meaning of *différence* [sic] emerges neither from the act of reference nor from the evaluation of semantic context, as is the case in linguistic functionalism. Instead it is an episodic figment, a violation of French orthography [p.8].

The trace, or the "present absence" of otherness in identity, is coexistent with the play of *différance*. *Différance* is a characteristically Derridean pun which picks up on the twin meaning (in French) of *différence* as the state of "difference" and the movement of "deferral" (the change from "e" to "a" in the final syllable of *différance* nicely illustrates Derrida's points both about writing and speech, and about absence and presence: the substituted vowel "a" can be read but not heard, and it only functions at all by virtue of its not being "e"—the force of the pun, therefore, lies very much in the *absence* of "e" and in the fact that the pun is recognised as a written mark, not as a spoken word[25]). *Différance* has a double sense. As "difference" it describes much the same condition of alterity-in-identity as "trace": Derrida in fact writes that "the (pure) trace is *différance*",[26] and so *différance* can be seen, like "trace", as

> that which threatens to interrupt the normal, unquestioned use of dichotomous terms, for it indicates the impossibility of the privileged term's self-representation.[27]

"Male", as we have seen, differs from "female", but this is as much a statement of common identity as it is of difference, since the part played by the radically other in defining each term is essential—"male" is only determined as such *because* it differs from "female", and this trace of perceived absence of female in male is essential to the condition of maleness. The difference between the two terms is critical to the identity of each, and there is a paradoxical sameness at work where each term is ontologically bound to its opposite:

> In the one case "to differ" signifies nonidentity; in the other case it signifies the order of the *same*....We provisionally give the name *différance* to this *sameness* which is not *identical*.[28]

But *différance* also carries the sense of "deferral", a kind of movement; so if self-present identity is a static condition, then the "sameness which is not identical" of *différance* can be understood as the flickering back and forth, or "play" (to use a key Derridean

---

[25] Cf. Derrida (1973), pp.131-37.
[26] Derrida (1976), p.62.
[27] Grosz (1989), p.31.
[28] Derrida (1973), p.129.

term) of differences within and between signifiers and concepts. Indeed, Saussure and Derrida both indicate that in the linguistic system there is nothing but this movement, and so *différance* describes the salient dynamic of language itself, involving

> syntheses and referrals which forbid at any moment, or in any sense, that a simple element be *present* in and of itself, referring only to itself....no element can function as a sign without referring to another element which is itself not simply present. This interweaving results in each "element"....being constituted on the basis of the trace within it of the other elements in the chain or system....*Différance* is the systematic play of differences, of the traces of differences, of the spacing by means of which elements are related to each other.[29]

The play of *différance*, then, shows that the stability of meaning in language is an illusory or incomplete notion. The meaning of a signifier can be provisionally located and fixed, but only at the expense of considering its "motion" or quality of endless deferral: this is the epistemological strategy favoured by logocentrism. Deconstruction, on the other hand, focuses on the differential nature of language, and yet seeks not so much to wipe logocentrism and Western metaphysics off the philosophical map (Derrida's own reliance on logocentric assumptions is freely admitted and will be discussed in the next chapter) as to indicate the kinds of repressions and biases on which the "metaphysics of presence" must rely to argue its case for the transparency of language and the existence of a unified conceptual order beyond it. So it is hardly surprising that deconstruction has been met in traditional philosophical, theological literary and biblical-critical circles with something less than rapturous acclaim: wherever a self-evident concept or truth is invoked, deconstructive criticism ushers in the "trace" of its negative, problematising Other, sets in motion the play of *différance* and thus generally vexes the order of Being:

> The ontology of presence is the ontology of beings and beingness. Everywhere, the dominance of beings is solicited by différance—in the sense that *sollicitare* means, in old Latin, to shake all over, to make the whole tremble. What is questioned by the thought of différance, therefore, is the determination of being in presence, or in be-

---

[29] Derrida (1981b), pp.26-27.

ingness....différance is even the subversion of every realm. This is
obviously what makes it threatening and necessarily dreaded by everything in us that desires a realm, the past or future presence of a
realm.[30]

In this respect deconstruction is profoundly anti-humanist, very
much a "poststructuralist" discourse as described in the previous
chapter. If all determinations of self-certain truth are disrupted by
showing that the "transcendental signified" (i.e. any stable guarantee
of meaning beyond language) is in fact "never absolutely present
outside a system of differences",[31] then we are bound to conclude
that the rational, self-aware "I" which constitutes the humanist subject, along with the experience of that subject, is in some way also a
part of that system. Appeals to experience or rational consciousness
as the source or still point of meaning cannot be justified if consciousness is itself determined by signifiers and traces of signifiers
across a range of discourses. And so "language" in its broadest
sense—denoting the complex interplay of signifier/trace and patterns of signification—creates and constitutes "textuality", which
Derrida sees as the fabric of all thought and experience. Deconstruction offers a perspective from which

> "textuality", the system of traces, becomes the most global term, en-
> compassing all that is and that which exceeds it,[32]

a statement expressed even more succinctly in Derrida's maxim *il
n'y a pas de hors-texte* [there is no "outside" to the text].[33]

---

[30] Derrida (1973), p.153.

[31] Derrida (1978), p.280.

[32] Alan Bass: "'Literature'/Literature" in Richard Macksey (ed.): *Velocities of
Change* (Johns Hopkins University Press, Baltimore 1974), p.349. Quoted in Atkins
(1983), p.23.

[33] Derrida (1976), p.158. *Il n'y a pas de hors-texte* is a difficult phrase to translate
adequately into English. The favoured formulation "there is nothing outside the
text" compromises the radical force of Derrida's claim in several ways. First, for
there to be "nothing outside the text" implies that the text *has* an outside; that there
is, in fact, an *hors-texte*, albeit one full of nothing. Textuality is thus conceptualised
in terms of inside/outside, and the play of differences between these binary poles is
foreclosed. More importantly, "there is nothing outside the text" hinges unavoidably (as does my own translation) on the copula *is*, the verb which above all others
invokes the realm of identity and the metaphysics of presence, and which Derrida
places *sous rature* (under erasure) in the first part of *Of Grammatology* (1976), to

It becomes clearly apparent here that deconstruction aspires to something beyond purely literary theory; nevertheless, Derrida's fascination with language, the fact that his own work consists largely of readings of (mostly philosophical) texts, and his emphasis throughout on such issues as writing and textuality, all combine to make literary criticism the discipline to which deconstructive practice is perhaps most obviously suited. Literary criticism of the more traditional kind (in which I include much biblical criticism) is also precisely the field in which deconstruction tends to meet its most fervent opposition. For those to whom the tradition of "great literature" embodies nothing less than the living tissue of civilised culture itself, and to whom criticism is, in Matthew Arnold's phrase, the endeavour "to know the best that is known and thought in the world",[34] the role of criticism as reverent handmaid-to-literature is unquestionable. For those who take a more formalist approach, to whom literary works exist in a state of "organic completeness",[35] unaffected by historical or cultural change, the ultimate aim of the critic is dispassionately to process and explain a text's rhetorical workings by means of strict objective analysis. In both cases, the meaning of any piece of literature is the truth which exists "behind", or is enclosed "within", the language of the text, and criticism seeks to give that meaning full presence by teasing it out of its formal structures and displaying it in unambiguous, transparent terms. Deconstruction, however, in positing language as a system of differences and shifting "traces" of meaning which can never be fully present, cuts meaning loose from the old mainstays of authorial intention and "the words on the page", displacing it somewhere, it would seem, in the direction of the reader. But the authority of subjectivity in determining meaning is also undermined by the fact that a reader can never be disinterested or fully self-aware; the "textuality" of conscious-

---

demonstrate its highly problematic nature. Derrida's French has more appropriate resonances: *il n'y a* avoids the use of the verb "to be", favouring an inflection of the less-directly-referential *avoir*, while *y* ("there" in the sense of place) suggests Presence figuratively, by means of a metaphor of spatial location. The determinate or referential sense of "there", in its negation by *ne....pas*, illustrates the paradox of displacement-in-identity which characterises *différance*.

[34] Matthew Arnold: "The Function of Criticism at the Present Time" in *Essays in Criticism: First Series* (Macmillan & Co. Ltd., New York 1900), p.16.

[35] Finley (1988), p.10.

ness or the subject means that no critic is a blank page devoid of
prejudices or presuppositions, and so while the thrust of any reading
is determined to a great extent by who and what the reader is, and
why she or he picked up the text in the first place, meaning does not
stop here. It does not stop anywhere; rather, it is a dynamic function
of the relationship *between* text and reader. This means that to read
is not to approach the still centre of a text's meaning, but effectively
to rewrite the text; meaning is not located or discovered like a seam
of gold in the earth, but produced, multiplied, always *re*created.

One important consequence of this insight is that essential or
qualitative differences between the activities of author, poet, editor
and critic become difficult to ground. Reading generates new texts
as it seeks to elucidate the primary one, and every "primary" text is
in some way a commentary on pre-existent texts or on the discourses which produce them, since interpretation and literary criticism "both inhabit a host-text of pre-existent language which itself
parasitically feeds on their host-like willingness to receive it".[36] In
short,

> [b]y replacing the rhetoric of consciousness with a rhetoric of textual-
> ity, deconstruction....obliterates the line between text and interpreta-
> tion.[37]

It is at this point that deconstructive critics really begin to provoke
their more traditionalist colleagues: the idea of the Critic-as-Artist is
no more popular now, in many circles, than it was when Oscar
Wilde first mischievously introduced the idea into modern critical
consciousness, as it involves the transgression of a kind of sacred
boundary, and makes literature vulnerable to being taught and written about by acolytes who deliberately and systematically mistake
themselves for priests. In addition to this, much deconstructive
criticism is open to the charge of wilful or even perverse obscurity:
certainly, Derrida's work is labyrinthine and tortuous to say the
least; his French is "full of wordplay, allusion and the tactic of an-
nouncing straightfacedly propositions he then overturns or sati-
rises",[38] and translation muddies the water even further. The stylistic

---

[36] Norris (1982), p.93.
[37] *Ibid.* p.96.
[38] Schneidau (1982), p.9.

excess (*jouissance* is the more positive term) of deconstructive "play" similarly characterises the work of Kristeva, Luce Irigaray, Hélène Cixous, Geoffrey Hartman, J. Hillis Miller, and a number of other Derrida-influenced thinkers who seek directly to illustrate the dynamic character of meaning and its ambiguous, undecideable quality in their own writing;[39] to their theoretical opponents, these critics are presumptuous and derisory in their attitude toward the texts they deal with.[40] And such objections cannot be passed off simply as aesthetic distaste or the shock of the new—although there is a certain amount of that about. Built on the deconstructive axiom that every signifier carries within itself the trace of its "other" is the more confrontational claim that every pattern of signifiers, every text, is in some way similarly divided against itself, and so deconstructing a text involves showing how its ruling rhetorical or logical structure relies on suppressed gaps or contradictions which undermine that structure—and to those who hold that literature means self-evidently what it says, or what its author wanted it to say, this amounts to a kind of harassment or interpretative violence which is suitable enough for, say, Dadaist poetry (which nobody understands anyway), but an outrage when brought to bear on the more well-bred texts of Shakespeare, Jane Austen or the bible. Even worse: if we are to accept Derrida's pronouncement that *il n'y a pas de hors-texte*, that textuality encompasses all structures of meaning, then all the metaphysical guarantees of truth (*ousia*, rational consciousness, God, whatever) are in fact textual processes, caught up in a web of ambiguity and contradiction. In other words, we have no access to

---

[39] Detailed discussion of the diverse styles and strategies of these writers could occupy a volume or two in itself. Cf. for example Julia Kristeva: *The Powers of Horror: An Essay on Abjection* trans. Leon S. Roudiez (Columbia University Press, New York 1982); Luce Irigaray: *This Sex Which Is Not One* trans. Catherine Porter and Carolyn Burke (Cornell University Press, Ithaca 1985); Hélène Cixous: "Sorties" and "The Laugh of the Medusa" in Marks and de Courtivron (1981), pp.90-98, 24564. These works are, in the main, discursive and deal with issues of gender, language and politics. For work of a more specifically literary-critical nature, cf. Geoffrey Hartman: *Criticism in the Wilderness* (Yale University Press, New Haven 1980); J. Hillis Miller: *Fiction and Repetition: Seven English Novels* (Harvard University Press, Cambridge 1982).

[40] Cf. Edwards and Woodard (1990), p.314.

any kind of "transcendental signified", and its effective absence "extends the domain and the play of signification infinitely".[41]

It is here, poised on the brink of interpretative chaos or anarchy, that I wish to leave deconstruction in its "pure" form (and it should shortly become apparent just how troublesome a term that is): the next chapter will take up the issue of whether or not deconstruction is in fact nihilistic, and whether or not deconstructive biblical criticism, with its denial of a transcendental signified, can be practised without a necessary denial of the conventional tenets of biblical faith—that is, whether or not a reader can be "religious" and deconstructive at the same time. For the remainder of this chapter, I wish to turn to an examination of deconstruction/Derridean thought in the light of feminist hermeneutics, and to assess the degree to which the latter might profit from a theoretical alliance with the former.

"Resexualised" Discourse: Derrida and the Female

A good deal has already been written on the implications of deconstruction for feminism. This has been due in part to the emphasis which Derrida, in a number of instances, places on issues of sexual difference and on the question of Woman—what she "is", where she stands, what she represents in the symbolic order of logocentrism. Derrida also, provocatively, uses terms such as "hymen" and "invagination" as metaphors to signal key strategies in his deconstructive practice. In the first case, Derrida's discussions of gender and sexual difference stem from the understanding that logocentrism, in its reliance on dualistic hierarchical thinking, has distinctively patriarchal overtones: Derrida's suspicion of fundamentals would keep him from stating—as I have—that sexist oppression is an *essential* or paradigmatic form of oppression in any society governed by binary-oppositional logic, but nevertheless his close equation of logocentrism with sexism is apparent in his coining of the term *phallogocentrism* to indicate "the complicity of Western metaphysics with a notion of male firstness".[42] Accordingly, the project

---

[41] Derrida (1978), p.280.
[42] Christie McDonald, translator's note in Derrida (1982a), p.69.

of deconstructing and providing alternatives to the "metaphysics of presence" is seen as a project which is in some sense marked "female":

> The concept of the concept, along with the entire system that attends it, belongs to a prescriptive order. It is that order that a problematics of difference, as sexual difference, should disrupt along the way.[43]

In the second case, Derrida's careful choice of such terms as "hymen" and "invagination" in his writing forms part of a strategy whereby the claims of philosophical/theoretical discourse to pure abstraction and sexual neutrality are disrupted. We have already seen that Western philosophy has tended to present itself as a disinterested, neutral discourse, carried out at the level of pure reason, while in fact its values of logic, rationality and dispassionate analysis have operated according to a "male" norm; it is this situation that Derrida refers to when he says that "according to a surreptitious operation that must be flushed out, one insures phallocentric mastery under the cover of neutralization".[44] His use of terms which denote, in their most commonly recognised senses, the most sexually-marked area of the female body indicates a reversal of this tendency, a deliberate emphasis on "resexualising" philosophy and theory.[45]

"Hymen", for example, indicates the moment at which two diametrically-opposed "beings" achieve a mutually-recognised fusion or identity, and in this respect it has a similar function to "trace" and *différance*. The dualism inherent in such concepts as inside/outside, or desire/satisfaction, ceases to operate as such where a consummation of both terms is achieved, and "hymen" represents this point of consummation—the two terms do not merge to form one unified, self-identical concept, but rather "it is the *difference between* the two terms that is no longer functional".[46] Each regards the other as its necessary condition for identity—and, paradoxically, the immediate consequence of this consummation (as of all consummations) is that the hymen itself as a present, tangible entity no longer exists. The genius of "hymen", then, is that it illustrates a critical move-

---

[43] Derrida (1982a), p.72.
[44] *Ibid.* p.72.
[45] *Ibid.* pp.74-75.
[46] Derrida (1981a), p.209 (my italics).

ment in Derrida's anti-dualistic project without coming to be seen itself as a stable fundamental or ground:

> the hymen, the confusion between the present and the nonpresent, along with all the indifferences it entails within the whole series of oppositions....produces the effect of a medium (a medium as element enveloping both terms at once; a medium located between the two terms). It is an operation that *both* sows confusion *between* opposites *and* stands *between* the opposites "at once"....The hymen "takes place" in the "inter", in the spacing between desire and fulfilment, between perpetration and its recollection. But this medium of the *entre* has nothing to do with a center.[47]

"Invagination" is more enigmatic, partly because Derrida's definition of it is less generously elucidated. In "Living On: Border Lines", the term weaves itself through a complex reading of two short stories by Maurice Blanchôt and Shelley's poem "The Triumph of Life", a reading in which the narratives of the French author are presented as reworkings or representations of Shelley's poem, and thus in which the boundaries between individual texts are seen as shifting and indeterminate. "Invagination" is described as

> the inward refolding of *la gaine* [sheath, girdle], the inverted reapplication of the outer edge to the inside of a form where the outside then opens a pocket. Such an invagination is possible from the first trace on,[48]

and it illustrates the way in which deconstruction questions the notion of a text's margin or edge. Any attempt to delineate a text's meaning or reiterability does so by setting a limit, a margin beyond which the interpreter cannot legitimately travel, and by relegating the text's inconsistencies and paradoxes out to that marginal space, away from the "central" meaning. "Invagination" describes the deconstructive manoeuvre of folding the edge back in toward the "centre", of showing that the text's marginal inconsistencies and paradoxes are as fundamental to meaning as its coherences. No reading is final or determinate, and so this deconstructive process is repeatable any number of times and in various ways: Derrida thus

---

[47] *Ibid.* p.212.
[48] Derrida (1979b), in Bloom *et al* p.97. Cf. also Leavey (1982), pp.55-56.

can speak of "double invagination", "crisscross double invagination", and so on.

The outline of these terms offered so far is necessarily simplistic. Neither term can satisfactorily be removed from its context: further discussion of "invagination" would necessitate closer examination of Derrida's reading of Blanchôt and Shelley, just as "hymen" is not completely to be understood outside the discussion of Mallarmé and Plato in which it appears. What should be apparent here is simply that Derrida's linguistic environment is a deliberately sexualised one, and one in which the feminist reader (or any reader seeking to venture beyond the limits of patriarchal discourse) might find landmarks which provide better orientation than those encountered in "phallogocentric" interpretation and philosophy.

But at this point it may be asked why Derrida, in his disavowal of philosophical neutrality, and in the space for greater subjectivity which deconstruction opens up, should choose as a male writer to render his discursive practice "female". The answer to this has been briefly hinted at above, where I indicated that deconstruction's challenge to Western metaphysics and logocentrism, given that logocentrism and patriarchy are inseparably meshed, must therefore also be anti-patriarchal—"feminist" in the broadest sense of the word, "female" by a further (and riskier) metaphorical leap. In the discussion of Nietzsche's *The Gay Science* offered in *Spurs*, Derrida locates in the German philosopher's notorious denunciations of Woman a kind of unwitting endorsement of feminism and the Female as providing an alternative "truth" to the dualism and logical closure of metaphysics. Traditionally situated on the disreputable side of the truth/falsehood opposition, woman has long been seen— and is enthusiastically endorsed by Nietzsche—as emblematic of guile and deceit. But "truth" in the Western tradition is ideally singular and fixed, an unquestionable unity of pure meaning: resisting the impulse to grope after this apparition is, of course, the Derridean theoretical imperative, and so Derrida is able to invert the patriarchal philosophical hierarchy by portraying Woman as non(metaphysical)Truth in a positive light, not as Nietzsche's liar/deceiver but as "a dissimulatress, an artist, a dionysiac".[49] Woman comes to

---

[49] Derrida (1979a), p.97.

represent the exploding of the myth of stable signification, as "she engulfs and distorts all vestige of essentiality, of identity, of property".[50] But this demythologising involves more than just the simple inversion of binary values, and Derrida accordingly goes on to deconstruct the opposition he has created between Woman-as-dissembled-Truth and metaphysical/phallogocentric Truth by means of a paradox which recalls that of the Cretan liar—the "truth" or essence of Woman lies in the problematising of truth or essences which constitutes her fundamental dynamic; that is, she is centred around a non-centre:

> There is no such thing as the truth of a woman, but it is because of that abyssal divergence of the truth, because that untruth is "truth".[51]

The result of this paradox is a kind of simultaneous affirming and erasing of the essential Female, and this constitutes a movement or dynamic similar to that which operates between the essentialism of radical feminism and the relativism of poststructuralist feminism, the dynamic of "identity politics" discussed in the previous chapter. Derrida is not explicit on this point in *Spurs*, but he does indicate elsewhere that both the affirmation of and resistance to the "truth" of what it means to be a woman are equally important in feminist practice, just as they are in deconstructive theory. Of the idea of a "woman's place", for example, he has said that

> I would be wary of such a description. Do you not fear that having once become committed to the path of this topography, we would inevitably find ourselves back "at home" or "in the kitchen" [the pun at work here in "at home" is significant: Derrida also uses *chez soi* to denote selfhood or self-identity]?....Why must there be a place for women? And why only one, a single, completely essential place?....It is without doubt risky to say that there is no place for woman, but this idea is not antifeminist, far from it; true, it is not feminist either. But it appears to me to be faithful in its way both to a certain assertion of women and to what is most affirmative and "dancing"....in the displacement of women.[52]

---

[50] *Ibid.* p.51.
[51] *Ibid.* p.51.
[52] Derrida (1982a), p.68.

In Derridean theory, then, woman is both located and displaced: located in that she represents a politically identifiable alternative to the logocentric order of patriarchy, displaced in that this alternative cannot be reduced to a female essence, *topos* or mode of Being— once again, Derrida invokes the play of *différance*, this time between the opposite poles of "a certain assertion" of the Female and her elusive, undecideable character.

Up until this point I have confined my discussion of deconstruction to its Derridean formulation, in fact it may be noticed that over the last page or so the focus has explicitly shifted from "deconstruction" to "Derridean theory". The distinction is important because deconstructive criticism could only be of limited use to feminist hermeneutics if it were to be understood as what Jacques Derrida alone had to say about language and reality. Derrida's "sexualising" terminologies, his interest in sexual difference and the importance he gives to the place (or displacement) of Woman in logocentric discourse all contribute to making his work relevant to feminist theory of all kinds, but this is not to say that the relationship between Derrida and feminism is unambivalent or uniformly comfortable. For a start, "Woman" could be said these days to be a rather overused metaphor: employed as she has been throughout literature and philosophy to represent life, death, truth, falsity, earth, heaven, creative inspiration, and so on; to see Woman now held up by a male French philosopher for close scrutiny as an emblem of textuality raises suspicions which subsequent talk of hymens, invaginations, desire and consummation does little to allay.[53] Furthermore— and perhaps more importantly—to assert that all good feminists must be deconstructionists, by which is meant card-carrying Derrideans, is to subordinate feminism to somebody else's pre-established agenda and deprive it of a large measure of autonomy, implying that feminists had been rather ineffectual and dithering in the wilderness

---

[53] Cf. Christie McDonald in *ibid.* p.71. Derrida's response to this point is that

"hymen" and "invagination", at least in the context into which these words have been swept, no longer simply designate figures for the feminine body. They no longer do so, that is, assuming that one knows for certain what a feminine or masculine body is, and assuming that anatomy is in this instance the final recourse [p.75].

until *Of Grammatology* arrived to disseminate systematic philosophical rigour among them.

The irony, then, of Derrida coming to be seen as the father of modern feminist criticism must be sidestepped at all costs, and this can best be effected by considering his work as prototypical rather than archetypal, as one form of deconstruction among many, illustrative of but not necessarily fundamental to various kinds of deconstructive practice. And indeed this must be the case: a critical programme like deconstruction which involves such scepticism regarding authorship, and which works from such an anti-hierarchical imperative, can hardly range itself into more or less "authoritative" formulations, and it is as well therefore to resist the temptation to evaluate any piece of deconstructive criticism according to whether or not we feel Derrida, de Man, Kristeva, Irigaray or anybody else would give or have given it official sanction.[54] Even terminology or jargon, that mainstay of systematic discourses, holds less sway within deconstruction than the foregoing terminologically-slanted analysis of Derrida might suggest; the "conceptual master-word"[55] is actually a dispensable or changeable entity throughout Derrida's work, provisionally defined and redefined according to context, and sometimes abandoned altogether—even with the name "deconstruction" itself Derrida has expressed a bemused dissatisfaction:

> the word "deconstruction" has always bothered me....this word which I had written only once or twice (I don't even remember where exactly) all of a sudden jumped out of the text and was seized by others who have since determined its fate.[56]

The point is not that deconstruction is some kind of radical anti-theory, an intellectual abyss without a name, a structure, a lexicon or even an authorial signature; but rather that all of these notions are provisional, and none provides a fixed ground or legitimising para-

---

[54] Cf. Culler (1987), p.227:

> Since deconstructive criticism is not the application of philosophical lessons to literary studies but an exploration of textual logic in texts called literary, its possibilities vary, and commentators are irresistably tempted to draw lines to separate orthodox deconstructive criticism from its distortions or illicit imitations and derivations.

[55] Spivak, in Derrida (1976), p.lxxi.
[56] Derrida (1985), pp.85-86.

digm for deconstructive criticism. This lack at the centre, concomitant with an undermining of all centres or metaphysical anchors, should ultimately lead us from a theoretical preoccupation with what deconstruction *is* to the more practical consideration of what it *does*. It is more useful to think of deconstruction (like *différance*, trace, invagination and so on) as a dynamic than as a conventional, stable "philosophical" concept, and thus understood, deconstruction provides a set of critical strategies or movements which are highly appropriate to what might be called a "hermeneutics of displacement"—the kind of hermeneutics best suited to feminist criticism.

Deconstruction, Feminism and Power

Perhaps the most significant thing, in the light of feminist hermeneutics, that deconstruction does is that it accommodates—indeed necessitates—a conception of the world as textually constructed. Derrida's insistence that *il n'y a pas de hors-texte* appears at first glance to court nihilism (there is *nothing* outside the text), or at least to indicate a bad case of philosophical megalomania, but to stop there is to read him only at face value. Literary critics who denounce Derrida as a terroristic Continental cynic often appear to think that he is trying to present reality as nothing but a mocking tissue of words; in fact, it is more accurate to paraphrase him as saying that reality is perceivable only through discourses or "processes of signification".[57] Nothing is known or experienced, in other words, that is inseparable from some kind of language or sign-system. The extension of textuality to include not just words on pages but all meaning and experience perhaps takes some getting used to, for those of us schooled (as we all are) in a metaphysical philosophical tradition, but its implications for feminist theory and critical practice are, I believe, largely positive. For a start, the notion of reality as textually or discursively constructed provides a good base from which to begin to dismantle patriarchal determinations of female

---

[57] Cf. Fulkerson (1991), p.55. Fulkerson's discussion deals broadly with poststructuralism and "discourse theory", but much of her argument (like a great deal of discussion concerning poststructuralism) could as well refer specifically to deconstruction.

nature. That women are "essentially" mothers, wives, irrational, unable to drive cars, dissembling, promiscuous, in love with their fathers, and so on is often asserted in the name of common sense or "the way things are"; these statements never appear, however, outside an identifiably *constructed* set of ideological presuppositions—a text, in one broad sense of the word. And texts which rely on putatively stable fundamentals (e.g. the passivity of women) can be challenged and reworked deconstructively to show that these univocal Truths are in fact fragmented, held in place only by marginalising the significance of deviations from the set norm (e.g. an independent, assertive woman is seen as somehow anomalous or unnatural), and really wield power "without any justification outside of the axioms operative in the [patriarchal] culture".[58]

The most immediate value, then, in a theory of radical textuality is that it undermines all claims of patriarchal ideology to its own self-evident, natural authority. It also steers feminist theory and criticism away from the essentialising impulse of cultural or radical feminism criticised in the previous chapter: with the significance of the female body or women's experience made relative and the concept of Woman seen as a provisional, historically-constructed notion—another "text"—feminism loses its fixed ideological centre, and thus women on the margins inevitably created by any notion of a centre (married women, uneducated women, working class women), whose access to the cultural feminist Logos has been denied, are resituated and their experience can be accorded full validity. Furthermore, a non-fundamental or textualised understanding of feminism enables feminist criticism to be reread/rewritten by other groups whose interpretative focus lies outside of gender issues but whose experience of oppressive hierarchical domination is just as urgently in need of attention as that of women. If we take into account the textuality of feminist theology, for example, we can read it both as culture-specific *and* as part of a wider range of liberation theologies, so that the feminist theological call for an end to the religious legitimation of patriarchal oppression can provide insights and strategies which serve the needs not just of women alone but of all oppressed groups.

---

[58] Jobling (1990), p.83.

If textuality encompasses not just black marks on white pages, but also the subjectivity of the person who deciphers them, then reading is a process of interaction whereby the text interrogates or "reads" the reader just as closely as the reader reads the text. That is to say, reading calls attention to who and what the reader is, and it does not serve exclusively to locate stable meaning in texts any more than writing serves to produce it: in both cases, meaning reflects to a great extent the shifting, discursive constitution of the reading/writing subject. The signified always has a historical moment and a social function, and so deconstructive criticism, which operates according to this understanding, thus "breaches the bounds of the 'literary' altogether, in a 'political' direction",[59] since it conceives of meaning not as neutral but always as biased, or as representing the interests of a particular group or individual. The deconstructive critic sees that

> [m]eaning is not created and does not exist for meaning's sake, but exists to create and shape a world which benefits one class, race or gender over another,[60]

and in reintroducing politics into the making of meaning, or rather in acknowledging that politics has been there from the beginning, deconstruction again constitutes a useful interpretative approach for feminist criticism, where the necessity of the political is explicitly avowed, and where the political/ideological interests behind patriarchy's "objective" discourses provide an important focus for analysis. In the first chapter of this book, I argued that the "rhetorical criticism" of Phyllis Trible was of limited value precisely because it denied the function of history, sociology or ideology in the texts it dealt with, and claimed instead to articulate the meaning of "literature in terms of itself": Trible employed what she called "proper analysis of form" to extract a "proper" reading of Genesis 2:4b-3:24 which was supposedly as concrete, self-evident and politically disinterested as a rabbit pulled from a hat, and yet which was at the same time supposed to reflect and further the political interests of a historically-specific group. This naive rupture between means and ends is avoided by deconstruction, which eschews no-

---

[59] *Ibid.* p.96.
[60] Craig and Kristjansson (1990), p.123.

tions of the-text-itself in favour of a more complex approach. Rhetoric is, after all, a means of persuasion, and accordingly deconstruction is not just a neutral divining-rod for the locating of some ideal or "proper" signified, but

> an ultimately *political* practice, an attempt to dismantle the logic by which a particular system of thought, and behind that a whole system of political structures and social institutions, maintains its force. [Derrida] is not seeking, absurdly, to deny the existence of relatively determinate truths, meanings, identities, intentions, historical continuities; he is seeking rather to see such things as the effects of a wider and deeper history—of language, of the unconscious, of social institutions and practices.[61]

The deconstructive tactic of questioning binary oppositions, for example, is particularly relevant to cases where the always (but not always admittedly) political issue of legitimacy/illegitimacy in interpretation surfaces. Where a conservative Protestant Christian reading of Gen. 2:4b-3:24 may assert itself as valid and authoritative over against a Marxist or feminist reading on the grounds of what the text undisputedly "says" (and a Marxist or feminist reading may ill-advisedly respond likewise), deconstruction redirects the argument toward a questioning of the binary distinction between the normal and the deviant both in the text's discursive framework and in its readings. The deconstructive reader does not look for some unambiguous kernel of authorising significance in the text, but instead focuses on its logical gaps and inconsistencies, considering the forces which suppress these inconsistencies as supposedly insignificant or marginal to the text's dominant rhetorical structure, and thus in a parallel fashion being led to interpret the "text" of his or her culture in a similar manner,

> to consider what are the processes of legitimation, validation or authorization that produce differences among readings and enable one reading to expose another as a misreading.[62]

"Meaning" is not thereby sent spiralling off into oblivion, nor is it now possible to read the Garden of Eden story confidently as being

---

[61] Eagleton (1986), p.148.
[62] Culler (1987), p.179.

about nostrils or figs—which is not, all the same, to dismiss out of hand the possibility that the cultural circumstances may one day arise which do permit such a reading. Rather, meaning becomes situated in the contentious realm of conflicting discourses or reading communities, and the *authority* of any reading of any text becomes no more than a function of the persuasive ideological force with which it is held in place by the readers who produce it. For feminist readers, this means that their critical practice can no longer be summarily dismissed as a violation of authorial intention or common sense, or in any other way consigned to the "negative" pole of the orthodox/ heterodox dichotomy—nor, for that matter, can one kind of feminist reading claim absolute legitimacy at the expense of another: deconstruction seeks not to fix new guidelines or parameters for interpretation, but to focus attention on the political or discursive forces at work both within the text, and in the relationship between text and reader. The significance of a group of texts such as the bible, then, is freed from the constraints of patriarchal religious dogma, and a deconstructive feminist hermeneutics has the critical advantage of keeping biblical meaning open to challenge and negotiation within and between cultures, working on the understanding that

> what is crucial to the function of texts is not some fictive "real meaning", but the discursivity of "communities" in which women read them.[63]

Another important advantage which deconstruction holds for feminist hermeneutics is that it renders dualistic thinking extremely problematic. We have already seen that patriarchal literature and criticism rely heavily on philosophical dualism, often labelling readings of texts as valid or invalid on the strength of the objective/ subjective argument: if a text has one central meaning, then that

---

[63] Fulkerson (1991), p.59. The concept of "interpretive communities" is a useful one for feminist criticism, and has been most fully developed (although not in a feminist context) in the work of the North American reader-response critic Stanley Fish. Cf. his collection of essays and lectures *Is There a Text In This Class? The Authority of Interpretive Communities* (Harvard University Press, Cambridge Mass. 1980). Cf. also Lentricchia (1980), pp.145-48; Eagleton (1986), pp.84-88; Ian McLean: "Reading and Interpretation" in Jefferson and Robey (1986), pp.140-43; Burnett (1990), especially pp.54-63.

meaning can be located either by appeals to rational sense, or (in the case of difficult texts) by the use of critical techniques which are themselves disinterested and scientifically functional; objective means to objective ends. Conflicting hermeneutical modes are regarded suspiciously as being contaminated with a high degree of subjectivity; psychoanalysis and feminism, for example, are relegated to the fringes of critical respectability (or beyond) because they represent the messy ideological pleadings of "special interest" groups and have little to do with the neat, clinical discipline of dissecting and analysing literature. The objective/subjective dichotomy (with the male positioned squarely in the former camp) is crucial to patriarchal interpretation, as it serves both to validate *one* reading of any text (i.e. the objectively-perceived one), and to mask the political imperative at work behind such a judgement:

> if patriarchy can continue the fiction of the singularity of meaning, it can also continue the fiction that patriarchal ideology is not *a* world view, in fact, not an ideology at all, but simply the way things really are.[64]

Deconstruction, on the other hand, offers a perspective from which text, critic and criticism alike, far from being objective or neutral, are all seen as inscribed with presuppositions and traces of presuppositions which, like the culture that inscribes them, are neither stable nor able to be neatly sectioned-off from the business of interpretation. Any feminist criticism which likewise openly fuses the literary and the political can thus be seen not as "an attempt to force the text into a predetermined mold",[65] but simply as the explicit practice of what patriarchal criticism really does under cover of objectivity: deconstruction validates, indeed demands, a healthy measure of self-consciousness in critical debate, and this is because it disrupts the objective/subjective opposition along whose lines political concerns have traditionally been deemed irrelevant to interpretation.

Every text has some kind of organising system, some kind of dominant logical order to which we refer when we speak of what the text is "about". But this structure, rather like the Ego in Freudian psychoanalysis, is dependent for its stability on the repression of

---

[64] Craig and Kristjansson (1990), p.122.
[65] Culler (1987), p.55.

those elements which contradict or threaten to undermine it: meaning is never unitary, and systems of meaning never exist in texts without such contradictory elements, but the text's ruling rhetorical structure is usually designed to marginalise these elements or keep them at the level of the text's "unconscious". Deconstruction sees these gaps and paradoxes as essential to any meaning, just as it sees any self-identical concept as in fact radically dependent on its Other, and part of the deconstructive challenge to logocentric reading is the way in which it directs its critical practice at the text's logical limits, showing that these limits are marginal in the same way that the text's "central" meaning is central—i.e. as the result of an internal power-structure of discursive coercion and repression, *not* as a given or transcendent truth. Gayatri Spivak refers to "the moment in the text that seems to transgress its own system of values" as the starting-point for deconstructive criticism, and shows how deconstruction counters the logocentric impulse to pin meaning down:

> The desire for unity and order compels the author and the reader to balance the equation that is the text's system. The deconstructive reader exposes the grammatological structure of the text [i.e. the text's "writtenness"], that its "origin" and its "end" are given over to language in general....by locating the moment in the text which harbours the unbalancing of the equation, the sleight of hand at the limit of a text *which cannot be dismissed simply as a contradiction*.[66]

In other words, the sociopolitical structure within which interpretations of texts are accepted or dismissed as valid/invalid is reflected (or better, generated) in the structures of texts themselves: in both cases, the indeterminacy of linguistic practice ultimately necessitates the exercise of power or persuasion in asserting the central and repressing the marginal, and the veiling of this strategy under cover of unquestionable reason is the most powerful ruse of logocentrism and patriarchy alike. Deconstruction first reverses the hierarchy, by presenting the margin as the necessary condition of the centre (the centre of the centre), and then takes the further step of similarly dismantling the "winning" or newly-dominant term's conceptual autonomy, dissolving the central/marginal opposition altogether.[67]

---

[66] Spivak, in Derrida (1976), p.xlix (my italics).
[67] Cf. *ibid*. pp.lxxvi-vii.

For feminist criticism, this means that no text is *essentially* sexist, and for feminist biblical criticism, it means that those texts
whose meanings are held to be fixed and prescriptive of the God-
given natural order of things—texts in which the interests of women
are often ignored or attacked—carry within themselves the seeds of
interpretation which in fact takes account of political struggle and
cultural change. Authorial intention, for example, becomes properly
situated within its discursive context: what the author (the Yahwist,
the Elohist, Isaiah, Matthew, Paul) "meant" can be seen as

> not something prior to the text that determines its meaning, but [as] an
> important organizing structure identified in readings that distinguish
> an explicit line of argumentation from its subversive other.[68]

This approach, of course, has both its advantages and its dangers.
Deconstructive criticism tends sooner or later to concern itself with
questions of power; the deconstructive critic is eventually made
aware that "power tends to totalize itself in a 'center', and to prevent
the accumulation of power elsewhere than the center".[69] Derrida is
clear on this point:

> [t]he function of this center [is] not only to orient, balance and organ-
> ize the structure....but above all to make sure that the organizing
> principle of the structure would limit what we might call the *play* of
> the structure.[70]

What deconstruction ultimately deconstructs, however, is "the accumulation of power in discourse",[71] targeting the strategies by
which the margin is marginalised and the centre centralised, and
thus opening up new possibilities for interpretation both within the
text and within the larger "texts" of academic/religious institutionalised discourse where each interpretation is required to plead its case.
With attention focused on the marginal, and the power of the centre
to retain its unquestionable centrality undermined, the inevitability
or slippage of "play" in interpretation is recognised, and hard and
fast rules for discursive analysis come to be seen as operative only

---

[68] Culler (1987), p.218.
[69] Jobling (1990), p.99.
[70] Derrida (1978), p.278.
[71] Jobling (1990), p.102.

within specific discursive contexts. Hermeneutical possibilities, therefore, are not foreclosed, and this has the advantage for feminist criticism of allowing room for experimentation: along with the need for the recognition of women's space in patriarchal culture goes the attendant need for the recognition of non-patriarchal space in interpretation where the limits of phallogocentrism are explored and transgressed. In biblical criticism this allows for a mode of exegesis which can be appropriated by oppressed groups of various kinds, as the equation of logocentrism with patriarchy here need not imply that anti-logocentrism equals only feminism; indeed

> the list of those who can claim deconstruction as their ally is endless....anything that has been cast to the underside of the good/bad configuration can now assert its rights.[72]

But asserting your rights and enabling increased plurality in "legitimate" interpretation is no more innocent an enterprise than closing off interpretation and oppressing the marginalised; it would be naive to imagine that deconstructing "the accumulation of power in discourse" was an undertaking which could be carried out without a certain amount of power accumulating around the deconstructor. Critics of Derrida have not been slow to realise this, and it has been asserted that deconstruction ceremoniously ushers metaphysics out the front door while smuggling it in again at the back—with Meaning identified as unarguably and without a doubt flowing through the text's "structure" of traces and deferrals, deconstruction can now be seen as the archetypal criticism, and the deconstructive critic apotheosised as the Platonic model of the ideal reader. Derrida to some extent deflates the argument by admitting that deconstruction does indeed partake of the same language of reference and logic as logocentrism; the complicity of deconstruction with metaphysics cannot be ignored and will shortly be examined in detail. But similarly, with regard to the question of power, it could be argued that deconstruction involves, for all its suave evasions, a process of domination/submission, with the reader acting on "a desire to reappropriate the text actively through mastery, to show the text 'what it does not know'".[73] A deconstructive awareness of the discursive

---

[72] Joy (1990), p.11.
[73] Spivak, in Derrida (1976), p.lxxvii.

power-play at work in reading, writing and interpretation (which involves the awareness that these three activities are in a radical sense
one and the same) carries with it its own potential for the kind of
critical guerilla tactics which are only interested in dispersing the
power of legitimate meaning out from the centre to the margin because the margin happens to be where the deconstructive reader
situates him/herself. Deconstruction "politicises" reader and text by
seeing both as related species of a larger family of "texts", but this
does not always result in a balanced or harmonious relationship:

> the politicized reader can still gain the upper hand over the text in the
> power game that reading has now become, can turn (as in Aikido) the
> text's force against itself, can rough it up, so to speak, until it says
> what is ideologically required by the interpreter's community. For
> whatever the text's *apparent* politics, it can always be made over....
> into the mouthpiece for the reader's own politics.[74]

This is a fair comment, but perhaps one made with more wit than
insight: it does seem (as I hope to demonstrate) that the more polar-
ised a text's apparent political position is, the more vulnerable the
text becomes to subversion by the ideological "other" lurking below
its rhetorical surface—but to imply that a text can signify in some
sense or another *anything* the reader wants it to is to err on the side
of transcendent *jouissance* and forget that textual indeterminacy is—
like all linguistic phenomena—only relative. Still, in a broader cultural sense it is true that "the domain and play of signification" are
infinitely extended by deconstruction: meaning, while it can never
just go anywhere it likes, never stops moving, and can never be
closed off. And the knowledge of this, as we have seen, confers a
certain power—but keeping power likewise on the move within the
larger cultural "texts" of society should be the ruling imperative of
feminist hermeneutics, as of any hermeneutics of resistance, and this
should be reflected in the way we read.

There seems to be no way around the paradoxical desire of deconstruction both to "reappropriate the text through mastery" and to
displace or decentre interpretative mastery as soon as it is achieved,
but then it should be clear by now that deconstruction rarely if ever
serves to point the way out of a logical impasse. I believe that the

---

[74] Felperin (1985), p.3233.

root of the problem lies in the question of what kind of "mastery" the interpreter is exercising—Gayatri Spivak to some extent defuses the deconstructive will-to-power by pointing out that if a text possesses no intrinsic authority of its own, if a critic has no control over the text's meaning or that of her own interpretation, and if the primacy of meaning itself is thrown into doubt, then "the possession of [the deconstructive] formula does not amount to much"[75] in the political/ hierarchical scheme of things. Spivak goes on to indicate more positively that if the deconstructive critic is inevitably subject to her own hermeneutical practice, if "her own text is necessarily self-deconstructed, always already a palimpsest", then what results is not mastery *over* the text, from a point somehow above the abyss of textuality and infinite deferral, but a certain freedom within it:

> [b]y inaugurating the open-ended indefiniteness of textuality....
> [deconstruction] shows us the lure of the abyss as freedom. The fall
> into the abyss of deconstruction inspires us with as much pleasure as
> fear. We are intoxicated with the prospect of never hitting bottom.[76]

Some would no doubt say that intoxication is only too evident in the work of some of Derrida's more mandarin disciples, but this does not mean that all deconstructive criticism must abandon all the constraints of rational thought and language at once or in every instance. David Jobling, in his study of deconstruction and liberation theologies, follows a number of commentators in likening deconstructive "play" to the positive subversion of carnival, an iconoclastic expression of political freedom which inverts, mimics, ironises and generally exploits to the full incoherences within the structures of social order or oppression, while still recognisably inhabiting those structures.[77] To deconstruct a text is to recognise from the outset that you enter and work within the text partly on its own terms; that is to say, you are partly bound by the order you subvert, particu-

---

[75] Spivak, in Derrida (1976), p.lxxvii.

[76] *Ibid*. p.lxxvii.

[77] Cf. Jobling (1990), pp.106-9. Cf. also Alfredo Fierro: *The Militant Gospel: An Analysis of Contemporary Political Theologies* (SCM Press, London 1977); Dominick LaCapra: *Rethinking Intellectual History: Texts, Contexts, Language* (Cornell University Press, Ithaca, N.Y. 1983); Mark C. Taylor: *Erring: A Postmodern A/Theology* (University of Chicago Press, Chicago 1984), pp.158-68.

larly as far as the logocentric project of establishing and fixing meaning is concerned:

> as she deconstructs, all protestations to the contrary, the critic necessarily assumes that she at least, and for the time being, means what she says. Even the declaration of her vulnerability must come, after all, in the controlling language of demonstration and reference.[78]

In the same way, the "play" of carnival is not an attempt by revolutionaries completely to demolish the social order and set themselves up as *nouveaux dictateurs*, but rather the reversal and confusion within the system of dominant/subordinate roles where "individual identities dissolve and social oppositions break down".[79] Such a procedure recognises—springs directly from—political injustice and struggle, and yet it undermines hierarchical power without appropriating that power for itself. Translated into deconstructive-critical terms, a "carnivalesque" hermeneutics allows the interpreter freedom to acknowledge, celebrate, and exploit indeterminacy in meaning, deploying a diffuse and experimental style which flickers elusively back and forth across a number of logocentrism's sacred boundaries—between the serious and the comic, the academic and the poetic, the self-evident and the ambiguous, and so on—but which is both grounded in the (seriously) political and itself open to further deconstruction. From the perspective of logocentrism, as from that of any autocratic social class, the carnivalesque inhabits a world governed by "the thinking of the utterly other":

> we might think of this "other" world as one where power does not accumulate but flows—and deconstruction as play is precisely a preenactment of such a world.[80]

In summary: I hope to have established by this stage that any hermeneutics of resistance, in that it relies on the existence of a social order to resist, must be in a broad sense deconstructive, since deconstruction ultimately brings us back again and again to the political, to the consideration of how power is claimed, denied, suppressed and directed within and between texts. But this inevitably

---

[78] Spivak, in Derrida (1976), p.lxxvii.
[79] Taylor (1984), p.15 (cf. note 77 above), quoted in Jobling (1990), p.107.
[80] Jobling (1990), p.106.

brings with it the need for the critic to accommodate herself to un-decideability and deferral, to realise that one's own political position is provisionally constructed, occupying a point in history which has no necessary correlative in the realm of the Immutable. In the prac-tice of feminist deconstruction, then, the interpreter claims the power to mean, or signify, while simultaneously relinquishing that power in the knowledge that the desired attribution of centrality or authority to her "egalitarian" discourse will serve only to marginal-ise somebody else's; she speaks explicitly for women in the knowl-edge that Woman, as a *determinate* concept, belongs to the pre-scriptive order of Being ruled by phallogocentrism and must itself be deconstructed; as a feminist she exposes and deconstructs patri-archal dualism in the knowledge that feminism too relies on its Other for existence and has no self-identical essence of its own. Not that relativism should become the order of the day; pure undecide-ability

> can compromise the political chances of feminism and serve as an al-ibi for deserting organized, patient, laborious "feminist" struggles when brought into contact with all the forms of resistance that a dance movement cannot dispel, even though the dance is not synonymous with either powerlessness or fragility....you can surely see the kind of impossible and necessary compromise that I am alluding to: an inces-sant, daily negotiation—individual or not—sometimes microscopic, sometimes punctuated by a poker-like gamble; always deprived of in-surance, whether it be in private life or within institutions.[81]

This "incessant, daily negotiation" (which recalls, perhaps, the maxim that the price of freedom is eternal vigilance) should under-pin an approach to hermeneutics which addresses the criteria for feminist criticism outlined above: a criticism which is not commit-ted to excessive rationalising, which can work with contradictions without necessarily trying to resolve them, which celebrates differ-ence, leaving interpretation open to contention, creativity and plural-ism, not confining feminism to fixed categories but allowing the formation of "temporary alliances and coalitions"[82] relative to spe-cific political intention and context.

---

[81] Derrida (1982a), p.69.
[82] Bach (1990), p.8.

Neutrality, Politics and the Politics of Neutrality

Up to this point I have dealt principally with the case *for* decon-struction, doubtless at the expense of giving fair consideration to the arguments against. It is time to redress the balance, and this is an appropriate point at which to begin, since we have arrived once again at the issue of politics in interpretation. If the return to the political which deconstruction effects is advantageous to feminist hermeneutics, as to any "liberation" hermeneutics, it should be kept in mind that this tendency is precisely what gives ammunition to some of deconstruction's most vocal opponents, particularly in bib-lical criticism. The argument that the bible is invulnerable to politi-cal inquiry is sometimes made on explicitly religious grounds—i.e. that it constitutes a collection of sacred texts whose meaning is fixed by Divine decree—and sometimes according to the assumptions of a particular style of literary criticism which holds that reading is a neutral, disinterested activity, and that ideological considerations serve only to disturb the (ideally) tranquil waters of interpretation. Of the former objection to politics in interpretation more will be said in the following chapter. An interesting example of the latter objec-tion, however, can usefully be considered here; an example provided by the General Introduction to no less authoritative a work than Robert Alter and Frank Kermode's *Literary Guide to the Bible* (1987). The *Guide* offers an ambitious book-by-book discussion of the literary qualities of both Old and New Testaments, an endeavour shared among twenty-six contributors, and the editors' defence of their choice of contributors is illuminating. They write:

> We have not imposed uniformity of method on our contributors, but all involved in this project share a broad consensus of purpose as lit-erary critics....the critic [is] someone who helps make possible fuller readings of the text, with a particular emphasis on the complex inte-gration of diverse means of communication encountered in most works of literature....Certain varieties of contemporary criticism are not represented here because we think they are not really concerned with reading in the sense we have proposed....Given our aim to pro-vide illumination, we have not included critics who use the text as a springboard for cultural or metaphysical ruminations, nor those like

the Deconstructionists and some feminist critics who seek to demonstrate that the text is necessarily divided against itself. The general validity of such approaches is not at issue here, only their inapplicability to our project as we have defined it.[83]

This falls somewhere short of being a tirade against "political" criticism, but here and elsewhere in the editors' Introduction can be found assumptions which relegate politics, or ideology, not just to the margins of their own programme but to those of critical orthodoxy altogether. Alter and Kermode are provisionally willing to accept the "general validity" of the modes of criticism they sideline, but state that deconstruction, some varieties of feminism, and "cultural or metaphysical ruminations" have little to do with reading as they define it. And to read, we are told, is "to parse the language of literature", an operation which involves close and expert attention to such properties as "syntax, grammar....genre, convention, technique, contexts of allusion, style, structure, thematic organization" and so on.[84] There is no doubt that reading which focuses on these kinds of literary characteristics is important, even essential, for a well-rounded understanding of biblical texts (it is also integral to the approach to literature adopted by many structuralists, deconstructionists, feminists, Marxists, etc.). But the kind of *privilege* which Alter and Kermode claim for "their" style of reading is perhaps not so self-evident. The editors make this privilege-claim when they speak of recent shifts in biblical criticism; the emergence of biblical studies out from under the influence of nineteenth-century source-criticism has, we are told, constituted a return to a less fragmented (i.e. more literary) kind of commentary, and "the interpretation of *the texts as they actually exist* has been revalidated".[85] The bible can, in other words, be approached to an extent objectively; to focus on its formal literary properties is to deal with the "actual" text, and accordingly the editors of the *Guide* have in mind an "actual" reader to whom their efforts are directed:

---

[83] Alter and Kermode (1987), pp.5-6.
[84] *Ibid.* p.5.
[85] *Ibid.* p.4 (my italics).

> We are writing to serve the interests of the educated general reader
> rather than those of some critical party.[86]

On one hand, therefore, we have the biblical texts "as they actually
exist" and a disinterested general readership; on the other, the texts
against themselves, read as "springboard[s] for cultural or metaphysical ruminations" by the members of various critical sects. The
problem with this view is not that it unfairly taxes deconstructionists, feminists and others with the stigma of vested interest; culture,
ideology and subjectivity are inevitably and openly on the agenda in
any discussion whose participants include critics of these persua-
sions. But what about the interests of Alter and Kermode? The editors of the *Guide* implicitly claim that they have none, that their
editorial politics are not politics as such, but simply objective
guidelines for distinguishing between ideological and non-
ideological modes of criticism, the latter being concerned rightly
and properly with the-text-itself. "Evidently we are to infer", one
critic has noted, "that the somewhat modified 'new criticism' [Alter
and Kermode] promote is not a critical party vested in publication,
position and normativity".[87] Similarly, we are asked to accept the
unproblematic existence of "the educated general reader", an entity
spinning calmly in a serene orbit of Platonic reasonableness, un-
touched by ideology and yet instilled, one strongly suspects, with a
literary sensibility congruent at all points with that of the critics who
invoke him/her.

It is little wonder, then, that the editors of *The Literary Guide to
the Bible* relegate deconstruction, with maximum dispatch, to the
sidelines of critical debate, as deconstruction seeks to unbalance
their objectivist stance and calls their "educated general reader" a
fabulous beast. One does not, of course, have to be a confessed de-
constructionist to see that education is by no means a value-free or
apolitical enterprise, or that objectivity is never in practice what it
claims to be in theory, but we have seen that deconstruction is one
approach to reading which foregrounds these objections from the
outset, and Alter's and Kermode's stated aim in the *Guide* is to close
off debate before such objections can be raised. Indeed, a perspec-

---

[86] *Ibid.* p.5.
[87] Long (1991), p,76.

tive from which one's own critical stance is seen as dealing with "the texts as they actually exist", as not being the posture of "some critical party", can only be adopted and maintained by keeping the likes of deconstructionists and feminists at bay, by seeing ideology as something which infects and obsesses commentators "out there" on the fashionably anarchic fringes of literary theory. But this kind of strategy, the establishment of criteria for normality (here, the literary-critical coordinates which situate the-text-itself at a point some distance above the grubby *mêlée* of politics and power),

> is itself a powerful and forceful conceptual practice that sublimates, disguises and extends its own power play through recourse to tropes of normative universality.[88]

In a more recent publication, Robert Alter performs this exclusionary manoeuvre in a way which invites close attention. The introduction to his *The Pleasures of Reading in an Ideological Age* is subtitled "The Disappearance of Reading", and in it Alter deplores an emerging state of affairs in literary-critical debate; more and more often, he says,

> [o]ne can read article after article, hear lecture after lecture, in which no literary work is ever quoted, and no real reading experience is registered....I strongly suspect that many young people now earning undergraduate degrees in English or French at our most prestigious institutions have read two or three pages of Lacan, Derrida, Foucault, and Kristeva for every page of George Eliot or Stendhal.[89]

Once again, Alter raises the banner of "real reading" in a way which suggests that whatever concessions may be granted to current critical trends, there still exists an approach to texts which is self-evidently normative and primarily legitimate. That this approach is purportedly untainted by ideology is implied in the title of his book, with its connotations of an Arcadian return to reading-for-pleasure amid the modern clamour of faddish "discourse"; that the desired approach is Alter's own becomes evident as his discussion unfolds.

The shift away from "real reading" is said by Alter to adopt two forms: one is a desire to blur the boundaries not only between litera-

---

[88] Butler (1992), p.7.
[89] Alter (1989), p.11.

ture and criticism, but between literature and other kinds of "non-literary" writing. The other is "a disquieting tendency to pitch critical discussion at one or two removes of abstraction from what actually addresses the reader in the literary text".[90] This self-absorbed critical abstraction is identifiable chiefly by its vocabulary; technical terminology has its uses, Alter allows, but

> [t]he promiscuous use of intellectual jargon all too frequently introduces real imprecision or serves as a cover for the lack of original thought, as one may readily see by scanning the current academic journals, whose pages are clotted with "discourse," "discursive strategy," "erotics of textuality," "diagesis," "foregrounding," "signi-fieds," "aporia," and much more of the same.[91]

Alter goes on to offer three examples of this kind of criticism, each one a short passage which "for reasons of simple decency" he leaves anonymous, but each of which is said to bear the unmistakeable hallmarks of an "addiction to sectarian cant".[92] It does not seem necessary to cite his examples here; suffice it to say that they are indeed notable for their terminological density, and very much characteristic of a certain style of poststructuralist literary-critical discussion. Alter's view is to be respected, and his dislike of the "bristling conceptuality"[93] of much contemporary theory does not, in itself, brand him an irredeemable reactionary. But what he seeks to *prove* by pillorying the excesses of the new theorists is less defensible.

His point is, basically, that the ground of literary criticism has shifted "from literature to some form of politics or metaphysics or politics and metaphysics combined",[94] that whatever the disciples of Derrida, Foucault *et al* are now doing, it does not come under the category of "real reading". What Alter conceives of as real reading, however, is perhaps no more easily comprehended than the grand but vague gestures of the theorists he denounces. Where Alter castigates the sectarians for their enslavement to "jargon and voguish imprecisions",[95] his own vocabulary when it comes to establishing

---

[90] *Ibid.* p.15.
[91] *Ibid.* pp.15-16.
[92] Cf. *ibid.* pp.16-19.
[93] *Ibid.* p.15.
[94] *Ibid.* p.19.
[95] *Ibid.* p.18.

the guidelines for literary activity could be a good deal tighter. Real reading is said to constitute, among other things, "passionate engagement in literary works"; "a sense of deep pleasure" in this engagement; intimate participation in "the imaginative life of the text",[96] and so on. Why these types of engagement and affinity are necessarily unthinkable in "politicised" criticism is unclear to me, almost as unclear as precisely what it is they involve. Alter has a well-developed, even rather forbiddingly complex, idea of what they involve: close attention to "modalities of literary expression",[97] to the intricate configurations of semantics, syntax and orders of textual organisation; to the rhetorical interplay of metre, alliteration, zeugma, mnemonics, linearity, congeries, the tension between structural narrative complexity and mimetic plausibility, and so on. All these terms are drawn from the pages of Alter's discussion of real reading; none of them, I wish to argue, is intrinsically less baffling in its technical specificity than discourse, diagesis, aporia, or the like. The difference is principally one of currency or familiarity, but Alter wishes to dignify only one set of criteria with the appellation "reading", while the possibility that "what actually addresses the reader in the literary text" might be discursive strategy or a-signification is vehemently disallowed.

Again, I believe it is irrelevant here to take issue with Alter's aesthetic distaste for "sectarian cant"; what concerns me is that his exclusion of certain approaches to reading from the inner sanctum of critical orthodoxy can only be achieved at the expense of a measure of self-scrutiny. Alter cannot acknowledge that there may well be a legitimate reading perspective from which his own terms appear arcane and rarefied, or from which, as we have seen suggested, his methodology appears to serve the professional interests of an established academic class. This lends an aspect of irony to his enterprise; for all his denunciations of politics and metaphysics in criticism, Alter's idealisation of "true" reading carries decidedly metaphysical force, while his attempts to prescribe the field of legitimate literary inquiry are, by his own admission, inspired to a large extent by his experience within the academy—generated, that is, within

---

[96] *Ibid.* pp.11-15.
[97] *Ibid.* p.19.

"the messiness of the social order"[98] and thus inextricable from political interests and influences. The *Dictionary of Biblical Interpretation* gives several lengthy paragraphs to its discussion of
"Ideology", during the course of which it cites *Ideologiekritik* as a
kind of meta-criticism which attempts to ensure that political consciousness maintains a prominent function in the business of interpreting texts. According to the *Ideologiekritik* enterprise,

> the ethics of reading and the sociology of scholarship as well as the
> reception of texts and the modes of their production are all part of the
> ideological scrutiny required of alert scholars. Methods of appropriat-
> ing texts may reveal or conceal ideological factors which should be
> part of the debate about the meaning and function of texts.[99]

What Alter singularly fails to do in *The Pleasures of Reading in an
Ideological Age* is to open the debate wide enough for such considerations, to bring his own ideological presuppositions (which may
be theological, professional/academic, ethical, etc.) into any clearer
view than that afforded by the rather opaque insistence that his favoured approach to hermeneutics is the one which, above all others,
reflects "real reading experience". Just as he rejects "voguish imprecisions" only to make room for his own more traditional abstractions, Alter decries ideology and politics in contemporary criticism
without apparently realising the extent to which his own interpretative stance evinces an earlier set of cultural criteria, a network of assumptions which owe much to the insights of the early twentieth-
century Leavisites (who drafted the canon of English literature as it
is studied today, and spoke of such qualities as "life", "vitality",
"moral seriousness", "sensibility" and so on as definitive of literature in the Great Tradition) and to the later New Critics of the
1940's and 50's (who conceived of the literary work as an organic
unity, capable of being grasped objectively and exhaustively by rigorous scrutiny of its formal characteristics[100])—critical parties de-

---

[98] Long *op. cit.* p.79.

[99] Robert P. Carroll: "Ideology" in R.J. Coggins and J.L. Houlden (eds.): *The
Dictionary of Biblical Interpretation* (SCM Press, London/Trinity Press International, Philadelphia 1990), p.311.

[100] Cf. F.R. Leavis: *The Great Tradition* (Chatto & Windus, London 1948); Ron-
ald Hayman: *Leavis* (Heinemann Totowa, London 1976); C.E. Pulos: *The New
Critics and the Language of Poetry* (The University Press, Lincoln 1958); David

nounced in their day as sectarian, and whose approaches to reading were as closely informed by ideology as those of any contemporary feminists or deconstructionists.

It should be noted at this point that Alter nowhere takes issue specifically or at any length with deconstruction *per se*, but his is partly what gives his argument its force—in conflating deconstruction with feminism, Marxism and other unspecified critical heresies, Alter erects an indistinct but huge target which he is then able to hit with unerring accuracy, and yet whose ultimate significance is dwarfed by the equally murky but even more massive spectre of the "educated general reader" for whom he speaks. It can be seen, however, that the ideological age whose dawn Alter witnesses with such dismay is undoubtedly that ushered in by the critical climate which has enabled the work of Derrida to be received and developed. We have seen that a key strategy of deconstructive reading is to trace the workings of power; power to signify or "mean" within the structure of the text under discussion, power to legitimise meaning within the broader context of the interpretative community, power to determine where meaning "within" the text ends and interpretation begins. Considerations of ideology, of the political interests at work in the activities of reading and writing, are unavoidably part of such an approach to literature. Robert Alter is correct when he remarks that criticism of this kind has important and immediate bearing upon the way in which literature is conceived of and taught within the academic institution;[101] his analysis of the situation falters, however, when he suggests that the way to resolve the inevitable confrontations is to return to what he sees as a disinterested, apolitical understanding of texts and textuality. To adopt such a solution is merely to veil the political beneath appeals to objectivity and reason, and thus to engender the kind of fixed, false consciousness that surely constitutes the worst kind of ideology.

In the above paragraphs, I have opened the case against deconstruction on what might be called typological grounds, principally with reference to the *kind* of reading that deconstruction involves.

Robey: "Anglo-American New Criticism" in Jefferson and Robey (1986), pp.73-91. Cf also Eagleton (1986), ch.2 "The Rise of English"; Felperin (1985), ch.1 "Leavisism Revisited".

[101] Alter (1989), pp.12-15.

This is a somewhat specious move, or at least an incongruous one, as I have also suggested in this chapter that generalisations or abstractions run counter to deconstructive criticism, that deconstruction is less a matter of theory than of practice. Talking "about" deconstruction unavoidably involves a fair degree of misrepresentation; one can, in the final analysis, only deconstruct. This opens directly onto the contradiction which lies at the heart of this study, the contradiction which lies at the heart of any theoretical approach to such a subject: that which exists between the theoretical and the practical, between the general and the particular, between metaphysics and its Other. This contradiction shall be discussed in the following chapter, which focuses on the problematic application and activity of deconstructive gestures in biblical interpretation, particularly with reference to their implication for reading communities whose interests in reading the bible are primarily religious.

CHAPTER FOUR

DISPLACEMENT AND FAITHFUL READING

> The problem with reason today is that it has become an instrument of discipline, not a mark of freedom, and that, when it is put to work, it is taken out of play.[1]

The present status of deconstruction in literary and biblical studies is far from settled. In the previous chapter, I left the elucidation of Derrida's work at the point where meaning came to be seen as fundamentally indeterminate, or at least fundamentally non-fundamental, and I indicated that many traditionalist literary critics have responded to this by denouncing deconstruction as an interpretative approach which outrageously and cynically violates the integrity or "meaningfulness" of the texts it deals with. Words like "outrage" do not exaggerate the pitch at which the debate over deconstruction has been conducted among academics in literary studies; one report has it that some scholars

> see Derrida as "immoral", corrupting young minds with nihilism, etc.: some phrases used are "the current critical scandal", "the failure of criticism", "literature against itself", and so forth....the rancour has infected a number of prominent universities, notably Yale and Johns Hopkins. A noted classicist now at the latter found a work of Derrida in his mailroom; so incensed that he failed to notice that the mailbox wasn't his own, he seized the book and tore it to pieces on the spot.[2]

This passage, however, which reads rather like a news dispatch radioed from the middle of a war zone, was written over a decade ago, and it is true that the literary-critical establishment has, in some quarters, since then relaxed its stance against deconstruction. The domestication of what was initially reviled as a subversive, irre-

---

[1] Caputo (1987), p.211.
[2] Schneidau (1982), p.7.

sponsible practice has become apparent in the rise to mainstream power and acceptance of such "deconstructive establishment"-figures as Hartman, Miller and the late Paul de Man; Derrida himself received his honorary doctorate from Cambridge University in 1992. One critic has described this process with reference to Kafka's parable of the leopards in the temple—leopards break into a temple and drink the water from the sacrificial vessels; they persist in this profane act until it becomes predictable, then sacralised and finally incorporated into the temple ritual.[3] So there is now a consensus of tolerant opinion which holds that deconstruction has its rightful and proper place in the history of literary criticism; the academic "assimilation of potentially destructive agents"[4] is well under way, even while those agents threaten and harass the institution which assimilates them.[5]

At the same time, however, there is no shortage of academics whose opposition to deconstruction is both bitter and influential: it should not be forgotten that Derrida's nomination for a Cambridge doctorate caused such a degree of controversy that the University was obliged to vote on the fitness of the award—the first vote on an honorary degree at Cambridge in nearly thirty years.[6] The nature and gravity of the accusations held against deconstruction vary—some objections reveal little more than a keen and profound ignorance on the part of the antagonist—but there is one complaint which is perhaps heard more often than any other: namely, that deconstruction is part of a perverse and derisory trend in criticism, one which fails to respect either the structural or the aesthetic integrity of the literary text, and which transforms the activity of reading into a kind of wanton iconoclasm. It is much the same objection as that which we have just seen levelled by Robert Alter at modern literary criticism in general. No reader worthy of the name, it is often argued, having

---

[3] Felperin (1985), pp.6, 45-6.

[4] *Ibid.* p.46.

[5] On the uneasy relationship existing between deconstruction and the academic institution, cf. Burnett (1990), pp.65ff.; Culler (1987), p.156-79; Felperin (1985), pp.216-23. Cf. also Emma Henderson: "Derrida and His Friends Deconstruct France's Universities" in The *Times Higher Education Supplement* (June 12, 1992), p.1.

[6] Henderson *ibid.* p.1.

seriously engaged with the subtle textures of, say, *Mrs. Dalloway*, or the rhetorical elegance of Ecclesiastes, or the sheer brutal power of *King Lear*, can justifiably subordinate the study of how those effects are achieved to the desire to pull the text apart and demonstrate that, in the final analysis, one rearrangement of the pieces is as good as any other—or worse, that any one *text* is as good as any other. The "new wave" critics have, with a kind of totalitarian Communist zeal, interrogated the privileging of meaning in texts, and texts in culture, to the point where privilege itself is no longer permitted, and thus they have forgotten what it is to practise the open-minded study of literature on literature's own terms. Exactly what those terms are, what it is that makes literature Literature, provides the subject for a good deal of lively debate;[7] suffice it to say here that for those who have made a career out of explicating the intrinsically Literary, structuralism and its hybrids amount to little more than a joyless sociology-of-ideas which would be more appropriately brought to bear on such phenomena as television, advertising, "bureaucratese" and pop culture—all species of a pernicious new "literature" which only too richly deserves the baleful attention of the deconstructive *mafiosi*.

The discussion which this controversy opens up is an important one, and a great deal more could be said here; I have introduced it, however, more or less by way of introduction to the issue to which the greater part of this chapter will be devoted: the issue of deconstruction in biblical interpretation and its implications for the "religious" reader. It could be argued that little of the above debate poses any insurmountable problems for those who believe that literary criticism is a kind of marketplace for interpretative methodologies where various permutations swing in and out of fashion and where deconstruction has, for the moment, ousted whatever came before it as the latest in radical chic. Shakespeare has, in the past, been variously put forward as a humanist, a formalist, a modernist, a feminist and a Marxist-historicist; to say now that his works self-deconstructively defer meaning in favour of *différance* and polysemy is merely to continue in a time-honoured tradition of hermeneutical innovation and affirm that the great classics of literature

---

[7] Cf. for example Eagleton (1986), ch.1 "What Is Literature?"; Alter (1989), pp. 13-14, ch.1 "The Difference of Literature".

eternally defy our attempts to explicate them exhaustively. When deconstruction turns its attention to the bible, however, matters tend to become more serious. This is because the bible, for many of us, is not "simply" literature but the one text above all others which does point to unassailable truth, and in this hope we invest a good deal of spiritual and emotional commitment which is a lot less flexible than our intellectual curiosity. For a religious Jew or Christian, the bible is in some sense the word of God. According to the tenets of deconstruction, the very idea of a transcendental Signified, of a source of meaning which is stable and resistant to the vagaries of language, is an outmoded presupposition of classical Greek metaphysics—which can of course be a roundabout way of saying that there is no God. Carl A. Raschke has enthusiastically articulated this unsettling aspect of deconstruction in terms whose glow borders on the satanic:

> deconstruction is the death of God put into writing....Deconstruction is the *descensus in infernus*, the venture into the underworld of limitless writing, the dismembering of all names and concepts....the dance of death upon the tomb of God....a kind of Bacchic fascination with the metaphysics of decomposition and death,[8]

and so on. Regardless of whether or not we feel Raschke overstates the case a little, his point is impossible to miss: the deconstructive exegete's first move must necessarily be to jettison all notions of a God who speaks from a single point somewhere behind, above or beyond the biblical text, because the *hors-texte* (along with any unitary guarantor of Meaning who might be said to inhabit it) simply does not exist as such. It is not to be wondered at, then, that deconstruction is not popular in those theological-exegetical circles where the bible is held to be the repository of truths which are essentially transhistorical: not only, it is said, does deconstruction undermine biblical faith and the sacredness of scripture, but it does so with the same kind of self-justifying circularity that raises the same sceptical questions over and over again without perceiving any need to provide constructive answers. The realisation that any concept of determinate truth is a product of discourse or culture rather than something extraneous to it provides the rather attractive temptation

---

[8] Raschke (1982), pp.27-8.

of taking a big stick to all metaphysical/religious claims, and then walking away leaving somebody else to pick up the pieces —a stale, flat and unprofitable kind of exercise, and one which forestalls objection to this by elevating the empty gesture to the status of philosophical *coup de théâtre*.[9] One could hardly conceive of a mode of criticism more antithetical to biblical scholarship, or quite simply more tedious: Frank Kermode has taxed deconstruction with the charge that "it is entirely absorbed in demonstrating its own validity",[10] and elsewhere Terry Eagleton states that much deconstructive criticism emerging from the universities of Britain and the United States bears witness to a kind of competitive macho ethic; everybody deconstructing everybody else's work and ridiculing determinations of meaning wherever they may be found, in a bid to see who can stare most resolutely into the abyss of a-signification and still come up smiling:

> [s]uch deconstruction is a power-game, a mirror-image of orthodox academic competition. It is just that now, in a religious twist to the old ideology, victory is achieved by *kenosis* or self-emptying: the winner is the one who has managed to get rid of all his cards and sit with empty hands.[11]

Of course Kermode and Eagleton are not primarily biblical critics, and it would be wrong to make a radical distinction between biblical interpretation and "secular" literary criticism, suggesting that deconstruction precipitates anguished existential wranglings in the former camp and differences merely of aesthetic opinion or academic politics in the latter. The truth is that there are markedly similar issues at stake in both fields, and in any case, it should be noted that just as there remain those scholars of literature who stand in passionate opposition to all things Derridean, so there exist biblical critics who make free and imaginative use of deconstructive manoeuvres in exegesis. For the time being, however, I wish to separate the two fields and look specifically at biblical criticism, not because I believe that exegesis is an activity far removed from other kinds of criticism, but because the main issue I wish first to deal with is one

---

[9] Cf. Eagleton (1986), p.144.
[10] Kermode (1983), p.6.
[11] Eagleton *op. cit.* p.147.

which lies closer to the surface of biblical-critical discussion: the issue of religious belief and whether, or how seriously, it is threatened by a hermeneutical strategy which questions all determinations of Presence and stable truth. As I indicated in the previous chapter, feminists who reject the bible and biblical faith out of hand as being irredeemably patriarchal may be only too happy to perform Raschke's "dance of death upon the tomb of God", given that the God underfoot is the God of the patriarchs of Israel, of Jephthah, of Ezekiel, of Hosea, of Paul, of Origen, Tertullian, Augustine and Aquinas. But for those who see the bible as revelatory of a God who is something more, or other, than the sum of a sexist tradition, deconstructive reading may leave too little to work with once it has inverted all hierarchies, blurred all distinctions and dethroned all metaphysical presuppositions. The question is: is deconstruction inevitably tied to a death-of-God theology, and thus only of limited use in biblical interpretation?

Some questions, it has been observed, "beget not so much answers as different ways of phrasing themselves".[12] Certainly, the question of whether or not deconstruction delivers the *coup de grâce* to all theological determinations necessitates reformulation, inquiring further into what God "is", what the "death" of such a being might be said to entail, and other such speculations. I hope to avoid becoming too perilously involved in such discussion here, partly because I am no theologian, but partly also because I believe that deconstruction, at least in its Derridean formulation(s), is not at all readily articulated in classical theological discourse. Derrida's maxim *il n'y a pas de hors-texte* appears at first glance to court a directly theological translation: there is nothing beyond textuality, everything is engulfed in discourse, there exists no guarantee or ground of meaning or truth outside the web of mutability woven by language and history—there is no God. But Derrida is well aware that "there is no God" is a manifestly theological statement, an assertion of metaphysical-religious truth, and he stresses on a number of occasions that his overarching claims for textuality are not to misconstrued as triumphalist metaphysics-in-disguise:

---

[12] Crossan (1982), p.39.

I try to keep myself at the *limit* of philosophical discourse. I say limit and not death, for I do not at all believe in what today is so easily called the death of philosophy (nor, moreover, in the simple death of whatever—the book, man, or god, especially since, as we all know, what is dead wields a very specific power).[13]

Derrida's deconstruction can be seen thus as neither onto-theological ("onto-theology" being the Heideggerean term appropriated by Derrida to denote the originary self-presence of anything, whether it be God, Being, Logos, soul, rational consciousness, philosophy or any master-discourse), nor as "a linguistically crafty existentialism which poises writing, in [Edward] Said's phrase, 'just a hair beyond utter blankness'".[14] Neither can such deconstructive movements as *différance* be said to operate according to the logic of "negative" theology, if Derrida is correct in seeing negative theology as the other side of the onto-theological coin:

what is....denoted as *différance* is not theological, not even in the most negative order of negative theology. The latter, as we know, is always occupied with letting a supraessential reality go beyond the finite categories of essence and existence, that is, of presence, and always hastens to remind us that, if we deny the predicate of existence to God, it is in order to recognise him as a superior, inconceivable and ineffable mode of being. Here there is no question of such a move....[15]

Whether or not Derrida's assessment of negative theology actually does justice to the subtlety of the tradition,[16] the above comments

---

[13] Derrida (1981b), p.6.

[14] Lentricchia (1980), p.171. Lentricchia quotes Edward Said: "Abecedarium Culturae: Structuralism, Absence, Writing" in John K. Simon (ed.): *Modern French Criticism: From Proust and Valery to Structuralism* (University of Chicago Press, Chicago 1972), p.385. Said's early work evinces a profound suspicion of structuralism and its offshoots: the idea of "man mired in his systems of signification" he sees as "a veritable nightmare utopia", and Derrida's work is said to constitute a "grotesque explication" of this outlook (cf. Said pp.349-85, quoted in Lentricchia pp.162-3).

[15] Derrida (1973), p.134.

[16] Cf. Crossan (1982), pp.37-9. Crossan is not so readily convinced that negative theology is "a simple strategy within onto-theology", and he considers it possible that "something more profound is going on within that marginal but magnificent strand of our [theological] tradition" than Derrida appears to allow. Derrida's reply to this objection somewhat contradicts his earlier position, but he stops short of detailed discussion:

taken as a whole sound the general warning that the ominous theological implications of Derrida's work are not as clear or direct as they might at first appear.

Deconstruction and Metaphysics

In assessing the viability of deconstruction within religious discourse, it is probably best to begin by widening or shifting the focus of inquiry from theology to metaphysics, assuming for the time being (in defiance of our moratorium on conceptual hierarchies) that one is a species or sub-genre of the other. "Metaphysics", as it is generally understood, refers broadly to that aspect of philosophy which deals with first principles: the decisive claim, or root assumption of classical metaphysical discourse is that there exists a sphere of primary being where knowledge, existence and meaning are originary and non-contingent. The metaphysical realm is, as its etymology suggests, that in which the sensual/linguistic/temporal apprehension of things is transcended; likewise, metaphysical realities

---

> [I] am quite convinced of the need for a rigorous and differentiated reading of everything advanced under this title (negative theology). My fascination at least testifies to this, right through to my incompetence: in effect I believe that what is called "negative theology" (a rich and very diverse corpus) does not let itself be easily assembled under the general category of "onto-theology-to-be-deconstructed" [p.61].

Whether or not—or how consciously, unconsciously, bravely, or perniciously—Derrida's deconstruction appropriates the movements of negative theology is a complex question, a question whose form depends on the kind of negative theology you have in mind when you raise it. Like "deconstruction", "negative theology" is a generic term which sacrifices difference to taxonomical convenience, and masks the fact that the *via negativa* follows no single, universally-recognised map:

> How to speak suitably of negative theology? Is there a negative theology? A single one? A regulative model for the others? Can one adopt a discourse to it? Is not one compelled to speak of negative theology according to the modes of negative theology, in a way that is at once impotent, exhausting, and inexhaustible? Is there ever anything other than a "negative theology" of "negative theology"? [Derrida, 1992, p.83].

Thus Derrida in ludic mode, and in his riddling attempt to demonstrate that deconstruction is *not* negative theology in disguise—which is what he is doing here—he rather confusingly indicates that the two movements of thought have at least a vertiginous resistance to definition in common. For fuller discussion on this topic, cf. the essays (three of which are Derrida's) in Coward and Foshay (1992).

consist of those certainties which are beyond empirical inquiry, both posterior and anterior to the shifting constructs of culture and history. It should be necessary below only to summarise briefly one or two particular forms in which the encounter between deconstruction and metaphysics has taken place, the general reminder being that where the dominant branches of Western philosophy, with their roots in Platonic/Aristotelian thought, have long taken metaphysics and metaphysical assumptions for granted, deconstruction's salient impulse is invariably to seek out, question and disturb such assumptions. In "White Mythology", Derrida's extended essay on metaphor, a much-quoted passage from Nietzsche is offered which illustrates with characteristic Nietzschean force the kind of perspective adopted:

> What, then, is truth? A mobile army of metaphors, metonymics, anthropomorphisms: in short, a sum of human relations which become poetically and rhetorically intensified, metamorphosed, adorned, and after long usage, seem to a nation fixed, canonic and binding; truths are illusions of which one has forgotten that they *are* illusions....coins which have their obverse *effaced* and now are no longer of account as coins but merely as metal.[17]

In Nietzsche's figure of truths as effaced coins, we are presented with the idea that eternal verities, or metaphysical assurances, whether religious, scientific or philosophical, are really no more than commonly-held understandings which have felicitously (but speciously) transcended communality. As a coin, stamped with its particular numerical value, is recognised as a token of exchange only within the economic community where it circulates, so truths start out as propositions whose validity is constrained by culture and history. Rub the face off a coin, and its value (in the absence of social determinants) becomes a question of "essential" worth, just as a communal belief whose existence as a cultural inscription is forgotten or denied may readily be put forward as Truth. Derrida sees the cultural/historical origins of Western metaphysics as having been erased in this manner, part of a philosophical strategy which seeks to

---

[17] Nietzsche: "On Truth and Falsity in Their Ultramoral Sense" in D. Levy (ed.): *CompleteWorks of Nietzsche Vol.2* (London and Edinburgh, 1911), p.180. Quoted in Derrida: "White Mythology" in (1982b), p.217.

elevate metaphysical certainties to the status of ground-and-object of
all discourses:

> Metaphysics—the white mythology which reassembles and reflects
> the culture of the West: the white man takes his own mythology, Indo-
> European mythology, his own *logos*, that is, the *mythos* of his idiom,
> for the universal form of that [which] he must still wish to call Reason.
> Which does not go uncontested....metaphysics has erased within itself
> the fabulous scene that has produced it, the scene that *nevertheless re-
> mains active and stirring*, inscribed in white ink, an invisible design
> covered over in the palimpsest.[18]

Metaphysics, in other words, by no means constitutes an unshake-
able structure, as it bears within itself the "active and stirring" traces
of its own fabrication, traces which are often invisible to philosophical self-scrutiny, but no less operative for that. We have examined,
in the previous two chapters, various ways in which deconstruction
questions metaphysical certainties and enables the making-visible of
covert cultural imprints; one approach is that mapped out in the
course of Derrida's sundry critiques of logo-centrism. Metaphysical
discourses, we have seen, tend to structure reality in terms of binary
oppositions (meaning/form, soul/body, etc.), elevating one term as a
fundamental grounding entity or principle over and above its conceptual opposite, which is held to be derivative or inferior. Logocentrism, or the "metaphysics of presence" (by which is meant any
system of thought or behaviour predicated upon this "hierarchical
axiology"[19]), is recurrent throughout the dominant Western philosophical tradition, "from Plato to Rousseau, Descartes to Husserl",[20]
and can even be identified in the work of such apparent anti-
metaphysicians as Nietzsche, Freud and Heidegger. It is this all-
pervasiveness that makes the metaphysics of presence "invisible", as
Jonathan Culler has cogently argued: knowledge itself, the making
of logical sense from disordered sensation, is effected by establish-

---

[18] Derrida *ibid.* p.213 (my italics).

[19] Derrida (1988), p.93.

[20] *Ibid.* p.93. Cf. also Derrida's various discussions of the work of key phi-
losphers—Derrida has written at length on Husserl (1973) and (1978), pp.154-68;
on Rousseau (1976), pp.97-316; on Freud (1978), pp.196-231; on Descartes and
Foucault (1978), pp. 31-63; on Hegel (1978), pp.251-77 and (1982b), pp.69-108;
on Heidegger and Nietzsche (1979a); on Plato (1981), pp.63-171.

ing fundamental conceptual yardsticks against which we measure variations, complications and perversions, and

> [t]he difficulty of imagining and practising different procedures is an indication of the ubiquity of logocentrism.[21]

Culler goes on to list some of the more familiar concepts whose elevation to the status of "fundamentals" relies on the notion of self-certain presence, or metaphysical priority:

> the immediacy of sensation, the presence of ultimate truths to a divine consciousness, the effective presence of an origin in a historical development, a spontaneous or unmediated intuition, the transumption of thesis and antithesis in a dialectical synthesis, the presence in speech of logical and grammatical structures, truth as what subsists behind appearances, and the effective presence of a goal in the steps that lead to it. The authority of presence, its power of valorization, structures all our thinking. The notions of "making clear", "grasping", "demonstrating", "revealing", and "showing what is the case" all invoke presence. To claim, as in the Cartesian *cogito*, that the "I" resists radical doubt because it is present to itself in the act of thinking or doubting is one sort of appeal to presence. Another is the notion that the meaning of an utterance is what is present to the consciousness of the speaker, what he or she "has in mind" at the moment of utterance.[22]

Another, we might add, is the idea germane to this study that the male, with his "masculine" attributes of rationality and objectivity, and his capacity for dispassionate analysis, provides the model for humanity, stands in the image of God, has intellectual access to Truth, and generally sets the standard against which female and "feminine" models of experience must be evaluated.

The problem is, of course, that none of these fundamental, determinate concepts has fallen from the sky, or from any other notional realm of pure Being. Each logocentric "first principle" can only function as such by virtue of its relationship to its binary opposite and to other "derived" concepts, and therefore each self-identical Presence can be shown to exist only as part of a *system* of differences and absences. Whatever is put forward as an instance of metaphysical Presence is in fact a product or construction, itself

---

[21] Culler (1987), p.93.
[22] *Ibid.* pp.93-4.

"dependent or derived in ways that deprive it of the authority of simple or pure presence".[23] We have seen that "mouse" is meaning-ful not in and of itself, but as a recognisable variation on similar-sounding arrangements of phonemes; likewise, what is signified by the term "Caucasian male" is sedimented with traces of everything that is neither Caucasian nor male—female, Asiatic, Negroid, even the genderless and non-human, each leaves its "trace", a trace which marks *absence* but yet which is definitive, in much the same way as the absence of heat determines the nature and degree of cold. Seen in this light, what gives definition to concepts and signifiers is not fixed identity, but the play of differences between them, the unde-cideable dynamic of *différance* which

> no more allows the opposition between [for example] activity and passivity than that between cause and effect or indetermination and determination, etc.[24]

If all such oppositions are illusory, if Presence is, in part, a construct of all things absent, then the metaphysical granting of originary status to anything at all involves inconsistencies and paradoxes which philosophy can suppress or rework but never ultimately avoid. The elevation of Nature, for example, to ontological or moral primacy over and against culture, can never be fixed or secure be-cause philosophical determinations of Nature are themselves effects which have historical/cultural causes. Similarly, I have outlined Derrida's argument above that the privileging of speech as being somehow closer to meaning than writing is dependent upon the at-tribution of certain unsavoury characteristics to writing which can, on close inspection, be shown in fact to characterise speech just as profoundly. Similarly again, patriarchal religion establishes God in terms of maleness and vice versa, but maleness can be seen as a concept inscribed with traces of all that it must exclude to claim in-dependent identity; indeed it can only function as a concept "insofar as it consists of such traces".[25] The repressions and exclusions neces-sary to establish Presence become, as it were, all the more conspicu-ous to the deconstructive mind by their absence: who says Nature

---

[23] *Ibid.* p.94.
[24] Derrida (1973), p.147.
[25] Culler *op.cit.* p.96.

says culture; who says Self says other; and so metaphysical determinations of all kinds can be read as evocative of what they seek to
exclude, as operating "according to the vocabulary of that very
thing to be de-limited".[26]

There is another way in which Derrida deconstructs metaphysics,
or shows how metaphysics deconstructs itself according to its own
principles. In the introductory paragraphs to "Structure, Sign and
Play in the Discourse of the Human Sciences",[27] Derrida examines
the history of the "centred structure", first establishing that all
structures traditionally *have* a centre, an organising locus or principle which controls "the play of its elements inside the total form
....even today, the notion of a structure lacking any center represents
the unthinkable itself".[28] The centre is the metaphysical "still point"
of the structure, that which grounds and situates everything else in
the structure:

> it is the point at which the substitution of contents, elements, or terms
> is no longer possible. At the center, the permutation or the transfor-
> mation of elements (which may of course be structures enclosed
> within a structure) is forbidden. At least this permutation has always
> remained *interdicted*....[29]

The centre, then, could be said (in linguistic terms) to be
"untranslatable". But the history of philosophy, the very fact that
there *is* a history of philosophy, shows that translating and substituting one determination of the "centre" for another has been precisely
the business of those most devoutly committed to its stability. In its
restless desire for metaphysical certitude, for a point of "fundamental immobility....which is itself beyond the reach of play", Western
philosophy has amounted to nothing so much as a play of substitu-
tions:

> the entire history of the concept of structure....must be thought of as a
> series of substitutions of center for center, as a linked chain of deter-
> minations of the center. Successively, and in a regulated fashion, the
> center receives different forms or names. The history of metaphysics,

---

[26] Derrida (1973), p.147.
[27] Derrida (1978), pp.278-93.
[28] *Ibid.* p.279.
[29] *Ibid.* p.279.

like the history of the West, is the history of these metaphors and me-
tonymies.[30]

Even as it strives for fixity, in other words, metaphysics *in its striv-
ing* inevitably participates in indeterminacy and flux. But it is here
that Derrida introduces an idea which is crucial to his discussion,
crucial to deconstructive thought in general—and yet crucially ignored by a number of deconstruction's fiercest critics. The idea can
be picked up at the point where Derrida writes of a "rupture" in the
history of Western philosophy, of the evolution of a kind of anti-
metaphysical school of thought which sees the putative structural
"centre", the determination of Being-in-presence, as "not a fixed locus but a function, a sort of nonlocus in which an infinite number of
sign-substitutions [come] into play". In this "rupture" meaning is
transformed from being something which exists behind the words
we use to describe it into a function of those words; historically, this
is seen as

> the moment when language invaded the universal problematic, the
> moment when, in the absence of a center or origin, everything became
> discourse....that is to say, a system in which the central signified, the
> original or transcendental signified, is never absolutely present outside
> a system of differences.[31]

Derrida traces this "rupture" through the Nietzschean critique of
Truth, through Freud's work on the fragmentation of consciousness
and the rational subject, through Heidegger's dismantling of Being
and onto-theology, and on. He goes on to assert, however, that each
of these thinkers can be shown to be caught in a philosophical double-bind; that is, that each and every attempt to dismantle metaphysical structures must necessarily, owing to the demands of philosophical argument, set up its own centred discursive structure and
establish its own determinate principles of reference and demonstra-
tion—principles which, in each case, we are persuaded to believe are
fixed and binding, and which therefore have the unmistakeable smell
of Presence about them:

---

[30] *Ibid.* p.279.
[31] *Ibid.* p.280.

all these destructive discourses and their analogues are trapped in a kind of circle. The circle is unique. It describes the form of the relation between the history of metaphysics and the destruction of the history of metaphysics. There is no sense in doing without the concepts of metaphysics in order to shake metaphysics. We have no language—no syntax and no lexicon—which is foreign to this history; we can pronounce not a single destructive proposition which has not already had to slip into the form, the logic, and the implicit postulations of....what it seeks to contest.[32]

Derrida's terminology is precise: there is "no sense" in doing without metaphysics, because all the most natural and immediate ways in which we make "sense" to each other involve appeals to Presence, invocations of stable, commonly-understood meanings to which our words direct the listener or reader. Any systematic refutation of Presence, insofar as it relies on a system, must make its own claims to truth and certitude, and these claims are, of course, "borrowings" from the proscribed field of metaphysics. Thus are the anti-philosophers incorporated into the history of philosophy:

every particular borrowing brings along with it the whole of metaphysics. This is what allows these destroyers to destroy each other reciprocally—for example, Heidegger regarding Nietzsche, with as much lucidity and rigor as bad faith and misconstruction, as the last metaphysician, the last "Platonist". One could do the same for Heidegger himself, for Freud, or for a number of others.[33]

It seems that the death of metaphysics, then, can only be heralded in terms which paradoxically secure its future good health, and which leave even the most scrupulous destroyer of Presence open to charges of negligent Platonism. And this of course has particular relevance not just to the work of Nietzsche, Heidegger and Freud, but to that of Derrida and all other deconstructive thinkers. What are we to make of a discourse whose practitioners assert that meaning is undecideable, that language defers truth, that metaphysics is the "white mythology" of the West, and yet who nevertheless continue to disseminate texts in the expectation that the language of those

---

[32] *Ibid.* pp.280-1.
[33] *Ibid.* pp.281-2.

texts will be "properly" or at least adequately understood?[34] In communicating structured ideas of any kind, we inevitably adopt to some degree the article of Platonic faith that there are such things as ideas, and that they can be communicated with relative success through language: where, then, does that leave deconstruction with all its anti-metaphysical subtleties?

In the answer to this question lies also the answer to the charge that deconstruction is a species of chaos or interpretative anarchy. For the philosophical double-bind, the inevitable complicity between metaphysics and anti-metaphysics that "ruptures" the logic of Nietzschean thought, is a double-bind in which deconstruction is no less inextricably caught; indeed, Derrida states that "we cannot give up this metaphysical complicity without also giving up the critique we are directing against this complicity".[35] For deconstruction to be practised as the all-relativising, apocalyptic gesture of nihilism its critics often make it out to be, would deprive it not only of any coherence, but also (more importantly) of its political efficacy, a point which Derrida makes with reference to feminist deconstruction when he speaks of the need to take into account

> the *real* conditions in which women's struggles develop on all fronts (economic, ideological, political). These conditions often require the preservation (within longer or shorter phases) of metaphysical presuppositions that one must (and knows already that one must) question in a later phase—or an other place—because they belong to the dominant system that one is deconstructing on a *practical level*.[36]

One significant hermeneutical corollary of this proviso is that deconstruction should (according to Derrida) be a practice which, in acknowledging its reliance on "the form, the logic, and the implicit

---

[34] For a closely-argued attack on deconstruction-as-"deceptive"-discourse, cf. M.H. Abrams: "How To Do Things With Texts" in *Partisan Review* 44 (1979), pp.566-88.

[35] Derrida (1978), p.281. Cf. also pp.288, 282:

> What I want to emphasise is simply that the passage beyond philosophy does not consist in turning the page of philosophy (which usually amounts to philosophizing badly), but in continuing to read philosophers *in a certain way*....The quality and fecundity of a discourse are perhaps measured by the critical rigor with which this relation to the history of metaphysics and to inherited concepts is thought.

[36] Derrida (1982a), p.70.

postulations" of metaphysics, accordingly "recognise[s] and respect[s]" the requirements of traditional criticism:

> The movements of deconstruction do not destroy structures from the outside. They are not possible and effective, nor can they take accurate aim, except by inhabiting those structures. Inhabiting them *in a certain way*, because one always inhabits, and all the more when one does not suspect it....Without this recognition and this respect, critical production would risk developing in any direction at all and authorize itself to say almost anything.[37]

For all Derrida's restless interrogating, dismantling and reconfiguring of Presence, nowhere does he claim to do away with metaphysical presuppositions altogether, and this is why Derrida situates his work at the "limit" of philosophical discourse and not beyond it. Deconstruction in its most fearfully *avant-garde* forms may well redefine the boundaries of conventional structures of meaning, but this is not the same thing as stepping out of structure and signification completely—this particular commentary on Derrida would be a good deal longer (had it indeed been attempted in the first place) if Derrida's texts did not possess their own internal logic, or make appeals to certain (precarious) fundamentals which could be discussed in some communicable form or other. Ideas and general principles, reason and logic; the bulwarks of metaphysics are the foundations of Western thought, and we can no more "escape" them than we can escape culture or language itself. It is the necessity of language that keeps deconstruction on this side of "the threshold of sense";[38] words may defer meaning but their "reasonable orders" are "just about all that we have, and are likely to have"[39] with which to signify anything at all—a realisation which is as crucial to an understanding of deconstruction as is the awareness of undecideability and "play":

> Derrida has argued....that our signifiers do not communicate being, but distance it and postpone its advent indefinitely. They are not the sacrament of presence, but the marks of an infinitely iterated absence. However, with equal clarity and vigor Derrida makes the point....that

---

[37] Derrida (1976), pp.24, 158.

[38] The phrase is John Llewelyn's: cf. his *Derrida: On the Threshold of Sense* (St. Martin's Press, New York 1986).

[39] Lentricchia (1980), p.209.

the *presumption* of presence is inescapable....We cannot speak a word
that delivers the presence of the signified. But neither can we speak a
word that does not claim to. The utterance of the word defers presence; the word uttered dissembles that deferment.[40]

Here lies an answer to those who claim that deconstruction is simply
literature's revenge on philosophy. To say that all philosophy is, in
the final analysis, "only" literature, that (for example) all concepts
are metaphors, obscures the fact that all notions concerning metaphor (e.g. the difference between literal and figurative language) are
conceptualisations, derived from the language and logical resources
of philosophy; this is Derrida's concern in "White Mythology".

So it is idle to maintain that philosophy comes down to a handful of
disguised or occluded metaphors *unless* one makes this further con-
cession: that metaphor itself is unthinkable outside a certain genealogy
of philosophic concepts.... it is precisely *from* philosophy—from the
terms and distinctions made available by analytic reason—that linguists have adopted their various ways of arguing their relativist
case.[41]

Derrida, then, far from relegating meaning in texts to some ware-
house of obsolete critical interests and establishing "a new transcendental signified called the abyss",[42] acknowledges the necessity of
relatively determinate truths even as he relativises them. These unstable "truths", of course, include the insights of deconstructive
criticism-in-practice wherever they appear: the simple necessity of
being read and understood (to say nothing of the desire to be employed and published) means that deconstructive readings of texts
must at some point, and in some form, adopt the language and logic
of metaphysics and traditional criticism, and this in turn means that
deconstruction is never a final, annihilating gesture, but a mode of
interpretation whose structures are shakeable from within—i.e.
"deconstructable"—and whose logical closures are secured not with
Truth but with rhetoric:

---

[40] Mackey (1983), p.269.
[41] Norris (1987), p.170.
[42] Lentricchia *op. cit.* p.182.

Deconstruction is a perpetually self-deconstructing movement that is inhabited by *différance*. No text is ever *fully* deconstructing or deconstructed. Yet the critic provisionally musters the metaphysical resources of criticism and performs what declares itself to be *one* (unitary) act of deconstruction.[43]

A deconstructive reading of a text, in other words, may make certain conventional claims to finality and "correct" interpretation, but these claims are themselves textually constituted, embodying their own indeterminacies and contradictions, and are able to be deconstructed in their turn. Just as deconstruction operates to a significant extent from *inside* metaphysics, just as the practice of deconstructive criticism borrows the "strategic and economic resources of subversion from the old structure" of the text under scrutiny, so every critique of logocentrism unavoidably makes its own appeals to Meaning, and deconstruction "always in a certain way falls prey to its own work".[44]

Deconstruction and Theology

The relationship between deconstruction and metaphysics, then, is not one of competitive opposition, but a relationship in which each carries the trace of the other: metaphysical formulations embody their own deconstructive *aporia*, deconstruction relies on metaphysics to the extent that it must be "thinkable" or able to be constructed as intelligible discourse—and it is at this point that the parallel between the metaphysical problematic and the theological becomes perhaps most obvious. God, as the transcendental Signified *par excellence*, is never fully present, and so our determinations of what God is, whether they be grounded subjectively (in religious experience) or objectively (in rational thought), always-already defer the Presence they invoke; even the deepest spiritual awareness of God requires interpretation if it is to be anything other than disordered sensation. At the same time, however, the attempt to "deconstruct" God in any final or negating sense will always be frustrated, in that to assert the absolute non-being of God is to invoke metaphysical

---

[43] Spivak, in Derrida (1976), p.lxxviii.
[44] Derrida (1976), p.24.

Truth, and to invoke metaphysical Truth in the name of even a non-existent God is to appeal to a supremely high authority—as Louis Mackey puts it: "the proposition that closed down theology would have to be a theological proposition".[45] So while deconstruction gives serious consideration to Nietzsche's claim that God is dead, it cannot fairly be said that deconstruction "does away with" God, any more than it does away with metaphysics. A deconstructive theology need not be atheistic or nihilistic; what it necessitates is a particular configuration of the notions of Being and Presence, a bearing-in-mind of certain understandings which are perhaps not as hostile, or even as alien, to theological discourse as has been in the past suggested.

The theology which deconstruction deconstructs is that of a Platonic divinity who exists as "a transcendent, a sovereign and an impassive God....an eternal and unmoving Being".[46] As we have seen, deconstruction holds that all such concepts are in fact constructs, metaphors inscribed in a chain of linguistic markers with no ultimate referents, signifiers which defer the presence of the Signified interminably:

> Derrida reminds us that if Being can be said in different senses (i.e. analogically), it is because being is not a unified origin, a proper and univocal name, and because analogy affects it from within. In effect, the "as-structure" is anterior to and makes possible this idealization, the concept of Being....God did not choose to "withdraw" in order to "represent" the world, but, rather, the anterior movement of analogy inaugurated the very universality of God as source concept. Like Being, God is a derived origin derived from metaphoricity.[47]

---

[45] Mackey (1983), p.269.

[46] Thomas J.J. Alitzer: *The Gospel of Christian Atheism* (Westminster, Philadelphia 1966), p.42. Quoted in Atkins (1983), p.42.

[47] Ash (1987), p.77. Cf. also Derrida's discussion of "play":

> Play is the disruption of presence. The presence of an element is always a signifying and substitutive reference inscribed in a system of differences and the movement of a chain. Play is always play of absence and presence, but if it is to be thought radically, play must be conceived of before the alternative of presence and absence. Being must be conceived as presence or absence on the basis of the possibility of play and not the other way around [Derrida, 1978, p.292].

In the beginning, to put it another way, is interpretation; the movement of analogy precedes its referent. Deconstructive theology asserts that there can never be a *hors-texte*; our experience of God, like the "unitary" subject which experiences it, is in fact fragmented and contradictory, in need of interpretation; the awareness of Divinity always demands "reading". Our sacred texts do not, by means of some sublime alchemy, translate language into Presence, but disseminate meaning across and through the unpredictable shifts and upheavals of history; readers of the bible are in dialogue not with God but with God-as-read by the Yahwist, the prophets, Qohelet, the Gospel writers, Paul, the Church Fathers, the Reformationists, the Counter-reformationists, and so on. Holy scriptures of all faiths are produced and received by those whose concern is "the explication of the significance of events and not the events themselves",[48] and, as Robert Detweiler has argued, the very holiness of scripture lies partly in its occult or inscrutable nature, conveying "the incomprehensible otherness of the gods"[49] and necessitating the exercise of hermeneutics. Louis Mackey has suggested that even Being-in-presence, the historical, bodily manifestation of Divinity which constitutes the great hope of Christian theology, is a text to be read. Orthodox Christology would have it that in Christ, the gulf between word and flesh, between signifier and Signified has been spanned; the transcendental *logos* has assumed the mantle of earthly existence and thus, incarnate, literalised once and for all every metaphor for the Divine. Mackey's admonition is that

> [w]hat Nabokov said of the word "reality" should also be said of a word like "Incarnation"....it should never be used except in scare-quotes.[50]

By this he means that even the Incarnation is a sign, and reasons that if we could somehow magically travel back through the ages to first-century Palestine and witness directly the birth, teachings, miracles, transfiguration, death and resurrection of Jesus, thus avoiding the historical/theological distortions of the Gospel writers, our experi-

---

[48] Zelechow (1992), p.163.
[49] Detweiler (1985), p.219.
[50] Mackey (1983), p.266.

ence would still fail to deliver immediacy, or the unmediated apprehension of Presence:

> Suppose we had been there, what would we have heard? Words which, like any other words, require interpretation, and which therefore do not by themselves deliver the intended meaning of their speaker. How often in the Gospels does Jesus feel that he has been misunderstood!....Suppose we had been contemporaries of Jesus, what would we have seen? Some very strange goings-on. Overwhelming proofs of the presence of God in this man? The presence itself? No. Just signs and wonders: signs calling for interpretation and wonders resisting it. If his deeds had been proofs of his divinity, the Christ could not have been rejected, and Jesus would not have appended to a list of his miracles the admonition: "Blessed is he that is not offended in me".[51]

What deconstruction necessitates, then, is a theology "without nostalgia for theological presence"[52] (and it is important here to distinguish nostalgia from desire: the former, with its connotations of yearning for the recovery of a Golden Age, implies that there was once a time when we had what we now lack; desire, on the other hand, can be nameless, unimagineable, and need not be rooted in any past experience, real or illusory). The scope of this book, however, does not allow for much more than a glance in the direction of deconstructive theology, and accordingly it is my aim only to look as closely at deconstructive theology as is necessary to indicate one or two of the directions in which it might develop—and, more pertinently, to show how such a theology might inform feminist biblical hermeneutics.

If we accept that there has always been a complicity between metaphysics and what we now call deconstruction, then it is not impossible that movements or ideas now called deconstructive can be read, at certain points, without any violent degree of misrepresentation into the existing Western theological tradition. In a recent paper published in *Christianity and Literature*, David Thomson examines the relationship between various medieval mystical texts and deconstructive criticism; he does not go so far as to say that the likes

---

[51] *Ibid.* p.265.
[52] Ash (1987), p.75.

of Teresa of Avila, John of the Cross and Julian of Norwich were "actually" deconstructionists *avant la lettre*, but he indicates nevertheless that these and other mystics were keenly aware of the shortcomings of language in determining Being-in-presence, and that they had a sense of the inevitability of deferral and interpretation which informed even their most immediate experience of the Divine. Thomson explores "this near paradox that those most involved in primary experience, the mystics, are the ones most likely to insist on the primacy of interpretation over experience", and in so doing he makes the decidedly Derridean-sounding claim that

> [i]t is not simply that words about God fall short of the glory of God and ought to be jettisoned to attain real presence, but that even the real presence, what Christians might call "very God", is itself merely another notion *about* God. God does not exist, for people, save as interpretation.[53]

Thomson sees this idea as a kind of theme which can be identified again and again at key points in the texts of the Christian mystics. From the writing of the twelfth-century theologian Richard of St. Victor, for example, we are presented with the following surprising admonition:

> if you already believe that you see Christ transfigured, you should not easily believe whatever you see....or whatever you hear from Him— unless Moses and Elijah appear with Him. For we know that every testimony stands firm on the word of two or three....[I do not] accept Christ in His glorification if Moses and Elijah do not stand beside Him.[54]

Here, even the direct evidence of the senses in apprehending Presence is to be rejected unless that evidence is accompanied by the interpretative "signs" of Moses and Elijah: Being cannot be guaranteed as such without commentary, and even before the gaze of the devout mystic, "Incarnation and interpretation arise together".[55] Similarly, Julian of Norwich can be found at many points throughout the *Revelations of Divine Love* to assert that the meanings of her vi-

---

[53] Thomson (1991), p.109.

[54] Richard of St. Victor: *The Twelve Patriarchs* trans. Grover A Zinn (Paulist, New York 1979), p.138. Quoted in Thomson *op. cit.* p.111.

[55] Thomson *ibid.* p.111.

sions are determined by what she considers to be authoritative commentary: "I shall always believe what is held, preached and taught
by Holy Church".[56] St. John of the Cross presents an even stronger
apologetic for interpretative discourse, affirming an absence-in-
Presence which relativises the significance of mystical experience,
and even renders such experience spiritually dangerous to those who
take its meaning as given:

> They think that, because of their awareness of the genuineness and
> divine origin of these visions, it is advantageous to admit and trust
> them. They do not reflect that, as with worldly goods, *failure to deny*
> *them can be a hindrance*, and cause attachment and possessiveness
> concerning them.[57]

Here, the recognition of the necessity to "deny" or contextualise
even the most convincing determinations of Presence is made explicit: mystical experience is, like worldly wealth, no more than a
sign of Divine grace, and we must be at least prepared or willing to
account it as nothing, as a trace, the repository of absence that *signi-*
fies Presence without delivering it. Thomson's paper is exploratory
and falls short of comprehensive analysis, and he does not claim that
the texts of the medieval Christian mystics are in fact congruent at

---

[56] Julian of Norwich: *Revelations of Divine Love* trans. Clifton Wolters (Penguin
Books, London 1966), p.75. Quoted in Thomson *op. cit.* p.114. We cannot, of
course, ignore the sceptical view that it would have been dangerous for Julian to assert otherwise—those who dreamed dreams and saw visions in fourteenth-century
England were only too liable to draw unwelcome attention to themselves, and by
far the safest course in "going public" was that of punctuating your discourse with
regular avowals of fidelity to orthodox doctrine—but this in itself can be seen as an
indication of the role played by political factors in all kinds of dogmatic statements
of belief. As it happens, there are many points in the Revelations at which Julian
appears to have strayed some considerable distance from "what is held, preached
and taught by Holy Church". The ambiguity which this introduces into the
"meaning" of the *Revelations* and the authorial intentions of the Norwich anchoress
provides a good example of the inseparability of the text from our commentaries on
it. On Julian and orthodoxy, cf. Francis Oakley: *The Western Church in the Later*
Middle Ages (Cornell University Press, London 1979); Brant Pelphrey: *Christ Our*
Mother (Darton, Longman & Todd Ltd., London 1989); Sheila Upjohn: *In Search*
of Julian of Norwich (Darton, Longman & Todd Ltd., London 1989).

[57] John of the Cross: *The Ascent of Mount Carmel* trans. Kieren Kavanaugh and
Otilio Rodriguez (I.C.S., Washington D.C. 1979), p.154 (my italics). Quoted in
Thomson *op.cit.* p.116.

all points with deconstruction. He does, however, demonstrate (at least to a degree of satisfaction which invites further study) that the theology of the mystics points the believer in much the same direction as might a deconstructive theology: toward a faith predicated upon (indeed, necessitated by) a displaced, deferred God; a God who is not "nonexistent" but absent, the desire for whom generates discourse, interpretation, the play of signs:

> Whether he is Being or the master of beings, God himself is, and appears as what he is, within difference, that is to say, as difference and within dissimulation.[58]

Logocentrism, the "tradition which esteems the self-presence of meaning in specific units of signification",[59] is what both Derrida (explicitly and exhaustively) and the Christian mystics (more suggestively) warn us against: it is the temptation to locate meaning in the signifiers we use to construct it,

> the tendency, endemic to religion, to mistake words for presence. And "words are presence" only in the essentially contradictory sense that words are the only presence there is. All is conceived in interpretation, even the Christ of Christocentrism. God is found by faith,[60]

and faith is groping in near-darkness, seeking out and reading the indistinct tracks and traces of God, traces which both signify and ceaselessly defer the object of the search.

A more "politicised" reading of deconstruction into theology is that outlined by James Evans in "Deconstructing the Tradition: Narrative Strategies in Nascent Black Theology". Evans' thesis is that the early texts of black American theology "called into question the intellectual hegemony of the white, male, Western theological tradition"[61] in a way which was both iconoclastic (questioning and rejecting the racial/cultural assumptions underlying the dominant theological tradition) and affirmative (forging a new theology and a corresponding biblical-hermeneutical matrix based on the shared experience of oppression), and which thus employed to great effect the

---

[58] Derrida (1978), p.74.
[59] Thomson *ibid.* p.118.
[60] *Ibid.* p.118.
[61] Evans (1990), p.101.

twin deconstructive gestures of "destruction and construction, man-
tling and dismantling".[62] Evans' analysis has considerable relevance
to the projects of feminist theology and feminist biblical hermeneutics, as it underlies the importance of experience in articulating a
theology of the marginalised—experience not as an interpretative
be-all and end-all, but as an indispensable means both of validating
one's own hermeneutical stance and of demythologising fixed, pre-
vailing ideologies. Evans argues that the experience of what it was
to be black and oppressed provided a grounding "subtext...an ex-
pressive and interpretative framework"[63] for subsequent theological
/hermeneutical activity and discourse, while the same awareness of
subjectivity or political interest in all texts provided a lever with
which to deconstruct the "Divine" authority of dominant white religion:

> the [prevailing] theological tradition was de-mystified by showing that
> black people are not "a people without a text", the Bible is not "a text
> without an author", and that European-American theology is not "a
> text without a point of view".[64]

Evans sees this demystification as having been an essentially deconstructive strategy, an example of how deconstruction's all-
textualising tendencies can have positive as well as negative potential; while the so-called objective authority of biblical and theological texts is undermined by showing that all writing is politically interested, subjective experience can be seen as a legitimate "text"
demanding critical attention and commentary:

> In a society where black people are considered to be "unproductive",
> i.e., unemployed or on welfare, black theology is built on the as-
> sumption that black people are the producers and the agents in their
> own histories. "Black power" was the name given to the self-
> validating force in black experience which undergirds that assump-
> tion.[65]

---

[62] *Ibid.* p.102.
[63] *Ibid.* p.104.
[64] *Ibid.* p.107.
[65] *Ibid.* p.106.

The parallel here between the "self-validating force" of black experience and that of women under patriarchy is clear. The roles, work and even the presence of women in patriarchal religious texts and teaching have long been devalued and sidelined; to read that experience of oppression now as itself a text, both as subversive commentary on patriarchal discourse *and* as primary narrative to be read and interpreted, is to adopt a hermeneutical approach which is usefully deconstructive not just in (feminist) theory, but also in that it is rooted in the particularities of women's lives. Experience is not thereby raised to the status of fundamental principle, but it is nevertheless justified provisionally as a necessary *a priori* from which to proceed. The danger of absolutising the validity of experience is indicated by Evans to have been realised at an early stage in the development of black theology:

> The question "Why a black theology?" is answered with the assertion that there is an infinite qualitative distinction between black and white theology. Initially, this aspect of black theology was criticised because it appeared to claim a kind of infallible privilege for black people, but it should be noted that this position was a necessary *starting point* for black theology because of the devaluation of black life and culture, and not the conclusion of the black theological task.[66]

The same attendant danger lurks on the margins of feminist theology: in both cases, a deconstructive awareness of the fragmented, textual nature of subjectivity and experience guards against the starting-point of the discourse in question becoming mistaken for its inviolate essence. Derrida's remarks, outlined above, on the necessity of a stable discursive "centre" which is nevertheless subject to the rule of *différance* are pertinent here—the need to establish relatively determinate principles of thought and experience does not accord "infallible privilege" to those principles; but, just as importantly for black and feminist discourses, the reverse also holds true:

> To deny the absoluteness of any given "center" is not to deny the possibility that it can function as a center.[67]

---

[66] *Ibid.* p.114.
[67] LaFargue (1988), p.350.

A deconstructive theology or biblical hermeneutics can thus accommodate the kind of creative self-definition and redefinition that
allows for changes in what it means to be black, or to be a woman,
in a changing society. In operating as a dynamic or gesture rather
than as an explicitly partisan hermeneutics, deconstruction follows
(or anticipates) the logic of "identity politics" which, as we have
seen, is itself a kind of deconstruction of the opposition between essentialism and relativism, and which thus provides a stable yet
flexible set of criteria for an identifiably black or feminist (or gay, or
lesbian, or working class, or Latin American) theology or hermeneutics.[68] The texts in which such a theology or hermeneutics might
find itself formulated should be creative and fluid rather than systematic or rigorously objective. In defining itself partly against an
oppressive tradition, any theology of resistance should feel itself
free from much of the weight of conformity to traditional modes of
discourse, and in feminist terms this should mean that patriarchal
dogma gives way to experimentation; abstract, analytical scrutiny to
a more experience-based approach to truth. In the context of early
black theology, Evans writes that

> the black theologian is a type of "bricoleur", an ingenious folk artist,
> whose work does not fit the mold of classical theological discourse
> because it is drawn from the cultural wellspring of African-American
> experience. This is a kind of creativity founded on the "stuff" of black
> life, its joy and pain, its victories and disappointments.[69]

Nascent African-American theology is thus understood as having
been an open-ended discourse within which all who participated in
"the stuff of black life" could be heard, and the black theologian as
one who pieced together various aspects of that experience into a
model of God which would be intelligible and relevant to all participants in the culture. The credentials of the theologian-as-folk-artist
were not established by education, gender or any other criterion
other than that he or she wished to give some form or utterance to
the experience of God in his or her particular cultural context. This
portrayal is perhaps a historically generous one, sketching as it does
a suspiciously Utopian community based on mutual respect and con-

---

[68] Cf. the discussion in chapter 2 of Alcoff (1988).

[69] Evans *op.cit.* p.111.

cern, and it does not take into account the reality of exploitation, oppression and power imbalances *within* black culture. But what Evans
wishes to demonstrate is simply that there is much creative power
and potential to be found in writing from perceived religious experience rather than from received theological tradition; more importantly, it is the only way forward for those whose received tradition
is one of bondage and humiliation. Once again, the parallel between
African-American theology and feminist theology does not need to
be spelled out in detail: nascent black theology, like emergent feminist theologies in patriarchal contexts, provides an example of
strategies which are integral to deconstructive criticism—strategies
of questioning dominant ideologies, and of textualising both ideology and experience; ways of formulating discourse which is not
simply critical of the old structure, but which also affirms the possibility of subversion, displacement, innovation and the creation of
positive alternatives.

Midrash: a Deconstructive Hermeneutics?

If deconstruction, in concerning itself with determinations of being
and presence, has direct relevance to theology, then the equal emphasis it places on such concepts as "writing" and "text" make it
equally relevant to biblical hermeneutics, if not more so. While it
may be reductive to pigeonhole deconstruction as a subgenre within
literary criticism, it is evident nevertheless that deconstruction has
had particular impact in literary-theoretical circles, and that a large
proportion both of Derrida's published writing and of other deconstructive texts consists of critical readings of literary and philosophical works. In the context of religious studies, then, it is difficult not
to harbour a certain tendency to see deconstruction as a practice
which has more natural and immediate bearing on exegesis than it
does on theology—although once again, to present these as separate
or opposed fields masks the fact that exegesis is never devoid of
some kind of theology, and that theology in turn is a form of reading
or interpretation. One arguable point of contact between the two is
that as with theology, so with biblical hermeneutics there exist significant strands within the existing tradition which can be shown to
have suggestive parallels with key deconstructive strategies, and

which indicate therefore that deconstruction is not so much a new and disruptive development in religious discourse as a radical re-formulation of certain historically-identifiable principles or approaches to understanding. The area of biblical interpretation with which the closest ties to poststructuralist literary theory have been established, and thus the tradition I wish to examine here, is that which arose in codified or "official" form out of post-70 C.E. Judaism: the tradition of Rabbinic midrash.

In midrash, we have one form of biblical commentary whose close relationship with modern criticism has been both asserted and refuted with equal degrees of enthusiasm. The arguments are complex on both sides, and accordingly on both sides a good deal of creative scholarship and imagination has been evident; indeed, the controversy over Rabbinic and poststructuralist hermeneutics is to be welcomed if for no other reason than that it focuses attention precisely on such issues as creativity and imagination in exegesis. The main points of the debate can be summarised as follows: on one hand, there is a growing body of opinion which holds that Rabbinic midrash in many ways anticipated the insights of poststructuralist criticism, or that "what modern literary theorists are now discovering about textual exegesis was already practised by the rabbis close to two millenia ago".[70] This is essentially the argument put forward by Susan Handelman in *The Slayers of Moses* (1982), a study which provides an ambitious step-by-step guide to exactly how and why the Rabbis were the hermeneutical forebears of such modern literary theorists as Derrida and Harold Bloom. Handelman begins by positing a radical division between Hebrew thought and Greek philosophy, and goes on to argue that from each of these matrices has evolved a distinct and particular kind of hermeneutics. She makes the point that the philosophy of Plato and Aristotle, with its suspicion of language as opposed to Form or Idea, is a philosophy of transcendence, designed

> to make the word suspect and to steer the seeker of truth away from language towards a silent ontology, or towards a purely rational sys-

---

[70] Halivni (1991), p.158.

tem of signs, an artificially constructed ideal language such as mathematics.[71]

This, according to Handelman, has given rise to an essentially metaphysical hermeneutics, a mode of interpretation which rests on the belief that "the central act of knowing is a movement *beyond* discourse",[72] a movement beyond signs and in the direction of an unambiguous Reality behind them. This hermeneutics has enjoyed spectacular doctrinal success in Christianity, a faith whose key sacred text, the New Testament, is both regularly punctuated with Hellenistic exhortations to distinguish between letter and spirit, and is itself enshrined as the one true and authoritative commentary on the Hebrew Bible—the final "reality" or fulfilment of the Old Testament's signs and prophecies. The miracle of Christ himself is that he embodies both sign and Spirit, signifier (in human form, the image of God) and transcendental Signified (God-in-Presence), a Platonic miracle if ever there was one:

> Behind the aspiration to the invisible, nonsensible world was the Greek desire to *see*, a concept of thought in terms of the image (*idea*, from the Greek *eidos*, image)....Hence, when the Christian deity was born in the cradle of the pagan world, he was, inevitably, a *physical* image of God, a mediator, and a *substitution*. He mediated the gap between sensible and nonsensible, thought and thing, by becoming both at once....the metaphysical transfer, which depended on the recognition of the tension between categories, the recognition that the metaphorical simultaneously "was" and "was not" what it "stood for", became itself literalized. As the first chapter of the Gospel of John puts it, "The Word became flesh and dwelt among us".[73]

Hebrew thought, however, is said by Handelman to operate according to an entirely different logic. In contrast to the binary-oppositional logic of language and idea, signifier and signified (a tension which Christianity attempts to resolve in the doctrine of the Incarnation), Hebrew implicitly postulates an "*original* unity of word and thing, speech and thought, discourse and truth",[74] a unity

---

[71] Handelman (1982), p.4.
[72] *Ibid.* p.7.
[73] *Ibid.* p.17.
[74] *Ibid.* p.4 (my italics).

expressed in *dabhar*. Where the Greek word for "word", *onoma*, also means "name" and thus resonates with the metaphysical notion that words are "names" for immutable Forms, the Hebrew *dabhar* means not only "word" but also "thing", "matter" and "affair"[75] (in addition to a host of related concepts such as advice, promise and decree[76]). Meaning, or reality, then, in the Hebrew tradition is very much coincident with the language in which it is thought, expressed, communicated and disputed: discourse and interpretation are not simply ways of accessing truth; to put it perhaps over-simply, they *are* the truth. This is the kind of epistemology which Handelman sees as having been inherited by the Rabbis and developed in Rabbinic midrash; an approach to knowledge which seeks always to generate interpretation rather than to transcend it or close it off— "[f]or the Greeks, following Aristotle, things are not exhausted by discourse; for the Rabbis, discourse is not exhausted by things".[77] Where Christianity has long celebrated the final and substantial manifestation of the Word, subordinating discourse to one "decisive act of presence",[78] Rabbinic Judaism is said to have celebrated *dabhar* itself, and to have developed a hermeneutics conspicuous for its lack of any commitment to transcending the linguistic order:

> For the Rabbis....the primary reality was linguistic; true being was a God who *speaks* and creates *texts*, and *imitatio deus* [sic] was not silent suffering, but speaking and interpreting....the infinity of meaning and plurality of interpretation [were] as much the cardinal virtues, even divine imperatives, for Rabbinic thought as they [were] the cardinal sins for Greek thought. The movement of Rabbinic interpretation [was] not from one opposing sphere to another, from the sensible to the nonsensible, but rather "from sense to sense", a movement into the text, not out of it.[79]

Rabbinic hermeneutics, thus understood, is an interpretative mode which pulls many and varied meanings out of the biblical text: the

---

[75] *Ibid.* pp.3-4.

[76] Cf. Francis Brown, S.R. Driver and Charles A. Briggs (eds.): *A Hebrew and English Lexicon of the Old Testament* (The Clarendon Press, Oxford 1906), pp.182-84.

[77] Handelman *op.cit.* p.8.

[78] *Ibid.* p.193.

[79] *Ibid.* pp.4, 21.

Torah, as the Word of God, is perfect and all creation is contained therein, yet at the same time it is "perpetually incomplete",[80] full of gaps and lacunae which require elucidation. But it is not only the gaps which call for interpretation: the very sacredness of Torah, its status as not just the product but the manifestation of a Divine intelligence, means that no aspect of it can be accidental or contingent; meanings are thus to be found in individual words, in the numerical values of their letters, in the crowns at the tips of the letters, in repetitions, omissions, even in aberrations of spelling and orthography. Nothing is irrelevant to the Rabbis' hermeneutical programme, nothing lies outside the concerns of reading and interpretation; there is nothing, to use a now-familiar phrase, outside the text.[81] This means, ultimately, that commentary itself comes to receive the same authoritative sanction as primary text. According to Rabbinic tradition, not only the written but also the *oral* Torah was given by God to Israel; the principles for interpreting the Word and applying interpretation to everyday life were as essential to the Rabbis as was the Word itself, and so the tradition of interpretation of the Law—oral Torah—was declared as holy as the Law itself: "all that a faithful disciple will expound in the future in front of his master was already disclosed to Moses at Sinai".[82] Commentary thus becomes retrospectively validated by the highest possible authority: that of direct revelation from God to Moses. This results, of course, in a certain blurring of any qualitative distinctions between text and commentary, between written and oral Torah. From the Rabbinic perspective, scripture exists less as a static, time-bound document than as a process, a ceaseless and sometimes cataclysmic unfurling of meanings,

> applicable not only to Biblical time and place, but to all time and place. Through proper interpretation, then, the application and meaning appropriate for any contingency is revealed. Thus interpretation is not essentially separate from the text itself—an external act intruded upon it—but rather the *extension* of the text, the uncovering of the

---

[80] *Ibid.* p.40.
[81] Cf. *ibid.* pp.38-39.
[82] Jerusalem Talmud *Peah* 6:2. Quoted in Handelman *ibid.* p.40.

connective network of relations, a part of the continuous revelation of
the text itself: at bottom, another aspect of the text.[83]

The broad parallels between Handelman's view of Rabbinic hermeneutics and contemporary literary criticism may by now be apparent,
and indeed Handelman's overriding concern is, perhaps too ambi-
tiously, to make those parallels explicit and consistent. From a detailed account of Rabbinic thought and interpretative methodology,
she proceeds to draw up a map of modern literary theory whose
main thoroughfare leads directly from the Rabbis, through Freud and
Lacan, and on to Derrida and Harold Bloom: her thesis is that these
latter theorists (all, with the exception of Lacan, Jewish) have inherited from the Rabbis and continued to develop a "complicated inter-
weaving of tradition, revision, and heresy"[84] in their approach to
texts. Freud, in his psychoanalytic science and his interpretation of
dreams, is presented as a kind of post-Enlightenment Talmudist,
reading the unconscious not in search of Platonic truth/ falsity, but
with a view to uncovering more and deeper meanings.[85] Every apparently arbitrary detail of the unconscious, whether manifest in
dreams, behavioural oddities, neuroses, slips of the tongue and so
on, condenses a "wilderness" of significance, a polysemous wilderness in which Freud, like the Rabbis before him, is portrayed as
having wandered; and this wandering is presented as a kind of exile
from the realm of rational, empiricist (read: Hellenistic) science. To
the Freudian mind,

> [i]nterpretation is not, in the Aristotelian sense, the distinguishing of
> truth from falsehood, but the relationship of hidden to shown: not ap-
> pearance to reality, but manifest to latent....Everything that logical
> consciousness rejects as nonsensical, useless, disconnected, contradic-
> tory and impossible has, in fact, a meaning; and to say that dreams in-
> deed have a meaning, Freud recognized, put him in opposition to
> every ruling theory....Freud was the "exegete who rediscovers the
> logic of the illogical kingdom".[86]

---

[83] Handelman *ibid.* p.39.

[84] *Ibid.* p.222.

[85] *Ibid.* p.146.

[86] *Ibid.* p.148. Handelman quotes Paul Ricoeur: *Freud and Philosophy: An Essay
on Interpretation* (Yale University Press, New Haven 1970), p.35.

Jacques Lacan, the intellectual who in the 1950's and 60's reread psychoanalysis in terms of poetics and linguistics, and announced that "the unconscious is structured like a language", is presented by Handelman as having played Joshua to Freud's Moses. It was Lacan who first perceived the connection between Freud and Rabbinic thought, and he saw the Jews overall as

> the interpretative people par excellence, developing their hermeneutic skills particularly in the crush of exile: "....ever since the return from Babylon, the Jew is he who knows how to read. This means he withdraws from his literal utterance so as to find an interval which then allows for the game of interpretation".[87]

Freud and Lacan are, in turn, shown by Handelman to have been read and appropriated by Derrida, "another in the line of Jewish prodigal sons",[88] whose deconstructive strategies involve

> an interpretative process in which attention is paid to the minute details of a text, to syntax, to the shapes of words—the dream's treatment of words as things. This is in effect a species of midrashic play.[89]

Handelman sees deconstruction-as-midrash as searching for meaning in much the same way as the Rabbis sought after God in Torah: the Signified is absent, deferred, perceivable only through the process of interpretation which yields up not Presence but further interpretation, the play of signs. As the prodigal son, Derrida is "unrepentant, enjoying his escapade",[90] affirming interpretation, a life of exile in the abyss of textuality, not as the curse or predicament portrayed in the Christian doctrine of a "fallen" world, but as the power and privilege of human existence:

> Let the commentary, then, says Derrida, the writing developed in the endless delay of exile, be all, and be playful. Let exile subvert being and logos entirely.[91]

---

[87] Handelman *op. cit.* p.154. Handelman quotes Lacan: "Radiophonie" in *Scilicet* 2/3 (Paris, 1970), quoted also in Mehlman (1972), p.32.
[88] Handelman *op. cit.* p.166.
[89] *Ibid.* pp.169-70.
[90] *Ibid.* p.175.
[91] *Ibid.* p.175.

Finally, Handelman turns her attention to Harold Bloom, the literary critic whose concept of hermeneutics as a kind of Oedipal power struggle relates back to the Rabbis insofar as Rabbinic interpretation, with its claim to the status of Torah itself, operates under Bloom's "anxiety of influence", the desire of the critic for mastery over the primary text, the will to wrest canonical privilege from the author under discussion. Also discussed is Bloom's interest in kabbalah, his notion that kabbalah is a kind of deconstruction of representational concepts of God, a "radical definition of God's absence and withdrawal as his presence".[92] In summary, Handelman reiterates that Bloom, Derrida, Freud and related theorists have all, in various ways, continued in the tradition of the "heretic hermeneutic" codified by the Rabbis in midrash. The tradition is manifestly Jewish rather than Christian, in much the same way as it is Hebraic rather than Hellenistic: exile, in many ways the definitive experience of the people of Israel,

> is resolved by making "exile" the precise metaphor for the act of creation and interpretation. This is a resolution in the Jewish mode, not as fulfilment of signs in the incarnate word, but as the raising of the Jewish historical condition into a paradigm of existence: to be is to be in exile; to create is to endure catastrophe; to make texts is already to interpret; absence is presence.[93]

Needless to say, the idea of Rabbinic hermeneutics as the precursory model for contemporary literary theory has not gone uncontested. To begin with, the underlying notion that there exists a fundamental antipathy between Hebrew/Rabbinic and Greek/Platonic systems of thought has been challenged by such scholars as David Daube and (more recently) Philip Alexander. Daube asserts explicitly that "Rabbinic methods of interpretation derive from Hellenistic rhetoric",[94] arguing that Hillel, the "great Pharisee" whose *middot*, or rules for interpretation of scripture, provided the technical framework for all subsequent *halakhah*, developed his hermeneutical laws from existing Graeco-Roman systems of rhetoric and jurisprudence.

---

[92] *Ibid.* p.217.
[93] *Ibid.* p.222.
[94] Daube (1949), p.240.

A "common Hellenistic background",[95] an irresistably Greek culture
in which Hillel and Cicero were contemporaries, is put forward as
having made it inevitable that the Rabbis would borrow heavily
from Greek philosophical thought. Daube sees Rabbinic interpretation as part of

> a science the beginnings of which may be traced back to Plato, Aris-
> totle and their contemporaries. It recurs in Cicero, Hillel and Philo —
> with enormous differences in detail, yet *au fond* the same. Cicero did
> not sit at the feet of Hillel, nor Hillel at the feet of Cicero....[but
> p]hilosophical instruction was very similar in outline whether given at
> Rome, Jerusalem or Alexandria.[96]

Philip Alexander shares Daube's extreme scepticism regarding the
validity of categorising Rabbinic interpretation as a peculiarly Hebraic hermeneutics. Like Daube, Alexander is unqualified in his insistence that "the hermeneutics of the Rabbis can be paralleled in all
essentials from the hermeneutics of the Graeco-Roman world", and
that having arisen from a strongly Hellenistic and Hellenising society, "Rabbinic hermeneutics is thoroughly of its time and place".[97]
He goes on to argue that the "fundamental and all pervasive form of
midrash"[98]—*lemma*, or quote from the primary text, followed by
commentary—corresponds to the characteristic structure of Greek
hypomnemata or commentaries on Homer, and that in both cases, a
key function of interpretation was to preserve the original text from
corruption. Like the Rabbis, the Greek commentators on Homer held
an overriding "*respect* for the received text", and tended "to leave
the standard text intact, and to confine their suggested improvements
to the accompanying notes".[99] Alexander also presents the gradual
institutionalisation of the Rabbinate within Jewish society as having
been directly influenced by the institutionalisation of the Roman legal system: issues of influence and authority were markedly similar
in both contexts, and the structure of the Rabbinic legal system is
said to have corresponded at significant points to that of the Imperial

---

[95] *Ibid.* p.257.
[96] *Ibid.* p.257.
[97] Alexander (1990), p.103.
[98] *Ibid.* p.104.
[99] *Ibid.* pp.105-6.

jurists.[100] The style of Rabbinic legal interpretation is similarly put
forward as showing traces of Graeco-Roman influence; overall, Alexander says, "Rabbinic halakhah [was] thoroughly at home in the
legal world of late antiquity".[101]

Thus is the tradition of the "heretic hermeneutic" rerouted from
the start: the challenge which deconstruction presents to logocentrism, which poststructuralist criticism in general presents to stability and univocity of meaning, is argued as having its genesis elsewhere than in some putative antithesis between Rabbinic thought
and Graeco-Roman philosophy. The connection between Rabbinic
hermeneutics and modern literary theory has been questioned on
other grounds: David Stern, in his review of *The Slayers of Moses*,
takes issue with several aspects of Handelman's analysis, questioning the intrinsic and inescapable "Jewishness" of the work of Freud,
Lacan and Derrida,[102] and suggesting that Handelman, in projecting
the concerns of latter-day critical theorists back onto the Rabbis (e.g.
where the Rabbis are said to harbour Oedipal resentment against the
authority of Torah), is guilty of forcing one or two "general correspondences" into the mould of systematic point-for-point parallels.
Stern wonders whether, in the final analysis, Rabbinic hermeneutics
can be said to bear more than a kind of coincidental generic resemblance to contemporary critical theory:

> the question remains whether these [general correspondences] reflect the
> revival of rabbinic hermeneutics in contemporary criticism, or whether
> they are simply functions of the fact that both midrash and criticism are
> species of commentary.[103]

Elsewhere, Stern addresses the issue of indeterminacy, and argues
that the interpretative "play" of such flamboyant *bricoleurs* as Lacan
and Derrida has no necessary relation to the polysemous exegesis of
the Rabbis. While indeterminacy, Stern reasons, "may still remain a

---

[100] *Ibid.* pp.109-17.

[101] *Ibid.* p.115.

[102] Stern (1984), p.199.

[103] *Ibid.* pp.203-4. Cf. Handelman's response to Stern in "Fragments of the Rock:
Contemporary Literary Theory and the Study of Rabbinic Texts" in *Prooftexts* 5
(1985), pp.75-95; and Stern's subsequent reply in "Literary Criticism or Literary
Homilies? Susan Handelman and the Contemporary Study of Midrash" in *Prooftexts* 5 (1985), pp.96-103.

significant category for understanding our own reading of midrashic discourse",[104] it is nevertheless a concept which was fundamentally alien to the midrashists' interpretative concerns. Stern sees indeterminacy of meaning in modern literary theory as a notion which stems from the sound poststructuralist premise that there is no stable or "correct" perspective from which to interpret language, experience or history; no objective hermeneutical methodology guaranteeing reading rinsed clean of ideology; no possibility of a transparent or universally understandable language.[105] Midrash, on the other hand, according to Stern is "predicated precisely on the existence of such a perspective",[106] i.e. a perspective from which all meanings coalesce into One. This is, of course, the Divine perspective:

> In contemporary criticism, textual meaning is often described spatially in terms of its position either "behind" the text (the traditional logocentric view) or "in front" of it (from the perspective of deconstruction). In the case of Rabbinic Judaism, the divine guarantee of meaning in Scripture might be described more accurately as coming from above, not in the sense of divine effluence or emanation, but literally from on high, from the top of Mount Sinai, from which, the Rabbis claimed, God gave to Moses not only Scripture....but also an "oral Torah", passed on by mouth from generation to generation.[107]

This "divine guarantee of meaning" effectively authorises the hermeneutical freedom of midrash by second-guessing it, and thus provides a preordained limit to the excesses of interpretation, no matter how apparently unrestrained they may become. To reverse Rabbi Akiva's famous dictum,[108] "all is open, and yet all is determined", and the paradox of building a fence around the Torah lies in

---

[104] Stern (1988), p.135.

[105] I am paraphrasing Geoffrey Hartman, who writes of

> the absence of one and only one context from which to view the flux of time or the empirical world, of one and only one method that would destabilize all but itself, of one and only one language to rule understanding and prevent misunderstanding.

Cf. *Criticism in the Wilderness* (Yale University Press, New Haven 1980), p.270. Quoted in Stern (1988), p.141.

[106] Stern *ibid.* p.141.

[107] *Ibid.* p.147.

[108] Cf. Mishnah *Avot* 3:19.

the fact that this operation is designed both to multiply meanings *and* to forestall (unauthorised) indeterminacy.

The discussion over Rabbinic hermeneutics and modern literary theory deals with areas of intersection between two enormously complex fields, and requires much fuller treatment than the foregoing broad analysis has allowed: I hope no more than to have outlined some of the important issues arising on both sides of a tangled and often rancorous debate.[109] We can, at the very least, now see that to present the Rabbis as nascent poststructuralists, or poststructuralist critics as modern-day Rabbis, is a decidedly problematic undertaking, and Stern's observation in particular should be kept in mind that "specialists in midrash too often find literary theorizing about midrash—even when most insightful—not adequately supported by the requisite familiarity with the material under discussion, that is, more wishful that knowledgeable".[110] At the same time, however, I believe that useful parallels can be established between midrash and modern literary theory (in particular deconstruction), parallels whose significance depends to a great extent upon the conclusions drawn from them. The critical success or failure of such an ambitious project as Susan Handelman's is a function of how skilfully and persuasively she can take certain similarities between two distantly-related hermeneutical fields, and build up those similarities into a detailed hermeneutical pedigree. To question or deny the success of her enterprise is not necessarily to deny that these suggestive similarities exist, or that they might yet prove in some other way enlightening.

David Stern complains that literary theorists who enthusiastically embrace midrash as the harbinger of poststructuralist criticism tend to base their arguments on insufficient knowledge of Rabbinic litera-

---

[109] For further reading on Rabbinic hermeneutics and contemporary literary theory, cf. Dauber (1985); Fisch (1986); José Faur: *Golden Doves With Silver Dots: Semiotics and Textuality in Rabbinic Tradition* (Indiana University Press, Bloomington and Indianapolis 1986). On more general literary approaches to midrash, cf. Hartman and Budick (1986); Goldberg (1990); Halivni (1991); Daniel Boyarin: *Intertextuality and the Reading of Midrash* (Indiana University Press, Bloomington and Indianapolis 1990); David Stern: *Parables in Midrash: Narrative and Exegesis in Rabbinic Literature* (Harvard University Press, Cambridge, Mass. and London 1991).

[110] Stern (1988), p.133.

ture. I believe this is a fair objection: if "midrash" is to be understood broadly as codified Rabbinic commentary on important religious and legal texts, then it covers a huge corpus of lengthy volumes, and to draw hard and fast conclusions concerning midrash's overall aims and purposes requires some close acquaintance with the history and texts of the Talmuds, the Targums and a proliferation of halakhic and haggadic commentaries on individual biblical texts—a body of literature so vast, spanning such long periods of time and shaped by such varied historical/cultural circumstances that it becomes risky, to say the least, to generalise too confidently about what "the Rabbis" thought (Susan Handelman's argument, for example, that midrash affirms the essential inseparability of text and commentary leads her to place allegory—the idea of a single "higher" meaning within the shell of a literal narrative—in the Hellenistic/Christian interpretative tradition.[111] This, however, is an overly-polarised view which implicitly—and wrongly—denies the significance of such *midrashim* as the *Song of Songs Rabbah,* which indulges freely in allegorical interpretation at points where the literal sense of the biblical text appears to offend religious or moral sensibilities[112]). But by the same token—and this is a point seldom raised—it should be considered whether or not Handelman, Stern and other participants in the debate have arrived at a sufficiently nuanced understanding of modern literary theory. Like "midrash", "modern literary theory" is a rubric which implies a greater degree of homogeneity than in fact exists, and yet the generalisation goes largely uncontested, as if the likes of Derrida, Kristeva, Bloom, Roland Barthes, Geoffrey Hartman and Mieke Bal (all "modern" literary theorists and, historically speaking, poststructuralists) were not as divided by difference as they are linked by similarity.[113] Even at the piecemeal level, misap-

---

[111] Cf. Handelman (1982), pp.14, 84-5.

[112] Cf. also Lawton (1990), pp.155-7 (on Targumic exegesis and its place in the history of the allegorisation of the Song of Songs); and Marvin H. Pope: *Song of Songs* (Doubleday, New York 1977), p.19.

[113] Judith Butler articulates the problem of exactly who can be held up as "paradigmatic" in contemporary critical discourse:

It may come as a surprise to some purveyors of the Continental scene to learn that Lacanian psychoanalysis in France positions itself officially against poststructuralism, that Kristeva denounces postmodernism, that Foucaultians rarely relate to Derrideans, that Cixous and Irigaray are fundamentally opposed, and that the only tenuous conprehension abounds. Stern's comment, quoted above, on the "spatial" location of meaning in modern criticism, is a case in point. He presents the idea of meaning "behind" the text as "the traditional logocentric view", and opposes it to "the perspective of deconstruction", from which we are told meaning exists "in front" of the text— i.e. where the reader sits. But this behind/in front dualism, baldly opposing deconstruction to logocentrism is, we have seen, simplistic; it fails to take into account the important and inevitable degree of complicity between deconstruction and what it deconstructs. Handelman is similarly reductive:

> As psychoanalysis was a species of parricide and giving of a new law, so Derridean deconstructionism will murder the father-founders of philosophy and disseminate a new writing ....Derrida's specific form of Jewish heresy is not metonymy become metaphor but metonymy run amuck, metonymy declaring itself to be independent of all foundations and yet claiming to be the origin and law of everything.[114]

Again, we have seen that "Derridean deconstructionism" in fact explicitly *disclaims* the "death" of philosophy and announces itself not as "the origin and law of everything"—a rather obviously ontological claim—but as the discursive Other to logocentrism which, like all Others, relies for its identity on its binary opposite, and which thus must question the primacy of all origins including its own.

It is when we consider deconstruction as consisting of interpretative gestures, movements or strategies—rather than as one systematic methodological programme with its central thesis and its stable philosophical principles—that we can best begin to assess its relationship to such forms of hermeneutics as midrash. It should perhaps be restated at this point that my aim in investigating this relationship is not to show that midrash somehow "is" deconstruction (or vice versa), but to identify some hermeneutical characteristics of midrash which parallel certain deconstructive movements and provide ex-

---

nection between French feminism and deconstruction exists between Cixous and Derrida, although a certain affinity in textual practices is to be found between Derrida and Irigaray....Do all these theories have the same structure (a comforting notion to the critic who would dispense with them all at once)? [pp.4-5].

[114] Handelman *op. cit.* pp.171, 174.

amples of how these movements in exegesis need not preclude religious commitment or faith on the part of the interpreter. One commonly-encountered objection to deconstruction in biblical interpretation is that it is too cynical and derisory a hermeneutics for the faithful to bring to bear on a sacred text; particularly in its commitment to "play", deconstruction amounts to a hermeneutics of mockery, of having "the last laugh" on the text. Michael Edwards recently lamented the paucity of biblical criticism "written in love and humility, severe and disciplined, unconcerned for self and devoted to understanding",[115] and suggested that if the bible itself is not enough for the community of faith, if we do in fact need secondary literature in addition to scripture, then the practice of writing and reading should be kept "thoroughly *serious*".[116] If this is to be taken to mean that *homo religiosus* and *homo ludens* cannot be one and the same species, and that a hermeneutics predicated upon interpretative "play" has no place in exegetical discourse, then it finds a sympathetic echo in this more pointed denunciation:

> A poem or prose narrative belongs first to its creator, and so it remains. Accordingly, deconstructionist "play" is incredibly presumptuous. If written criticism, belonging of course to its author, proposes to illumine another's work, how can it do so while denying the personal origin/authorship of the text under consideration? If ignoring the authority of source is legitimate, no deconstructionist has an ontological basis for defending her own critique.[117]

There are a number of fundamental misunderstandings here which lie outside our immediate area of concern: it could be said in passing that a critic who conceives of deconstructive reading as "*ignoring the authority of source*", or who holds that deconstructive criticism seeks legitimation on "ontological" grounds, is a reader whose actual encounters with deconstruction must have been brief and unfortunate. The notions of "play" and "seriousness" at work here, however, are worth a closer look. Michael Edwards' concept of serious exegesis is linked to a pessimistic view of interpretation in general: we should interpret, he argues, in the realisation that hermeneutics is

---

[115] M. Edwards (1989), p.64.

[116] *Ibid.* p.76 (my italics).

[117] B.L. Edwards and B. Woodard (1990), p.314.

the grim necessity of a fallen existence. Exegesis should be a serious undertaking because it confirms the Adamic curse of exile from the presence of God: "theology and criticism, for the same reason, are a necessary evil; they belong to our vanity".[118] Deconstruction, on the other hand, operates according to a view of interpretation as *jouissance*, as pleasure in the endless flux of textuality. The deferral of meaning, the movement from sense to sense is to be understood not as the result of an expulsion from Eden, but—quite the opposite—as liberation, "a way out of the closure of knowledge".[119]

There seems to have been a similar view of interpretation at work in midrash. The ceaseless activity of reading, the wandering in the wilderness of interpretation, was not, in Rabbinic Judaism, the unhappy consequence of primal disobedience[120] but a means of continuous revelation which had its genesis at Sinai. In the aftermath of the destruction of the second Temple and the subsequent scattering of Palestinian Jewry, the Torah became the centre of Jewish religious life, and as such it was called upon to answer the needs of small communities in various cultural contexts. Interpretation became an intensely practical concern, dominated not by abstract theorising about Meaning but by immediate questions of behaviour and social practice. It is hardly surprising, then, that the compilations of biblical commentary which make up "oral Torah" are notable for their diversity: the pages of the Talmuds consist of biblical text surrounded by a confusing juxtapposition of interpretative voices from various places and times, in what amounts to a discussion between Rabbis from different points in history, and the student of Talmud is expected to survey the various interpretations and draw his or her own conclusions. Similarly, in other *midrashim* such as the Rabbinic

---

[118] M. Edwards *op. cit.* p.75. It should be noted that in his discussion of Derridean thought in an earlier publication, Edwards is by no means as antagonistic to deconstruction in exegesis as his comments here might imply. Cf. his *Towards a Christian Poetics* (The MacMillan Press Ltd., London 1984), pp.217-31.

[119] Spivak, in Derrida (1976), p.lxxvii.

[120] On the "light" view of the Fall in Rabbinic Judaism, cf. Hayman (1984). It should, however, be noted that Derrida does not necessarily—or at least certainly not in his earlier work—subscribe to the notion that the Rabbis themselves happily equated interpretation with *jouissance*. Cf. his comments on the "irreducable" difference between "the rabbi and the poet" in (1978) p.67; also the translator's note on p.311.

commentary on Genesis, what the reader finds is not doctrinal closure, not *the* meaning of scripture, but a seemingly endless series of
interpretations which sit side by side in often contradictory attitudes,
carried forward at various points by the formulaic introduction *dabhar 'acher*, "another interpretation".

This is exegetical play at work, "play" in several senses of the
word. There is play in midrash in a kind of mechanical sense;
meanings are not fixed or static, but are allowed a certain looseness,
the licence to range over various texts and issues in a manner which
redefines the rules of interpretative logic. In expounding Genesis
2:16, for example, where God commands *ha-'adam* to keep away
from the tree of the knowledge of good and evil, R. Levi draws six
commandments out of the one prohibition under scrutiny, each
commandment being triggered by verbal association with other
scriptural verses.[121] The meaning of the Edenic prohibition is thus
not concretised but made diffuse, existing in the various relationships which R. Levi establishes between the *lemma* and other pieces
of scripture. Furthermore, these relationships are established not
through rational argument or dialectical reasoning, but by means of
a kind of word-game: Gen. 2:16 is linked to Exod. 22:27 by the
presence of the word *'elohim* in both verses, the word *le'mor* connects Gen. 2:16 with Jer. 3:1, and so on. Calling such patterning
"playful" does not deny the seriousness of the Rabbis' hermeneutical task, nor does it call into question their respect for the biblical
text, but it does serve to indicate that their style of interpretation operates according to an approach which traditional logocentric exegesis has relegated to the margins of "serious" criticism.

At one significant point in midrash, the notion of play is quite literal. The Rabbinic commentary on the first words in the Torah,
beˀreˀshit baraˀ 'elohim ("in the beginning [when] God created...."
Gen. 1:1), links this phrase to a passage in Proverbs where another

---

[121] Cf. *Beˀreˀshit Rabbah* 16:6. The Genesis verse begins *wayeˀtsaw YHWH 'elohim
'al ha-'adam le'mor*. R. Levi connects *YHWH* here to the appearance of the Tetra-
grammaton in Lev. 24:16 (*weˀnoqebh shem-YHWH mot yumat*, "and he who blas-
phemes the name of the LORD shall be put to death") and thus finds a prohibition
against blasphemy in the Genesis verse. Similarly, *ha-'adam* here is connected to
ha-'adam in Gen. 9:6 (*shophekh dam ha-'adam*, "he who sheds the blood of a
man...") and so the Edenic commandment is stretched to include the prohibition
against murder.

genesis is related. In Proverbs 8:22, *chokhmah*, the personification
of Wisdom, speaks of having been created at the beginning of all
things (*YHWH qanani re'shit dar^{e}ko*, "the LORD created me as the
outset of his work"), and so the Rabbis quote *chokhmah* here in
B^{e}re'shit Rabbah as having been present with God at the creation of
the world.[122] And at this unutterably solemn moment, *chokhmah*, according to Rabbinic exegesis, plays. The intersecting verse in
B^{e}re'shit Rabbah is Prov. 8:30:

> And I was beside him, a little child
> And I was [his] delight, playing before him always.

The Hebrew *m^{e}sacheqet*, (playing/rejoicing) is from *sachaq*, to
laugh, rejoice, exult; and this is what the midrash portrays hyposta-
tised Wisdom as having done at the moment of creation. Midrash
thus, in this instance, "not only plays with words; it points to the
idea of such play at the beginning of the discussion".[123]

It can be seen, then, that midrash, being part of a tradition which
esteems the activity of interpretation as a Divine sanction (as opposed to one which conceives of it as exile from Presence, the result
of a curse) provides many examples of how exegetical "play" need
not signal a departure from rigorous reading or from "serious" or
devotional respect for the text. For the Rabbis, Torah was so holy it
defiled the hands, and yet this holiness stemmed not from the fact
that it enshrined one unitary meaning or system of signification, but
from the infinity of ways in which it spoke to its readers. But can we
today call the Rabbis' exegetical "play" deconstructive? On one
hand, the freedom with which midrash takes its interpretative cues
from puns, word-associations and apparent intertextual coincidences
looks very much like the hermeneutical licence which characterises
deconstructive criticism. Like deconstruction, midrash is also constrained by the text it interprets; it works from *within* scripture[124] and
thus cannot say simply whatever it likes:

---

[122] *Ber. Rab.* 1:1.

[123] Fisch (1986), p.230.

[124] Cf. Rachel Salmon and Gerda Elata Alster (1992) on the "participatory stance"
of midrash, p.180.

Noah in his ark, Joseph in the pit, Ezekiel lying on his side for three hundred and ninety days, Jeremiah in prison, Jonah in the belly of the fish—all these are images of hermeneutic constraint....what we have... in midrash is the recognition of unlimited possibilities but also of the unlimited authority inhering in a prime text.[125]

On the other hand, however, midrash is fundamentally committed to the concept of a transcendental Signified, of God the divine Guarantor of meaning, and so in this respect it is perhaps not as wildly deconstructive as it appears. When Moses, according to Rabbinic legend, ascended into heaven and found God tying crowns to the letters of scripture for Rabbi Akiva later to untie,[126] he witnessed a securing of control over meaning which implied that the Author (blessed be He) fully anticipated every one of His readers—not by any stretch of the imagination a Derridean vision of the Almighty. But the way in which this story continues is revealing. Moses is transported forward in time to R. Akiva's academy, where he is dismayed to find he cannot understand a word of what Akiva is teaching to his students. And yet one of the students, upon asking the Rabbi to explain a particular teaching, receives the reply: "it is a *halakhah* of Moses from Sinai". Moses, in other words, finds his own *halakhah* incomprehensible when expounded in an unfamiliar historical context; this is because the practical meaning of the *halakhah* is determined by that context and not by any timeless kernel of significance.

What we seem to have in Rabbinic Judaism is a God who, as we have just seen, instigates and anticipates interpretation, but who is both subject *of* and subject *to* his own hermeneutical laws. This kind of interpretative circle or paradox appears in the midrash on Genesis 1, where the phrase "in the beginning [when] God created" is expounded. The first verse of the Torah, relating the beginning of creation in the past tense, could be said logically to have been written some time after the event; it is a commentary on the Divine *fiat*.

---

[125] Fisch *op. cit.* p.232. It should be noted that in fact Fisch makes this point to demonstrate what he sees as the essential *dissimilarity* between midrash and modern literary theory. Although his discussion does not deal specifically with deconstructon, he too (along with such critics as Handelman and Stern) appears to conceive of "modern literary theory" in general as being characterised by unrestrained relativism.

[126] Cf. Babylonian Talmud *Menahot* 29b

But in the midrash we find that commentary also somehow precedes
and determines the event: "the Holy One, blessed be He, consulted
the Torah when He created the world".[127] So too, in another well-
known Rabbinic legend, it is Torah rather than God who can never
be caught napping. Rabbi Eliezer and the Sages are disputing the ritual cleanness of an oven:[128] R. Eliezer, in support of his argument,
miraculously invokes a host of signs and wonders—a tree uproots itself, a stream flows backwards, a building leans sideways—all to defend his assertion that the oven in question is clean. The Sages stub-
bornly reject these phenomenal displays of proof and insist that the
oven is unclean. Finally, a heavenly voice intercedes in R. Eliezer's
defence, but even this is rejected as evidence by the Sages on the
strength of their reading of Deut. 30:12: "it [i.e. the Torah] is not in
heaven"—that is to say, the Law has already been given once and
for all time at Mount Sinai, and so even a voice from heaven may be
disputed with if the received text can be interpreted to support the
disputation. God's response to this is neither the wrath of an outwit-
ted tyrant nor a blast of irrefutable counter-doctrine, but good-
humoured acknowledgement—perhaps even celebration—of the infinite divisibility of the Word. The Torah is one book which might
be expected to instil some respect in the devoted reader for the
authority of signs, wonders and the heavenly voice, but the Sages in
this case are determined to read the "text against itself", insisting on
the equal status of (their) interpretation with direct audible revelation and thus making a claim for the inscribed/written sign over
against the notional immediacy of the spoken word. God, who after
all created Derrida, can only take pleasure in the manoeuvre: "God
laughed and said: my children have defeated me, my children have
defeated me!"

In the former of these two stories, God is presented as the Creator
both of Torah and of all its readings, but as Moses is led to realise,
these readings rely on the unfolding of cultural/historical circum-
stance to become apparent, and later interpretations may contradict
or reconfigure earlier ones to the extent that little common sense can
be established between them. The second tale depicts a God who,

---

[127] *Ber. Rab.* 1:1 (2).
[128] Babylonian Talmud *Bava Metzia* 59a-b.

having delivered Torah to Israel and set the process of interpretation in motion, happily finds himself challenged by a group of canny critics and responds not with anger but with laughter. In both these stories, deferral of meaning is affirmed as the chief characteristic of Holy Writ, and in the second tale God is a God who cheerfully, playfully, relinquishes his privilege to have the final word, because there *is* no final word. Or rather, the Word is a text which, in embracing all history, is in one sense final and determinate, but which within the continuum of time and mutability contains many truths, dependent on many contexts. It is this realisation that leads the Rabbis to allow meaning in midrash to be plural and ambiguous, to allow truth to be "principally discursive",[129] and to proclaim, in the case of contradictory readings or rulings, that "both these and these are the words of the living God".[130]

Midrash and Feminism

To draw clear parallels between midrash and deconstruction, therefore, necessitates a certain selectivity of emphasis on both sides: the playful, discursive aspects of midrash must be (and certainly can be) foregrounded, while the kind of "deconstruction" spoken of must be that which accords the respect of close, rigorous reading and constant return to one primary text, rather than the more pathologically eclectic style which makes commentary a *harlequinade* of dazzling intertextuality—serious, or devoted "play" rather than its more iconoclastic variety. Also, an important point to which little or no attention has been paid is that reading midrash as deconstruction involves, in a critical sense, deconstructing midrash. The Rabbis may have tolerated interpretative freedom amongst themselves, but the

---

[129] Goldberg (1990), p.61. Stern (1988) draws attention to stories in Rabbinic tradition which connect "polysemy with the original revelation [at Sinai]". According to one legend, the Law was given in "seventy tongues". Elsewhere, God is said to have appeared to Israel at various times and places in various forms which, taken as a whole, bore "a family resemblance to the polysemous meaning of Torah" (p.148). When God spoke to his people, the story has it, "each Jew said: it is to me that the voice is speaking" (*Peskita de-Rab Kahana* 1:223-24, quoted in Stern, p.148).

[130] Mishnah *'Erubim* 13b; *Gittim* 6b. Cf. Magonet (1992), p.24.

complexity and importance of the *middot*, and the way in which the Rabbis claimed authority for their own hermeneutical program, all indicate that they certainly distinguished in a broader sense between proper and improper articulation of meaning, and that the difference between the two was a matter both of reading competence and of a certain fidelity to method[131]—the first step in reading midrash as deconstruction must surely be to identify and exploit moments in the text which undermine this correct/incorrect dualism.[132]

If midrash must be deconstructed to appear as deconstruction, then this operation is even more important if we are to make useful connections between Rabbinic hermeneutics and *feminist* deconstruction. The exegete wishing to put together a feminist reading of Genesis 2-3 and consulting the midrash for hermeneutical tips may well be dismayed to find that the Rabbis at several points cite the biblical text in support of nakedly misogynistic claims; even as apparently disinterested a scholar as Jacob Neusner cannot help drawing attention, in his translation of *B^ere'shit Rabbah*, to "[t]he powerful and unrelieved anti-feminist bias of the document's framers".[133] I

---

[131] Cf. Green (1987):

> For rabbis, the credibility of scripture's discourse was guaranteed only by proper acculturation and training, in short, by rabbinic discipleship [p.159].

Cf. also Babylonian Talmud *Qidd.* 49a (and Tosephta *Meg.* 3:41):

> One who translates a verse literally, misrepresents [the text]; he who adds to it is a reviler and a blasphemer. So what is meant by translation? Our translation.

[132] Cf. Green (1987), pp.155-60.

[133] Neusner (1985), p.192. Although the Rabbis' pessimistic view of women is perhaps not as "unrelieved" as Neusner indicates, plenty of evidence exists to justify his claim, especially as far as the role of the woman in the Garden of Eden story is concerned. Cf. for example *Ber. Rab.* 17:7-8; 18:2 (Neusner's translation pp. 186-8; 191-2). Cf. also Richard L. Rubenstein's comment on the masculine bias in midrash, in *The Religious Imagination: A Study in Psychoanalysis and Jewish Theology* (The Bobbs-Merrill Company Inc., Indianapolis/Kansas City/New York 1968):

> There was an enormous overestimation of the status and prerogative of the male throughout rabbinic Judaism. The reasons for this must have been extremely complex. No explanation which fails to include the stresses of defeat, conquest and minority status upon male Jews will have any degree of adequacy. Jewish masculinity was decisively challenged by defeats of Roman times and perhaps earlier. After defeat by the Romans and the alienation of the Jewish community from its ancestral territory, Jewish

have already argued that there is no such thing as pure or exemplary deconstruction; there are, rather, particular instances informed by different historical/cultural contexts and political intentions, and so perhaps it is not surprising that Rabbinic "deconstruction" of the bible (insofar as it can be labelled thus) shares little ground in its codified or canonised form with whatever the results of feminist deconstructive exegesis might be—the exegetical aims in either case are completely different. It is not my intention here to deconstruct midrash with the aim of reading it as a feminist document: such an undertaking would be both too difficult—the corpus of literature is so huge and diverse that no manageably-sized piece could be said to be truly representative—and too (deceptively) simple, in that the logical gaps and textual *aporia* from which deconstruction works are legion throughout midrash; the invitation to deconstruct is bewilderingly open, and one would be hard pressed—*pace* Neusner—to find a systematic logical order to subvert (indeed, I believe that part of the reason midrash has been so enthusiastically appropriated by some poststructuralist critics and so fiercely defended by more traditional scholars of Judaism is that it is supremely tractable, able to be read convincingly in contradictory ways). Rather, I am interested in making the point that the Rabbis' approach to reading arose out of a set of cultural circumstances which had suggestive correspondences with the position of women in patriarchal societies—and that ultimately, discourses of feminist deconstruction of biblical texts could be enriched by close and creative attention to the hermeneutics of Rabbinic midrash.

I have concluded each of the previous three chapters with a comment on the kind of hermeneutics that feminist exegesis necessi-

---

men lacked the capacity to defend or assume possession of their own [*sic*] women ....the Jew reacted to the external threat to his masculinity by asserting it with extra insistence within his own community [pp.52-3].

Elsewhere (and more recently) Leilah Leah Bronner examines the attitudes to women evident in Talmudic literature, and finds that misogyny is prevalent but often countered by dissenting voices. Cf. her "Biblical Women in Talmudic Perspective" in *Proceedings of the 10th World Congress of Jewish Studies, Division C, Vol. 1* (World Union of Jewish Studies, Jerusalem 1990), pp.25-32. For a largely sympathetic account of Rabbinic teachings on female sexuality, cf. Blu Greenberg: "Female Sexuality and Bodily Functions in the Jewish Tradition" in Becher (1990), pp.1-44.

tates: a politically explicit hermeneutics which resists ideological closure and the imposition of orthodoxy; which embraces polysemy and conceives of meaning as a process rather than as an ahistorical entity; which accords integrity to subjectivity and imagination in interpretation, maintaining an awareness of the limitations of rational logic and "scientific" reading. At a glance, midrash appears to embody these characteristics to a great extent. We have seen that in its discursive style it celebrates the multivocal nature of interpretation, and conceives of commentary itself, the *process* of reading and expounding, as primary religious experience, liberating "the life of meaning from that of historical-geographical contingency".[134] Midrash also defers closure in interpretation and avoids the "authoritarian imposition" of final significance[135] within its own textual boundaries; it foregrounds hermeneutical means rather than ends, being concerned less with fixed doctrine than with "an interpretative stance, a *way* of reading the sacred text".[136] Midrash's commitment to the "omnisignificance" of the biblical text means that the creative imagination of the interpreter is called upon to explain "the unique significance of each and every linguistic element";[137] a rich variety of parables, fables and linguistic games weaves itself through such haggadic *midrashim* as the commentary on Genesis, and the arrangement of this material tends on the whole to defy our expectations of editorial logic:

> Similar arguments are often attributed to different authorities, and the textual evidence adduced in support of an argument is seldom arranged according to Western logical or chronological standards. This is not to say that the Midrash ignores logic, but to say that it employs logic, in such a way as to foreground its limitations.[138]

---

[134] Steiner (1989), p.40. Cf. Stern (1988):

> the activity of midrash does not....constitute an act of directly interpreting God, as though the text itself were literally divine. Instead, one could almost call midrash the interpretation of Torah as a figure or trope for God [p.150].

[135] Goldberg (1990), p.161.
[136] James L. Kugel: "Two Introductions to Midrash" in Hartman and Budick (1986), p.91 (my italics).
[137] Salmon and Elata-Alster (1992), p.186.
[138] *Ibid.* pp.186-7.

Midrash also in a sense foregrounds its own political stance. If, on one hand, the Rabbis' claim that their interpretation was given by God at Sinai can be seen as a claim to objective truth, it is apparent all the same that a high degree of subjective interest was at work, and this is partly what gives midrash its distinctive character. The Rabbis' broad political concern was to keep Israel holy or distinct among the various nations throughout which its people were scattered, and in the absence of a Temple cult, this meant making Israel a Torah-centred nation—which meant overall that a large amount of interpretative energy went into finding biblical proof to support the notion that Israel's (and more specifically the Rabbis') increasingly diverse concerns were still the particular business of one God and one all-embracing sacred text. Throughout both haggadic and halakhic midrash, the reader finds explicitly Rabbinic preoccupations read back into the biblical text: the serpent in Eden is judged not just by God but by a full Sanhedrin,[139] Cain and Abel engage in learned Pharisaic dispute over the afterlife,[140] the binding of Isaac is ascribed to the same calendar date as the future coming of the Messiah,[141] God rewards the study of scripture more richly than any other good work and Himself consults the Torah when creating the world.[142] The reader of midrash is never for a moment unaware that this is *Rabbinic* exegesis, and this is because the urgent practical and political demands which fuelled the midrashists' literary activity take precedence in the text over the impulse towards abstraction and scholarly neutrality.

It is clear enough that these surface similarities between Rabbinic and feminist modes of exegesis exist; what is less obvious is their significance, or the depth to which they may be pursued. If a model of correspondences were to be made, it would be structured around the affinity, which we have observed, between patriarchy and logocentrism (Derrida's *phallogocentrism*) and the inevitably Hellenis-

---

[139] *Ber. Rab.* 20:4.

[140] Targum Pseudo-Jonathan on Gen. 4:8 (trans. Michael Maher, T&T Clark Ltd., Edinburgh 1992, p.33).

[141] Targum Neofiti 1 on Exod. 12:42 (French trans. Roger Le Déaut, Les Éditions du Cerf, Paris 1979, pp.96-8).

[142] For other examples of this kind of interpretation, cf. Magonet (1992), pp.13-16; Plaskow (1991), p.29.

tic-philosophical tenor of this relationship, as opposed to the alter-
natively anti-patriarchal, anti-logocentric stances of feminism and
midrash respectively. But such a model could only stand, or be centred, on the relegation to marginal significance of such troublesome
details as the Hellenistic influences at work in midrash, the inextricability of logocentrism and anti-logocentric discourses, the patriarchal nature of Rabbinic Judaism and so on. The problem is essentially one of identity: systematic equations and models such as the
one outlined above rely on identifying the definitive characteristics
of their constituent elements, but we have seen that resistance to
definition is an important strategy both for feminism and deconstruction; even logocentrism and metaphysics are not, as deconstruction shows, entirely what they claim to be, and the current
conflict over midrash and modern critical theory is, for the greater
part, an unresolved debate on what Rabbinic interpretation "really
is".

This constant questioning of ontologies gets in the way of argument, and this is probably why it is often dismissed as a bad habit, a
kind of poststructuralist itch. But it could be that this same restless-
ness is what provides the most important link between midrash and
feminism. Issues of identity and difference have always been crucial
both to Judaism and to feminism, and in both cases this has had
much to do with the experience of marginality. In discussions of
Jewish identity, it is not uncommon to encounter the argument that
to be Jewish *is* to be an outsider. Statements to this effect range from
the direct:

> [t]wo thousand years of living as a minority people under the power
> structures of other societies and religions have helped form many of
> the characteristics seen as Jewish[143]

to the hyperbolic:

> [i]t is axiomatic for a Jew that it is better to suffer in hell as a member
> of a persecuted minority than to enjoy the pleasures of heaven as a
> member of a persecuting majority,[144]

---

[143] Magonet *op. cit.* p.9-10.
[144] José Faur: "Jewish and Western Historiographies: A Post-Modern Interpretation" in *Modern Judaism* 12:1 (1992), p.36.

and they rest on the underlying assumption that the "Jewish condition" has traditionally been that of marginality, often at the cost of freedom and life. Herbert Schneidau sees marginality as having been written from the very beginning into the Jewish tradition: in his discussion "The Hebrews Against the High Cultures",[145] he argues that the "Hebrew vision" informing the Old Testament is a critical, demythologising one,[146] that of a disenfranchised minority railing against the grandiose pride and hubris of dominant urban culture. On the margins of *Hebrew* culture are those whom the biblical narratives present as assimilating and becoming Egyptians, or Canaanites, or Babylonians; at the centre are the dissenters. The biblical record of Israelite history establishes this pattern at an early, crucial stage:

> The stage was set for Exodus by migrations of Semites to Egypt, in search of food perhaps, and many prospered there; but deep hostility to Egyptian life kept some—the ideological nucleus of the Hebrews— from immersion and disappearance in the population. They kept their character, significantly, by insisting that they were shepherds, "for every shepherd is an abomination to the Egyptians" (Gen. 46:34); they retained their identity at the cost of being stigmatized....The pastoral badge that allowed these Hebrews to evade the sacralized social system bespoke not only an alien's occupation, but also a religious declaration of noncompliance: it was itself a demythologization.[147]

Whether we can accept Schneidau's implicit assumption here that the Hebrew Bible offers a more-or-less accurate account of Israelite history, or whether we hold that the biblical texts were compiled by an exiled intellectual class wishing to shore up its claim to legitimate inheritance of the Yahwist covenant,[148] the point still stands: the Hebrew Bible tells the story of a people whose definitive condition, as depicted in the story, is that of alterity. The Hebrews, entering Canaan under Joshua, are portrayed in the biblical account as "the natu-

---

[145] Schneidau (1976), pp.104-73.

[146] *Ibid.* p.110.

[147] *Ibid.* p.111.

[148] The argument over who wrote the bible when, and why, is not one which I am qualified to enter with any great degree of authority. Cf. for further (introductory) discussion Morton Smith: *Palestinian Parties and Politics That Shaped the Old Testament* (Columbia University Press, New York and London 1971); Philip R. Davies: *In Search of "Ancient Israel"* (JSOT Press, Sheffield 1992).

ral enemies of the Canaanite city-states";[149] the books of the prophets
later denounce the power-political ambitions of Israel by calling on
"the Yahwist heritage of ambivalence toward culture and all its
works";[150] still later, the book of Daniel, with its narrative relating
the humiliation of a powerful despot, is written with the intention of
rallying Jewish opposition to the tyrant Antiochus Epiphanes;[151] finally, the Jews in Roman Palestine are shown as

> a recurrent plague to the Caesars, infecting the eastern part of the em-
> pire with disorder; for they could see Rome as only one more in the
> series that began with Akkad and ran through the Seleucids.[152]

Many of the key narratives in the Hebrew Bible also develop the
theme of spiritual and physical affinity between the people of Yahweh and the wilderness. The desert, the "marginal space" that
formed a kind of no-man's-land between the ancient Near Eastern
city-states, provides the venue for several crucial events in the formation of Israelite religious consciousness. The people of Yahweh
are not depicted as being completely at one with the wilderness environment, but nevertheless the wilderness is a place of refuge and,
frequently, theophany, in spite of the dangers it affords; the prophets
can be found at times to speak of the period of wandering immediately following the exodus from Egypt as "a period of special inti-
macy, a honeymoon, between Yahweh and his people".[153] Even in
the wilderness, however, the centre of Israelite identity is deferred:
the people of Yahweh do not live *in* the desert but are led *through* it,
by a God whose most notable characteristic is displacement. Yahweh speaks but is never seen; his signs may be natural phenomena
(flood, plague, famine) or unnatural (a burning bush, a "still, small
voice"), but the sign is never itself Being-in-presence, never a full or
perfect manifestation, and even in the desert, the place in which he
most dramatically reveals himself to his people, Yahweh is always
somehow absent or "elsewhere":

---

[149] Schneidau *op. cit.* p.115.
[150] *Ibid.* p.115.
[151] *Ibid.* pp.115-6.
[152] *Ibid.* p.116.
[153] *Ibid.* p.127. Cf. Jer. 2:2; Hos. 2:16-17.

Yahweh, unlike the nature gods of the pantheons, is fittingly found in the wilderness, as opposed to the cities, marketplaces, or grain-fields: the unearthly landscape of the desert is not God's "home" but a scene appropriate to him, for he too is unearthly. It may be that *djinn* and other desert demons are relevant to the ideas behind certain biblical passages (especially Exodus 4:24-26, where Yahweh tries to kill Moses), but Yahweh is not a "desert god", for he is not localizable anywhere.[154]

Thus at the centre of the biblical construction of Hebrew identity, both political and religious, can be found the concept of marginality and displacement, and it is not difficult to see how this relates to midrash. Several centuries after the Babylonian exile, the people of Yahweh were a handful of communities scattered throughout Palestine and outlying regions, a people with neither a political nor a cultic centre, for whose religious leaders the necessity to adapt, to survive in exile, was answered partly by the development of a diffuse and elastic biblical hermeneutics. George Steiner has observed that "there is a sense in which all commentary is an act of exile",[155] and this statement is surely never more apposite than when applied to midrash, a form of commentary which arose out of displaced communities, and which presents meaning not as residing in any fixed place or time, but as a process of signification coincident—from the human perspective—with changes in historical and cultural context. The "exile" Steiner refers to is exile from the stable presence of the Word, from any unitary source of unambiguous signification, and it is a condition palpable throughout midrash, reflecting among other things "the Rabbis' apparent lack of interest in making a theologically coherent whole out of their disparate beliefs".[156]

I wish to suggest that there is a certain symbolic affinity between Judaism and feminism, an affinity which has considerable relevance to the project of feminist biblical hermeneutics. As in Judaism, so in contemporary feminism, marginality and displacement are crucial issues, because they have always been central to the experience of women under patriarchy. By definition, patriarchy is structured around a male norm; male-identified characteristics are held to be

---

[154] *Ibid.* p.142.
[155] Steiner (1989), p.40.
[156] Stern (1988), p.146.

desirable and natural, while those identified with femaleness represent either lack (e.g. intuition, passivity) or dangerous excess (e.g. carnality, emotion). Women's roles and interests are, as a result, first determined according to an androcentric ideal, and then given marginal or secondary status; men dominate the "public" domain of political power and influence, while women are relegated to the more silent, less visible sphere of domestic, family-oriented activity—a situation which pertains even in these enlightened "post-feminist" times.[157] This also gives rise to the problem of women's identity. We have seen in chapter two how in patriarchal dualistic thinking, the male and only the male possesses autonomy and self-identity; woman is derivative, defined not as Self but as Other, having her identity delineated for her in the negative sense of "not-man". The qualities allocated to the realm of the Female by patriarchy are, on the whole, derived negatively from their corresponding masculine virtues, and can usually be termed accordingly—inactive, irrational, illogical, unspiritual, and so on. As Other, therefore, woman in patriarchal society is perpetually "displaced", having no essential characteristic, role or self-image that has not been assigned to her by the patriarchal order (this displacement is what Julia Kristeva refers to when she says that woman "does not....belong in the

---

[157] The "post-feminist" argument is gaining currency: women, it is held, now have access to jobs, wages and social positions that were formerly only available to men, as well as being protected by a proliferation of positive-discriminatory laws. Feminism has thus done what it set out to do, and has had its day—it is even suggested in some quarters that gains made in the name of women have been far outweighed by the damage feminism has done to relations between the sexes (cf. Neil Lyndon: *No More Sex War*, Sinclair-Stevenson, London 1992). Apart from being statistically untrue—"equal opportunity" is still very much in its infancy—this portrayal of women in society focuses exclusively on the experience of a narrow, unrepresentative selection of middle- to upper-middle-class professionals, women whose opportunities have had much more to do with their economic and class status than with revolutionary advances made under the banner of feminism. The argument largely ignores the experience of working-class women, or women in non-Western societies, as well as failing to take into account sexist ideologies prevalent in religion, law, education, advertising and so on. For rather sobering (and tellingly-entitled) assessments of the state of contemporary feminism, cf. Susan Faludi: *Backlash: The Undeclared War Against Women* (Chatto & Windus, London 1992); and Marilyn French: *The War Against Women* (Hamish Hamilton, London 1992).

order of being"[158]). Thus I believe it is not overstating the case to describe the condition of woman in patriarchal society as a form of exile, as life in an environment where she is defined as Other, as alien, by the guardians of the dominant culture, and where she therefore finds that "belonging" is achieved only by speaking and behaving in ways which do not disrupt or challenge the given order.

There are links, then, which can be made between alterity in Jewish experience and in women's experience, aspects of commonality which have been noticed by such feminist writers as Gail Shulman, who sees her Jewishness as being at the very root of her struggle against patriarchy; it is in her identity as a Jew that Shulman finds "the readiness to live in opposition".[159] Marcia Falk is similarly aware of the ways in which Judaism and feminism have both been shaped by marginality:

> the psychology of anti-Semitism has much in common with that of sexism. And indeed, there is a significant Jewish teaching that focuses on the imperative to treat others as one would the self, and to empathize with all outsiders on the basis of one's own experience as a stranger.[160]

Identity is also a crucial issue in Judaism and feminism alike. Edmond Jabès has written that the most pressing question at the heart of Jewish experience is:

> "What justifies my considering myself Jewish? What makes my words and actions Jewish words and actions?"
> Thus a double questioning forms and develops in [the Jew]: his certainty challenging his doubt, and his doubt, his certainty.[161]

This tension is similarly perceivable in feminist thought and experience: "what does it mean to be a woman?" is a question whose answer oscillates, we have seen, between the "certainty" of essentialism and the "doubt" of relativism. The fact of biology makes a

---

[158] Cf. chapter 2, note 29.

[159] Shulman (1983), p.108. On historical similarities between the persecution of Jews and women, and the "demonising" of both groups, cf. Ruether (1975), pp.89-114; also Norman Cohn: *Europe's Inner Demons: An Enquiry Inspired by the Great Witch-Hunt* (Sussex University Press, London 1975).

[160] Marcia Falk, in Setel *et al* (1986), p.122

[161] Jabès (1986), p.353. Cf. also Shulman *op. cit.* p.105.

strong claim against those who would argue that gender is purely a social construct, while those who hold to that claim and say that biology somehow determines the Female ignore the role of discursive "play" in fragmenting and destabilising all human subjects, regardless of gender. While biological determinism does not figure in Judaism except as part of the most nightmarish of historical recollections, the concept of Divine "chosenness", of holiness as being set apart, can perhaps be seen as the corresponding factor underpinning certainty of identity in Jewish religious experience. *Qadosh*, with its connotations of sacredness and special relationship to God inextricably linked with the idea of withdrawal or separation, is a definitive element in Judaism, and as such it poses problems for Jewish feminists who perceive a conflict between *qadosh* as a religious imperative and the "feminist value of relationship".[162] This, however, is a conflict not just *between* Judaism and feminism but also within each. To assert separateness, or difference, is necessary for any sense of identity, but separateness is also what determines otherness, and otherness is crucial to the logic both of anti-Semitism and sexism. Relationship, or a sense of radical connection with all life, on the other hand, restores the balance that separatism too easily upsets, but this in turn contradicts the claim for distinctiveness which has protected both Jewish identity in exile and women's selfhood under patriarchy. As Catherine Keller puts it:

> in this experience of the double threat of oppression and absorption, Judaism shares as much with feminism as it does with patriarchy.[163]

Identity, then, is a problem which lies at the heart of both Judaism and feminism, an issue rife with contradictions for which there are no simple resolutions. Feminism (at least of the non-separatist variety), stresses the need for difference to be simultaneously celebrated and kept in check, while in an increasingly pluralistic world, the concept of *qadosh*, integral to Jewish religious identity, becomes similarly fraught with ambiguity:

---

[162] T. Drorah Setel, in Setel *et al* (1986), p.113.
[163] Catherine Keller, in *ibid.* p.119.

in the last two hundred years, the concept of chosenness has been almost endlessly refashioned as Jewish thinkers have tried to find ways
to discard and retain it at the same time.[164]

At the risk of establishing naively simplistic oppositions, I would
say that this problem of self-identity has influenced the development
of feminism and Judaism in a way that cannot, on the whole, be held
as characteristic of patriarchy or orthodox Christianity. According to
patriarchal logic, the male is supremely, confidently independent
and self-determining, while doctrinal declarations of Christian
identity traditionally necessitate a statement of unambiguous belief
in one Word, one Incarnation and one resurrection, one determinate
Truth beyond doubt or interpretation. Patriarchal discourses have
always had much to say about what is and is not natural or proper,
and similarly the concept of heresy, of being fundamentally "in error" has played a particularly prominent role in the history of the
Christian Church: in both cases, determinations of the acceptable
and the unacceptable have served to delineate and consolidate a
power-base. Feminism and diaspora Judaism, on the other hand,
both politically marginalised, share common ground insofar as they
evince a tendency to be "suspicious of single-minded approaches to
truth":[165] the varied modes of experience of women under patriarchy
and of Jewish communities in diverse cultural contexts have given
rise to an awareness of *difference*-in-being; even monotheism, the
belief in one God, can be construed as a spiritual allegiance to an
all-inclusive unity:

> Judaism....contains such tendencies in its discussions of the deity's at-
> tributes (Justice and Mercy), in discussions of relationship between
> deity and its Spirit (*ruah ha kodesh*) or Presence (Shechinah), both of
> which are feminine, and most particularly in Kabbalistic discussions
> of the deity's ten modes.[166]

Christianity, of course, is also officially monotheistic, and the
Christian Trinity is a theological construct which similarly embraces
unity-within-Oneness. The point I wish to make, however, is that
Christianity has, in the course of its history, tolerated less diversity

---

[164] Plaskow (1991), p.100.
[165] Falk (1987), p.40.
[166] Rita M. Gross, in Setel *et al* (1986), p.130.

in what its theological determinations are said to signify, or how they might be applied, than has Judaism—and the periods of most extreme Christian intolerance have, significantly, been those periods at which Christianity has functioned as a state religion, with the means at its disposal of mobilising the "secular arm" of power in defence of its interests. Rabbinic midrash, for example, allowing that biblical authority is vested partly in the interpretative community, accounts for subjectivity and historical contingency in its determinations of Truth, and so in the Jewish interpretative tradition, "belief" in Holy Writ necessitates an awareness of difference and an openness to change. In the Christian tradition, however, which leans more in the direction of placing biblical authority *outside* the human/cultural sphere, belief involves obedience to an inscrutable Divinity, and to this extent Christianity (like patriarchy) assigns determinate Truth to the realm of a dominant impersonal order—a manoeuvre which, when effected under the aegis of political power, all too easily serves to legitimate oppression.

A history of marginality and minority status, on the other hand, a history such as the one we have seen outlined by Schneidau, has given a different character to the concept of truth in Judaism, and this has had an important bearing on hermeneutics. Judith Plaskow has recently argued that Judaism is a religion rooted in memory, "living, active memory that continues to shape Jewish identity and self-understanding", memory which is "not simply a given but a religious incumbent on both Israel and God".[167] God sends the rainbow as a sign that he will remember the covenant made between himself and "every living creature among all flesh" (Gen. 9:15), and in return the primary religious obligation of Israel is that of remembering—and this memory, notably, is the memory of marginality, of "the experience....of slavery and redemption".[168] The great commandment of Moses is that Israel should "remember this day, in which you came out from Egypt, out from the house of bondage" (Exod. 13:3); the first commandment at Sinai is similarly an injunction to remember ("I am the LORD your God, who brought you out from the land of Egypt", Exod. 20:2); the same memory of oppres-

---

[167] Plaskow *op. cit.* p.29.
[168] *Ibid.* p.29.

sion gives rise to the ethical obligation not to "wrong a stranger or oppress him, for you were strangers in the land of Egypt" (Exod. 22:20).[169] This memory, Plaskow says, has shaped the Jewish understanding of religious and political identity down to the present day, and

> [i]t has fostered among some Jews an identification with the oppressed that has led to involvement in a host of movements for social change—and has fuelled the feminist demand for justice for women within Judaism.[170]

The past has the power in Judaism to shape present reality to a profound degree: "it is in telling the story of our past as Jews that we learn who we truly are in the present".[171] Remembering, however, is not a matter of simple cultural identification with this historical figure or that historical event; the cultural diversity to which Judaism has had to adapt since biblical times has resulted in the development of what might be called a historical imagination. This, we have seen, is the kind of imagination which characterises midrash, a point which Plaskow does not fail to make:

> It is because of the past's continuing power in the present that, when the rabbis profoundly transformed Jewish religious life after the destruction of the second Temple, they also reconstructed Jewish memory to see themselves in continuity with it. So deeply is the Jewish present rooted in Jewish history that changes wrought in Jewish reality continually have been read back into the past so that they could be read out of the past as a foundation for the present.... The point is not that such rereadings were a conscious plot to strengthen rabbinic authority—though certainly they would have served that function—but that it was probably unimaginable to the sages that the values they lived by could not be taught through the Torah.[172]

The Rabbis, as the religious leaders of communities which were on the whole politically marginalised, or at least displaced from the cultural environment which nurtured the development of their sacred text, were called upon to exercise a mode of biblical interpre-

---

[169] Exod. 22:21 (RSV).
[170] Plaskow *op. cit.* p.30.
[171] *Ibid.* p.29.
[172] *Ibid.* pp.30-1.

tation which made identification with the past more a matter of
creative reconstruction than of historical accuracy. It was an article
of Rabbinic faith that they were the inheritors of Israel's religious
tradition following the fall of Jerusalem; that being the case, they
were constrained to read the literature of that tradition as being in
many ways "about" them. It is in this sense, Plaskow says, that the
Rabbis adopted an interpretative stance which is being taken up today by many feminists. The infrequency of women's stories, and the
marginal significance accorded to women's experience in biblical
narratives, is at odds with the experience of contemporary Jewish
feminists who take it as given that their lives and their experiences
as women in the community of faith are as integral to Judaism as are
more traditional patriarchal concerns. This incongruity necessitates
a particular approach to reading and interpretation:

> To accept our absence from Sinai would be to allow the male text to
> define us and our connection to Judaism. To stand on the ground of
> our experience, on the other hand, to start with the certainty of our
> membership in our own people is to be forced to re-remember and
> recreate its history, to reshape Torah.[173]

Monique Wittig, in a much-quoted passage has said: "There was a
time when you were not a slave, remember that....You say there are
no words to describe this time, you say it does not exist. But remember. Make an effort to remember. Or failing that, invent."[174]
This exhortation does not deny the value of feminist historiography,
but it implies that where historical memory has been erased, creative
memory must take on the work of recovering a past for women that
is not appropriated by patriarchy. The program of modern feminist
exegesis, then, is markedly similar to the task which confronted the
Rabbis in the early centuries of the Common Era: that of making the
bible address the particular concerns of groups whose experience
has little or no apparent link with the explicit narrative concerns of
the biblical text. The Torah shows us no Rabbis, yet the Rabbis were
able to read it as a document which addressed them directly. Feminist biblical interpretation requires a similar leap of the exegetical

---

[173] *Ibid.* pp.27-8.
[174] Monique Wittig: *The Warriors* trans. D. Le Vay (The Women's Press, London 1979), p.89.

imagination, a hermeneutical approach which, like that of the midrashists, opens the text to new, often unexpected readings, conjuring meaning "to rise out of the white spaces between the letters"[175] of the biblical text and be shaped according to the needs of the interpretative community.

We have come a long way, it seems, from Derrida and the metaphysicians. But the main points of this somewhat lengthy argument can be summarised without too much difficulty. It should first be noted that in drawing comparisons, as I have, between deconstruction and feminism, deconstruction and midrash, and (finally) midrash and feminism, I have attempted—no doubt at the expense of clarity—to keep those comparisons as far as possible from crystallising into strict identifications-and-oppositions. Derrida has shown, perhaps above and beyond anything else, that things have always persisted, will always persist, in differing from what they "are", just as they maintain a perverse and radical identification with what they "are not": thus does the binary thinking of logocentrism catch itself out. Even deconstruction differs from itself; Derrida and many others have stressed that far from being a concept or a method, deconstruction is something you *do*, and that to explain it in fixed conceptual terms is

> to set aside the detailed and specific *activity* of deconstructive reading in favour of a generalized *idea* of that activity, an idea assumed to comprehend all its differences of local application.[176]

Accordingly, I have tried to avoid slipping too comfortably into the logic of typology: there is a fine difference between arguing that midrash is a type of deconstruction (or worse, that midrash is a type of feminism) and pointing out some ways in which the Rabbis anticipated modern feminist and deconstructive concerns, but it is a difference which I hope to have made more or less consistently.

The principal concern, however, of this discussion has been to show that deconstruction—whatever it might "be"—as a reading activity need not preclude, when it is brought to the bible, a biblical faith of some kind. Philosophically speaking, deconstruction's reli-

---

[175] Gottlieb (1983), p.273
[176] Norris (1987), p.20.

ance on the postulations of metaphysics provides evidence of one
way in which a deconstructive theology need not—cannot—give the
lie to determinations of transcendent Truth in any absolute or un-
compromising fashion. But what about the more practical business
of hermeneutics? It has been argued that there is no place for God in
the deconstructive reader's mind, and I would go along with this to
the extent that I believe God is much more dynamic than something
as static as a "place" would suggest. But if God is to be conceived of
(like reading) as a Verb, a process, as "I Will Be What I Will Be"—
and such formulations are notably prevalent within Rabbinic Judaism and feminist theology—then the thought of deconstructive exegesis is perhaps not so much scandalous as necessary. John Caputo's
comments on religion are worth quoting at length here, as he speaks
of the inevitability of reading and interpretation at the very heart of
faith, in terms which suggest a "deconstructive" awareness:

> Religion is a way of coming to grips with the flux, a struggle with the
> powers of darkness, which is "authentic" only so long as it "owns up"
> to the contingency of its symbols. Faith makes its way in the dark,
> seeing through a glass darkly, and it is genuine only to the extent that
> it acknowledges the abyss in which we are all situated, the undecide-
> ability and ambiguity which engulfs us all....The believer is not some-
> one who has been visited from on high by a supervenient grace but
> someone who, like the rest of us, does what he can to construe the
> darkness, to follow the sequence of shadows across the cave, to cope
> with the flux. To invoke grace from on high is just one more familiar
> way of bailing out on the flux—just when we are needed the most. It
> is one more way to say that one has gained an exemption from the
> human condition, that God has privileged a few with a lifeline that He
> has not thrown out to others—which would be comic if it were not so
> dangerous.[177]

This is very close to Derrida's idea of the "Nietzschean affirmation", the kind of thinking that resists the neat equation of non-Truth
with falsity, which "determines the noncenter otherwise than as the
loss of the center".[178] I would say that the affirmation of this kind of
faith is more easily read into the Jewish exegetical tradition than
into that of Christianity, at least to the extent that Christianity has

---

[177] Caputo (1987), pp.281-2.
[178] Derrida (1978), p.292.

invested more of its official theological capital in the Platonic ideal of access to Presence, of direct, unmediated and miraculous communion with God in the body of Christ. But even Christ is a sign that calls for interpretation, and, as Stephen Finley has remarked, deconstruction in Christian exegesis offers the opportunity to discover the regenerative possibilities in the way that texts, like the incarnation of the Word itself, "suffer and break".[179]

All this suggests no more than that a deconstructive *approach* to reading the bible can be a faithful one; we are left still with the question of what kind of readings such an approach might throw up. Critics of deconstruction often demand to know "where it will all end", what kind of horrors might be spawned in the name of biblical hermeneutics if the deconstructionists are left to pursue their diabolical master-plan through to its logical conclusion. Of course, logical conclusions are not necessarily the business of deconstructive readers, but Derrida himself adopts an uncomfortably apocalyptic tone at least at one point where he speaks of "the formless, mute, infant and terrifying form of monstrosity"[180] that may be emerging as the *différance* of presence and absence takes shape in the philosophical consciousness of the West. More pertinently, however, it seems that for all the theorising taking place over deconstruction in biblical interpretation, there still seems to be proportionately little deconstructive exegesis actually being carried out, and what there is offers little solace to those who fear that to deconstruct means to throw off every last vestige of critical respect for the text. If "play" equals limitless intertextuality, a dissolution of conceptual clarity into labyrinthine verbal esotericism, then those who are old-fashioned enough to want to read the bible in search of meaning quite justifiably want nothing to do with it.

What I hope to have demonstrated, however, is that midrash is one kind of exegesis which devotes itself seriously to the business of close reading, and yet which evinces a species of interpretative play not entirely unrelated to the play of signification that deconstruction exploits. Not that "exploitation" here should be understood in the perjorative sense of the word: deconstruction should not be a process of coercion brought to bear on the text from a point outside

---

[179] Finley (1988), p.14.
[180] Derrida (1978), p.293.

it, but rather a rigorous working-through of possibilities within it; an operation that begins in the space "between rhetoric and logic, between what [the text] manifestly *means to say* and what it is nonetheless *constrained to mean*".[181] This, I have argued, is how the Rabbis read their bible: as a text which spoke to them through gaps and fissures, which addressed them directly, eloquently, "in spite of itself", i.e. in spite of its literal silence regarding the specific questions they brought to it. So too, the project of reading the bible as relevant to feminist religious concerns involves a similar—perhaps even more radical—deconstruction of its ruling logic, in this case patriarchal logic.

Daphne Hampson, speaking of Christian feminism, has pointed out that those feminists who have retained their avowedly Christian beliefs have tended to be "historians and exegetes", while those who (like Hampson herself) count themselves as "post-Christians" have on the whole been "trained in philosophy or theology".[182] This, I believe, testifies to the fact that feminist Judaeo-Christianity depends for its future development very much on a radical commitment to issues of reading and writing, of textuality. Accordingly deconstruction, as a means of reading patriarchal texts "against themselves", from the margins inward, and in legitimising the broadening of critical focus to take into account the political stances of both author and reader, provides perhaps the most useful approach to a feminist biblical poetics. To place deconstruction and the insights of Derrida at the centre of the argument and proceed synchronically (disregarding for the moment the problem of anachronism—itself a logocentric anxiety), we can see midrash as one among numerous kinds of outworkings of certain reading strategies discussed, shaped by its own particular concerns—religious faith not being the least among them—and characterised by myriad deformations of what could be called "true" deconstruction if such a thing existed. Another outworking could be feminist exegesis, a critical practice which would, in many respects, be related to midrash—and which would undoubtedly stand to gain much insight from close attention to Rabbinic readings of scripture—but which would be somewhat

---

[181] Norris (1987), p.19.
[182] Hampson (1990), p.109.

inured to the ironies of such a relationship by constant, creative reversion to the supreme irony: that of reading the sacred texts of Judaeo-Christian religion as affirmative of the full humanity of
women. It is an irony of the kind which deconstruction most closely
investigates, to whose implications the deconstructive reader is most
closely-attuned, an irony of the kind whose full and fully-articulated
exploration is no less pressing for feminism than it is for any other
liberation movement.

CHAPTER FIVE

GENESIS 2:4b-3:24: YAHWEH AND THE SEXUALITY OF RHETORIC

> What is found at the historical beginnings of things is not the inviolable identity of their origin, it is the dissension of other things. It is disparity.[1]

The discussion offered over the past four chapters has been principally theoretical, and I hope to have paid at least adequate attention to the contradictions which result when a theoretical approach is taken either to feminism or to deconstruction. Indeed, I have indicated that deconstruction's resistance to neat categorisation as a "methodology" or a "concept" makes it a suitable set of strategies for a feminist hermeneutics. What remains to be provided is some idea of how a practical instance of "feminist deconstruction" might look when actually exercised on a piece of literature—particularly on biblical literature which has for so long been read and reread as enshrining Meaning beyond all question, and as validating the monolithic doctrines of patriarchal religion. I should immediately add that what follows will not be an attempt to piece together a critical reading which illustratively puts into practice all the theory discussed so far. David Jobling writes that as far as liberation theologies are concerned, there is still a measure of "swallowing the negative" to be done before we can proclaim the advent of a new egalitarian order,[2] by which I take it he means that as long as repressive social structures are maintained, an essential task of any movement for change must be to analyse and dismantle the old while forging the new. A cautionary indicator of the relevance of this observation to feminist hermeneutics can be seen in the work of Phyllis Trible, whose "positive" feminist hermeneutics is undermined by insufficient attention to the mechanics of patriarchal discourse. Accord-

---

[1] Foucault (1977), p.142.
[2] Cf. Jobling (1990), p.107.

ingly, my aim at this point is not to come up with an example of definitively "feminist" deconstruction, still less to try to formulate a
paradigm for it; rather, I hope to offer one example of how a patriarchal text can be read against itself.

Deconstruction, we have seen, firmly contextualises linguistic
practice. If textuality is all-encompassing, then to write is not to
pluck an eternal verity from a point outside culture and present it to
the world embodied in "literary " language; to read is something
other than the progressive apprehension of an invariable Presence.
Rather, meaning is produced, displaced, modified and contended
with as part of an infinitely dense and complex web of cultural assumptions and social codes. Subjectivity—the "discursive constitution" of the reader—therefore plays a large part in the process, particularly in biblical criticism where the vested interests of the interpreter are often bound up with religious faith; the questions we ask
of the bible at an intellectual level tend to have answers provided for
them at the more intuitive level of "belief" before we even open the
book, and so in matters of exegesis,

> the kernel of "timeless truth" which remains after the chaff is stripped
> away usually turns out to be very much like what the scholar hoped to
> find.[3]

This means that when we interpret, we often say as much about ourselves and our society as we do about the text at hand, and it is
partly in this sense that criticism has been dubbed "the only civilised
form of autobiography".[4]

With this in mind, deconstruction and other reader-oriented interpretative modes have been attacked for cluttering the discursive
field of criticism with too much subjective baggage and relativising
the focus of critical inquiry to the point of absurdity: if the meaning
of a text is something read into it rather than drawn out of it, and if
every reading of any text is really just a reflection of the reader, and
if even the reader is an ephemeral, culture-specific entity, then in
what sense can "the text" be said to exist at all? Some critics are

---

[3] Sakenfeld (1975), p.228.
[4] Oscar Wilde: "The Critic as Artist" in *Intentions* (Methuen & Co. Ltd., London
1927), p.140.

content to remain agnostic on this point;[5] my own tentative answer
would be that the text, with regard to the comments above, continues
to exist in a rich and varied array of forms; indeed, rather than re-
ducing the text to *no more than* a function of interpretation, deconstruction opens, multiplies and reproduces the text in as many forms
as there are readers of it. It is true that in critical discussion there is
no authoritative *arche*-text against which to measure the validity of
this or that reading (the only "pure" text is that which has not yet
been read), but complete incoherence in interpretation is curtailed by
what Frank Kermode has elegantly termed "the tacit knowledge of
the permitted range of sense"[6] in the discursive community. And so
in the absence of any pure, self-evident or "uninterpreted" text, to
deconstruct is—as the term implies—to question the text *as it is
constructed* and take issue not with the supposed text-itself but with
its readings, a movement prefigured in what the deconstructive
reader identifies as the text's own contentious rhetorical structure:

> [c]ritical disputes about a text can frequently be identified as a dis-
> placed re-enactment of conflicts dramatized in the text, so that while
> the text assays the consequences and implications of various forces it
> contains, critical readings transform this difference within into a dif-
> ference between mutually exclusive positions. What is deconstructed
> in deconstructive analyses attuned to this problem is not the text itself
> but the text as it is read, the combination of text and the readings that
> articulate it.[7]

My interpretation of any biblical text, then, should make no pretence
to being innocent or without presuppositions, as my social/historical
environment is saturated with pre-existent biblical readings and
traces of readings which profoundly influence how *I* read—and indeed why I read the bible at all. This dilemma—should I wish to
perceive it as such—is particularly acute in the case of Genesis
2:4b-3:24, as there is perhaps no other piece of biblical narrative (in
the Christian tradition, at any rate) so deeply sedimented with layers
of cultural discourse. It is probably impossible, in Western society,

---

[5] Cf. Eagleton (1986), pp.85-88 on Stanley Fish.
[6] Kermode (1983), p.171.
[7] Culler (1987), p.215.

to read the Old Testament creation-and-fall narrative without some sense of engagement or identification:

> we all (or most of us) confess that, although we do not read Genesis 2-3 as a factual/historical account, we nonetheless find in it elements of a belief system, an ideology, that has strongly informed our own, so that in the millennia-long dialogue with this text we locate a good part of our cultural identity.[8]

The story has been passed down from generation to generation, interpreted and reinterpreted to the point where Adam and Eve must surely head the roll of *dramatis personae* in the Western religious imagination, and none but the most isolated individual could be ignorant of at least one rough version of what happened in the Garden of Eden. But if the outline of the narrative is familiar, this should not imply that its meaning can easily be grasped: everybody "knows" the Garden of Eden story, but who in all its countless explications and analyses has finally determined what it is about? It seems safe enough to say that like any respectable creation-myth, the story is about origins, but this is not particularly helpful when we consider that the "origins" it deals with have variously (and persuasively) been put forward as being the origins of sin, sexuality, knowledge, death, male moral primacy, female moral primacy, patriarchy, sexual equality, civilisation, barbarism, religious faith, atheism, and so on. All these readings are valid enough, yet none of them is final or complete: evidently what we have here is a supremely enigmatic and elastic text,[9] and one in which the spaces between structural elements can accommodate endless varieties of exegetical filling-in. In fact, it is a text whose gaps and inconsistencies are so wide that the inevitability of interpretation becomes more apparent the closer we read—that is to say, a text which ultimately draws attention to its own indeterminacy.

---

[8] Detweiler (1988), p.137.

[9] This elasticity reflects not just authorial but editorial activity. Cf. Herbert Silberer: *Hidden Symbolism of Alchemy and the Occult Arts* (Dover, New York 1970):

> [The book of Genesis] itself is welded together from heterogeneous parts ....Displacements, inversions, and therefore apparent contradictions must naturally lie in such material.

(Quoted in Cunningham (1991), p.121).

In all this, Gen. 2:4b-3:24 could be said to be a fairly typical piece of Hebrew biblical narrative, faithful to a genre whose chief characteristics are

> the externalization of only so much of the phenomena as is necessary for the purpose of the narrative, all else left in obscurity; the decisive points of the narrative alone are emphasised, what lies between is nonexistent; time and place are undefined and call for interpretation; thoughts and feeling remain unexpressed, are only suggested by the silence and the fragmentary speeches; the whole....remains mysterious and "fraught with background".[10]

So fraught with background is this narrative, however, that even its "decisive points" are obscure: out of all its indeterminacies and silences, the Garden of Eden story's most puzzling inconsistencies emerge precisely at those points where we might expect to have things spelled out for us in no uncertain terms. The story appears at a simple sequence-of-events level to be about good and evil, knowledge and death; but by the end of chapter three, the questions which most obstinately remain unanswered are: what is the nature of "good and evil" that is supposed to have been made manifest to us? what kind of "knowledge" have we really acquired? and what kind of "death" has everybody been talking about?

So many unanswered questions raise the possibility of the indeterminacy of meaning and the need to interpret at a very early stage in the Garden of Eden narrative, and this is a paradoxical state of affairs in the light of orthodox readings of Gen. 2:4b-3:24 which would have it that the story deals with concrete, prehistoric certainties and the Divinely-prescribed consequences of mythic acts. Such interpretations, however, depend upon the willing suspension of hermeneutical scepticism and accept the text's apparent rhetorical structure as given: the story is a myth dealing with, say, sin and sexuality, and elements within the story which contradict this logic must be harmonised or interpreted into line with what we think we know is the myth's basic narrative thrust. Myths tend, after all, to be told and retold but not fundamentally questioned by the society at large in which they circulate; their shared symbolic significance is partly what makes them myths, and to tamper with a myth in such a

---

[10] Auerbach (1953), pp.11-12.

way that this communal significance is disrupted and becomes disjointed or internally divided is not "reading" but a marginal specialist activity requiring the obscure formal-analytical skills of the likes of anthropologists, antiquarian linguists and source critics.

But just how ineffably "mythical" is the Garden of Eden story? It is now generally recognised by all but the most hardline fundamentalists that what we have in the Judaeo-Christian creation-myth is in fact two stories—the so-called Priestly creation account of Genesis 1-2:4a, and the Yahwist text of 2:4b-3:24—and even a brief comparison between them throws up points which could serve as helpful indicators when considering the problematic distinction between myth and fiction. The Priestly account is altogether a more measured, austere piece of work; with its liturgical rhythms and its patterned, repetitive structure, Gen. 1-2:4a has all the ponderous solemnity appropriate to an account of the *in illo tempore* of sacred prehistory. The Priestly tale is ritualistic in tone and its structure seems to encourage, or at least to facilitate, word-for-word reiterability—in short, it looks and sounds like a myth. More significantly, it describes a sequence of events which take place in what Plato might have called the realm of the Ideal. Indeed, rather than "events" we might call them successive Beings: God's first creative act is to signify, to form an utterance, and in this utterance is Presence made manifest. God says *y^ehi 'or*, "let there be light", and the immediate consequence of this is *'or* brought into being. The necessarily linear sequence of the narrative implies that some kind of time-lapse is involved—"God said, let there be light, and (then) there was light"—but this is an inevitable result of the textual attempt to describe a pre-textual state: what is in fact referred to is a direct, atemporal and substantial correspondence between the Word and what it stands for. Language in the Priestly creation account is not differential but perfectly referential; issuing from the mouth of God, each signifier *is* a signified. Light, *'or*, is brought into being as an unambiguous, self-identical phenomenon, and God pronounces it good (*tobh*) as such before instituting the play of difference and setting the alternation of day and night in motion. This pattern continues over the six "days" of creation; God utters the world and everything in it into being, all of it is *tobh*, none of it is translatable or could have been said in any other way (each Divine linguistic *fiat* is sealed with the emphatic, finalising formula *wayᵉhi khen*, "and it was so"). The terseness of the narrative suits its subject:

> [c]reation is depicted as so complete and so good in Gen. 1:1-2:4a that little room is left for narrative movement and development.[11]

Things are very different, however, from the opening sentence of Gen. 2:4b-3:24, different in that the Yahwist creation narrative opens onto a world of difference. The narrative introduction to this story ("on the day that YHWH-God made earth and heavens") corresponds to yet differs from the beginning of the P-text in four significant instances.[12] The first is that the scene is set in 2:4a by *bᵉyom*, "on the day", rather than *bᵉreꞌshit*, "in the beginning", and where the latter refers to a single, indivisible point of ontology, *bᵉyom* is situated in the realm of change and deferral, of day and night.[13] Secondly, the act of creation itself is denoted in the Yahwist or J-text by a form of the verb *ꞌasah*, a verb which carries the sense of doing or making on a human, social level, and in this it differs significantly from P's *baraꞌ*, a word used exclusively throughout the Hebrew bible to describe the creative activity of the Divine. Next we meet the Creator himself, *YHWH-ꞌelohim*, not the mythic, all-in-One God of the P-text but the more historical/political Yahweh, God of the Israelites who is One and yet differs, who *is not* Baꞌal, Asherah or any of the other Gods in the Canaanite pantheon. Finally, what is created by God at the beginning of the Priestly account is precise and unambiguous (*hashshamayim wᵉ....ha-ꞌaretz*, "*the* heavens and *the* earth"), while in the Yahwist account, creation is described without the definite article *ha-*, and this signals a shift in the direction of a more indeterminate environment, the fictional landscape of *ꞌeretz wᵉshamayim*.

In addition to this, creation is described in the following verse in terms of lack or absence:

---

[11] Miscall (1990), p.3.

[12] Cf. *ibid.* p.2.

[13] It should be noted that *yom* throughout the Garden of Eden story refers to a more literal, twenty-four-hour time-frame than the mythical "days" of Genesis 1. Cf. 2:17, 3:5, 3:8, 3:14, 3:17.

no wild shrub was yet on the earth, and no herb of the field had yet
sprouted, for YHWH-God had not yet caused it to rain upon the earth,
and there was no earth-creature to till the earth [Gen. 2:5].

We are presented here not with self-identity and plenitude, but with
a partially-written script to be worked on, something that needs to be
added to; in particular the adverb *terem*, "not yet", resonates with
the admonition that in this tale, creation is signified as much by
what is deferred and still to come as by what is demonstrably present, and indeed further on in the story, Yahweh's first outright
judgement on his own handiwork is to be *lo'-tobh*, "it is not good
[that]....". There is no *wayᵉhi khen* here; this is a world of contingency, of absence-in-presence which "infects the narrative"[14]
throughout. This is not to say that the Priestly creation-myth is
somehow immune to the indeterminacy which is the condition and
result of its own textual constitution,[15] but in its concise rhetorical
structure it is not so clearly "about" deferral and textuality in quite
the dramatic way that the Yahwist account is.

Yahweh is not the speaking God of Genesis 1-2:4a. He creates
ha-'adam by hand rather than by Word, modelling *ha-'adam* from
ha-'adamah and thus (from the reader's perspective) making a linguistic connection, but regardless of whether or not Yahweh himself
is aware of this connection—and he is not, as we shall see, the Hebrew speaker *par excellence* of Genesis 1—he saves his breath for
the task of animating his earth-creature. At this point, Yahweh's acts
are effective and possessed of a relative sort of finality; he success-
fully creates and gives life to *ha-'adam*, plants and cultivates a garden, places the earth-creature in it. And then Yahweh speaks—and
in so doing, he effectively initiates the dissolution of ontological
certainty or Being-in-presence. If the Garden of Eden story docu-
ments a "Fall", this is the point at which it occurs:

> And YHWH-God laid a command upon the earth-creature, saying:
> "You may freely eat from all the trees in the garden, but you may not
> eat from the tree of the knowledge of good and evil, for on the day
> that you eat from it, you shall most certainly die" [Gen. 2:16-17].

---

[14] Miscall *op. cit.* p.2.
[15] Cf. Greenstein (1989), pp.45-46. Greenstein reads the Priestly creation account
as beginning—and concerning itself throughout—with relativity and difference.

A Divine utterance, as Gen. 1-2:4a demonstrates, is one in which signifier and signified merge to form a perfect unity; it is fundamentally uninterpretable. But the Creator's first speech act in this story is quite manifestly a text, recognisable as such by the hallmarks of textuality: inconsistency ("you may freely eat from *all* the trees....but you may not eat from one of them") and rhetoric (*mot tamut*, "you shall *most certainly* die"). The P-text shows us that the Divine creative attribute above all other Divine creative attributes is the ability to speak "substantially", to possess immediate and absolute control over the meaning of any utterance, and the words of the Priestly Elohim are presented as being intrinsically Meaning-full. In the J-narrative, however, language is not so stable. Yahweh himself is granted a certain diplomatic immunity with regard to interpretation: in a world where the ability to name constitutes a powerful privilege, his own Name is a grouping of consonants and thus defies utterance. He speaks, but cannot be spoken, being in a profoundly literary sense "above" criticism, and in this he perhaps represents the satisfaction of his author's most deep-seated desires. George Steiner has observed that the Judaic prohibition against giving utterance to the consonantal designation *YHWH* has much to do with the desire to keep the sacred Name from passing into "the contingent limitlessness of linguistic play". Just as Israel's God is (as we have seen) often to be encountered *in* the desert without being identified as a God *of* the desert, just as God intervenes in Israelite history while at the same time transcending historical determination, so it must be ensured by the biblical authors and redactors that "in natural and unbounded discourse God has no demonstrable lodging".[16] A fundamental tension may be observed here between deferral as theological virtue—Yahweh's spatial/temporal displacement sets him apart from the more localisable gods of Israel's idol-worshipping neighbours—and deferral as a force by which the Divinity must not be seen as influenced; it is a tension equivalent to that between the sense of *'ehyeh 'asher 'ehyeh* (Exod. 3:14) as (literally) "I will be what I will be" and its common translation as "I

---

[16] Steiner (1989), p.57.

am who I am",[17] the latter denoting a God undefinable on any terms other than his own, terms which are inscrutable and which pertain above and beyond "the anarchic ubiquity of possible discourse".[18] But "possible discourse", or interpretation, the realm of linguistic play which Yahweh in Eden seeks to control without inhabiting, is something which in fact determines his very nature, by virtue of his agency in the biblical narrative. He is a character in someone else's story, and although he seeks to exercise authority—the privilege of unquestionable authorship—by prophesying dire consequences for failure to obey his command, this is not quite the same thing as speaking Truth.

The Rabbinic commentators on Genesis show a certain sensitivity to this sort of idea. Throughout Rabbinic literature, the Holy One appears as a character who can usually be disputed with, and occasionally persuaded to change his mind; his language is predominantly discursive. Indeed, on at least one occasion, his attempts at self-sufficient, substantial Utterance are comically frustrated. The creation of woman (Gen. 2:22) in *B^ere'shit Rabbah* depicts Yahweh as a kind of bumbling spell-weaver, piecing the woman together and repeating over and over again the words *'ishshah tsanu'ah* ("woman, modesty!"), only to complain later that *'ishshah* turns out in fact to be frivolous, licentious, prying, jealous, thieving and flighty.[19] Obviously, part of the Rabbis' intention here is to make some familiar observations concerning the behaviour of women. They also, however, show not only that even Yahweh's determinations of female nature fail to hold, but that they fail because Yahweh's language is not a determinative medium.

In Gen. 2:16 (to return to the prohibition concerning the tree of the knowledge of good and evil) we are told not *wayyo'mer*, "[Yahweh] said", but *way^etzaw*, "he commanded", the latter verb denoting not plain utterance but persuasion or even coercion. What Elohim says, is; Yahweh, on the other hand, has less control over discourse and so he is more authoritarian, wishing to establish in-

---

[17] Thus the King James, Jerusalem and Good News Bibles, and the Revised Standard and New International Versions, all of which relegate the "incomplete" sense of *'ehyeh 'asher 'ehyeh* to a footnote.

[18] Steiner *op. cit.* p.53.

[19] Cf. *Ber. Rab.* 18:2.

controvertibly and beyond question that what he says "goes"—but in
the light of subsequent events, we see that where it goes turns out to
be only the common destiny of all language: out into the wilderness
of interpretation. In the Priestly creation account, God said "let there
be light" and there was light; there was no gap between the Divine
Word and what it signified. But here, Yahweh says "let there be
obedience", and we find that he creates something quite different.
This is because the prohibition is encoded as language, and language
in the Garden of Eden is an entirely worldly affair, offering not the
primal certitude of pure reference, but Derrida's "systematic play of
differences, of the traces of differences". In Eden, what is present
carries the trace of its Other, and so when Yahweh demands obedience, he invokes not some luminous, incorruptible reality but the deferral of meaning between what is and what is not. *Ha-'adam* may
well have been created in a state of innocence, but as soon as Yahweh tells him he must refrain from doing something or face mortal
consequences, he confers upon the earth-creature not just the power
to choose between one course of action and another, but the awareness that one course of action is to be preferred above the other. I
would call this a rudimentary knowledge of good and evil; *ha-'adam*
does not yet see it in those terms, but he already has a theoretical
version of the knowledge that has been forbidden to him.[20] Yahweh,
for his part, does not see that his own commands are fatally vulnerable to the vagaries of the language in which they are handed down,
and that humanity, required to recognise and obey the "essence" of
Divine ordinances, is in fact doomed to read them subjectively and
act accordingly.

So it is ironic that while the verb "he commanded" here is introduced—and authority is thus invoked in a way that is not necessarily
the case with *'amar*, "he said"—the command itself defies its auth-
or's power to enforce it as he would wish. There is a similar irony in
the pronouncement "you shall most certainly die": Yahweh announces with a rhetorical flourish "*mot tamut*", employing a sono-

---

[20] Cf. Greenstein (1989), p.50:

> Meaning....is always already the product of difference. When Adam and Eve chose to
> disobey God and eat from the Tree of Knowing, they applied a sense of discrimination
> that was not to be theirs until they had already eaten from the Tree.

rous double-root verbal form which again carries particular stress and helps to create an "overdetermined context"[21] around the prohibition—the narrative strategy seems to be to make the reader sit up and take notice, and maybe to anticipate a really satisfying death for *ha-'adam*, the tragic hero. Once again, however, we are to find that Yahweh's authoritative certainties slide inevitably into ambiguity.

Enter the serpent, who so shrewdly—and so notoriously—recognises and exploits this weakness. His first words to the newly-created woman are deeply sceptical: *'aph ki-'amar 'elohim*, "did God really say....?" This is anything but a straight question:[22] its surface form indicates that the serpent is merely asking for clarification of the Divine command, but given his legendary subtlety, we might well expect to find more to his words than meets the eye. For a start, he says he wants to know whether or not Yahweh said *lo' to'kh\u1d49lu*, "you [plural] shall not eat"; what was in fact said was *lo' to'khal*, "you [singular] shall not eat", and the serpent may possibly be drawing attention to this, suggesting in his oblique fashion that the prohibition was laid upon the undifferentiated earth-creature alone, and so that the woman's responsibility in this matter is far from clear. The reader might also notice that *'aph ki-'amar 'elohim* carries a verbal trace of *wayyo'mer 'elohim*, the formula used in the Priestly creation account to herald God's creative activity, the Divine Word-in-Being: what is gradually becoming clear in this story, however, is that Yahweh's power of signification is not that of *'elohim*, and his utterances are not the substantial Sayings of Gen. 1-2:4a. While the serpent does not quite see things from the modern reader's perspective (if we accept that his role as a character in the J-text denies him the critical distance from which to compare his world with that of the P-text) he nevertheless knows that in the Gar-

---

[21] Lanser (1988), p.75.

[22] Indeed, in the Masoretic Hebrew text it is not a question at all. The absence of the interrogative particle *ha* before *'aph ki-iamar 'elohim* has, reasonably enough, been commonly ascribed to haplography; the final letter of the preceding word (*'ishshah*) has coalesced with the interrogative *ha* owing to scribal error. Taken at (textual) face value, the serpent's words are translatable as "God indeed said you shall not eat from any of the trees in the garden", a statement which makes him both blatantly mendacious and somewhat less subtle in persuading the woman to show her hand. I choose, therefore, to treat his utterance as a question.

den of Eden, linguistic practice in itself is not a window onto the way things really are, and he will go so far as to question whether, or how effectively, Yahweh said what Yahweh said.

The woman's reply to the serpent seems to indicate that she does not trust her sly interrogator:

> We may eat the fruit from the trees in the garden, but of the fruit from the tree which is in the middle of the garden, God said "you shall not eat it, and you shall not touch it, lest you die" [Gen. 3:2-3].

As far as we know, Yahweh said nothing about touching the tree, but the woman may sense that there is a power-play going on in this conversation, and it could be that she seeks to fix the meaning of the original decree as she understands it, to protect her reading from the onslaught of counter-interpretation which she feels may be imminent —significantly, it is at this point in the Genesis text that the Rabbinic commentators cite Proverbs 30:6 ("do not add to [God's] words, lest he rebuke you, and you be found a liar"), and they continue with a salutary (if from a certain point of view ironic, given that this is midrash) admonition not to make the interpretative "fence" taller than the textual foundation permits.[23] On the other hand, her information may have come from *ha-'adam* who, having named her as he named the animals, sought to exercise a little dominion over her and supplied his own interpretative addendum to the command, laying his reading down as law in the inscrutable name of *YHWH-'elohim* and thus providing the first recorded example of "phallogocentric" exegesis. In either case, it is evident now that Yahweh's prohibition is a text, subject to the law of semantic deferral, and beginning to differ from its original formulation in that "you shall not eat" has been read as "you shall neither eat nor touch", while the tree of the knowledge of good and evil has become "the tree in the middle of the garden"—a tree which, according to Gen. 2:9, is actually the tree of life, and so in addition to interpretative embellishment we are dealing at this very early stage with an error in transmission.

But the serpent is not a rhetorical critic, at least not in the sense that he is interested in manipulating the text-itself to come up with

---

[23] *Ber. Rab.* 19:3.

"proper articulation of meaning". He is a close reader: when he says to the woman "you shall most certainly not die", his words are *lo'-mot t^{e}mutun* (3:4), a phrase which echoes and perhaps parodies the extravagant verbal form used by Yahweh back in chapter two. But the serpent's critical approach is to examine the strategy of the prohibition, not to chase after its meaning; he offers no alternative reading, but throws the text open to any number of possible interpretations which undermine the authority of the "original", and along the way he raises some uncomfortable and very pertinent questions concerning the motives of the Divine author:

> God knows that on the day that you eat from [the tree], your eyes will be opened and you will be like God [gods?], knowing good and evil [3:5].

The well-known Hebrew pun on "subtle/naked" begins to resonate here. The serpent is subtle indeed; his own utterance is decidedly enigmatic, difficult to "read" in that we have no idea as to either his motives or the source of his knowledge—but in another sense, his words are as open and nakedly true as they could possibly be, as we are to find that the eating of the fruit does indeed gain for the human couple a faculty of perception which, by Yahweh's own admission, is Godlike, rather than the more-or-less sudden death that was originally threatened. The woman could be said to be "naked", innocent and vulnerable in the face of this conflicting source of authority; on the other hand, it could be that she is more than a match for the serpent, acting on her own initiative and employing her own rhetorical subtlety in defensibly elaborating on Yahweh's command. The latter explanation is that favoured by Phyllis Trible when she confers upon the woman the composite title of "theologian, ethicist, hermeneut, rabbi",[24] but this is a generous view, given that the serpent does in fact get the better of her; and interpretations of this part of the narrative which present the woman as *freely* and courageously choosing maturity over innocence tend uniformly to ignore the fact that the woman is persuaded to act against what appears to be her better judgement. At the end of her brief dialogue with the serpent, the woman is faced with what amounts to a choice between two very different interpretations of scripture: one (her own) predicated upon

---

[24] Trible (1978), p.110.

what Yahweh's words "really mean", and a more politically-oriented one which examines what the words are being used for, taking
into account not what the author means but what he knows. Interest-
ingly enough, her choice is determined by factors which are subjective, extrinsic and which should, by rhetorical-critical standards,
have no bearing upon "the text itself": the fruit has strong aesthetic
and sensual appeal, and like many an accomplished theologian, the
woman decides what she wants in advance and chooses to favour the
interpretation of scripture which best supports her decision.

In the confusion which follows, what is most clearly apparent is
that nobody has quite spoken the whole truth. "On the day that you
eat you will die", Yahweh threatened, but as the evening breezes
begin to blow he finds the human couple alive and well. "Your eyes
will be opened and you will be like God[s]", the serpent said, but all
they see is their own nakedness, and they perceive it not as a Divine
characteristic but as a kind of absence or incompleteness. Where
sexual difference had been an inevitable and functional aspect of the
creation of man and woman, secondary to their common humanity,[25]
it now assumes exaggerated importance and becomes a source of
anxiety, and it seems that the "knowledge" gained by the human
couple is in fact a skewed awareness of opposition, an entry into
Yahweh's dualistic thought-world governed by the good/evil dichotomy. Where the poem in 2:23 had celebrated *identity*-in-
difference ("this at last is bone of my bone and flesh of my
flesh...."), what is now perceived is non-presence, the other side of
the coin: man and woman see themselves in their nakedness as
lacking, as different from each other in a way that must be rendered
covert and unspoken; hence the sewing together and wearing of the
fig leaves. In this atmosphere of uncertainty and fear, it is not surprising that the man and the woman are reluctant to enter into conversation either with the authoritarian Yahweh or the subversive

---

[25] Cf. Derrida (1982a), p.73. In the course of a brief discussion of Emmanuel
Levinas' reading of the Garden of Eden story, Derrida remarks that

> [s]econdariness....would not be that of woman or femininity, but the *division* between
> masculine and feminine. It is not feminine sexuality that would be second but only the
> relationship to sexual difference. At the origin, on this side of and therefore beyond
> any sexual mark, there was humanity in general, and this is what is important.

serpent, both of whom seemed to speak plainly, but neither of whom apparently said what they meant. When called to account for themselves, what each of the human couple has to say is revealing. The man implicitly blames Yahweh for giving him the woman, more clearly blames the woman for giving him the fruit, and thus provides an account of the human condition which will later become known for centuries as the foundation of orthodox Christian anthropology:

> The woman whom you gave to be with me, she gave me [the fruit] from the tree, and I ate [3:12].[26]

In this statement we hear the firing of the first shot on the battlefield of sexual politics, and characteristically it is the man who tries to establish himself as independent and autonomous. He presents himself as the object of two acts of giving: Yahweh *gave* him the woman, the woman *gave* him the fruit, and in both instances his professed relationship to the "given" is passive and uncommitted. He no longer recognises that the woman is nothing less than the condition of his identity, that it was only when and because she was formed that "he" passed from an undifferentiated, ungendered earth-creature to *'ish* who differs from *'ishshah*, and so that the woman was not "given" to him but created with him. Like the proto-patriarch he is, the man projects his maleness back onto the sexually ambiguous point of human origin, existing by his own account in intrinsic relation to nothing and nobody, participating in no being but his own, and no doubt deeply regretting his "flesh of my flesh" speech back in 2:23.

The woman, on the other hand, perhaps in spite of herself gives a more perceptive account of what happened; she too is labouring under a misapprehension, but one which paradoxically reflects the truth:

> The serpent deceived me, and I ate [3:13].

Whether or not we can legitimately accuse the serpent of deception, as the word is commonly understood, is unlikely; the course of

---

[26] Cf. an influential New Testament gloss on this passage:

> For Adam was formed first, then Eve; and Adam was not deceived, but the woman was deceived and became a transgressor [1 Tim. 2:13-14].

events is beginning to show that the serpent in fact accurately predicted the outcome of the eating of the fruit. The RSV Bible translates the Hebrew *hannachash hishshi'ani* as "the serpent beguiled me", and this is a more suggestive translation, implying not that the serpent baldly lied, but that he used guile, charm or persuasion—all species of rhetoric—to win the woman over to his way of thinking. She indicates, rightly enough, that her action was the result of her entering into dialogue, a relational state of psychological interconnection between subject and object where the contradictory play of identity and difference takes place—identity in that dialogue involves, however imperfectly, a meeting of minds and a language shared; difference in that any understanding reached is incomplete, leaving room for the deferral and obscurity of meaning that "beguiling" inevitably entails. We have seen that the serpent's speech is largely unfathomable, "fraught with background" of the most irrecoverable kind, and in the absence of hard evidence to the contrary it is difficult not to assume along with a host of other interpreters that he appears in the Garden as a catalyst for discord. But we have also seen that his words to the woman were less manifestly deceptive than traditional exegesis has made them out to be. The serpent is an exploiter of meaning and has not spoken the whole truth, but neither has he lied, and so it could be said that his "critical reading" of Yahweh's prohibition, more clearly than the prohibition itself, constitutes in its curious moral and semantic indeterminacy a paradigmatic or exemplary linguistic performance—if language is inseparable from intention, and if words unavoidably defer final signification rather than yielding it up, then discourse involves the manipulation of *relative* degrees of truth and falsity, and "beguiling" is inevitably what we do whenever we speak.

To read the Garden of Eden story with this understanding in mind is to adopt a perspective from which the "conflicts dramatised in the text" appear as conflicts that stem from the intersection of language, interpretation and power. Adopting this perspective can usefully serve a more specifically feminist approach to the text, as it can help to gain some insight into how patriarchal language and power defines, asserts and ultimately defeats itself. Yahweh, for example, is unmistakeably a male God, a father-figure to his creatures. Materially and psychologically, his relationship to the human couple is patriarchal and evinces patriarchal authority, working exclusively from the "separated" or physically distanced side of the generative equation:

> The father is at no time physically united with the child. His psychological orientation toward the child tends to be one of confrontation rather than coincidence....When fatherhood is applied to God, it is characterised by the parallel concepts of creation out of nothing—i.e. the father's own substance is not committed to the offspring—and of relations of the will, such as covenant, obedience, loyalty, and faith.... An aura of contingency colours the whole relationship, with at least some hint of threat in the background.[27]

"Fatherhood....*applied to* God": a helpful phrase to keep in mind as it reminds us that Yahweh himself is a fictionally constructed character, whose personality and actions reveal the controlling hand of an author or editor (this in turn has a suggestive bearing on his name: *YHWH-'elohim*, not so much a name as a political title, denoting *YHWH* the historical God of the Patriarchs of Israel who has attributed to him the mythical power and unapproachability of *'elohim*, absolute Godhead[28]). It could be argued that Yahweh's inspiriting of *ha-'adam* with the breath of life involves a direct physical relationship, but this act in fact prefigures the patriarchal-biological theory that the male's role in fertilisation is to quicken or animate "inert" (female) matter, and in no sense is Yahweh substantially immanent in his creature, or vice versa.

In addition to this, there is the issue of identity, a crucial element in any patriarchal power-structure. I have argued above that the

---

[27] Bruteau (1974), p.97.
[28] Cf. the cry of the humiliated prophets of Ba'al in 1 Kings 18:39—*YHWH hu' ha-ielohim*; not an epiphany, but a politically expedient confession (which, as it turns out, does them little good) attributing supreme hierarchical authority over all other Gods to the God of Israel. In this context, Yahweh appears not as God but as Yahweh-the-God, one who has, as it were, had divinity thrust upon him. So too in Gen. 2:4b-3:24, we should understand Yahweh as *provisionally* Divine, the (fictional) signifier of Godhead characterised—and therefore compromised—like any signifier, by lack or absence of plenitude:

> If [the divinity of God]....is lacking, if only imperceptibly, then God is already no longer at issue—but rather "God", who by his quotation marks is stigmatized as an idol [Marion, 1994, p.579].

opening words in this creation account, $b^e yom$ '*asot YHWH-'elohim*, place Yahweh *already* in the world of history and time (as opposed to the $b^e re' shit\ bara'$ '*elohim* of Genesis 1-2:4a which begins, as it were, at the beginning); again, this aptly symbolises his "writtenness" or constitution within a pre-existent text. There are many other factors in the story which similarly indicate that Yahweh is more a literary character than a Divine Author, and thus that his power and authority are no more absolute than the meaning of his words. The Garden of Eden, for example, understood as the Divinely-established scene of an aetiological drama, might be expected to occupy some kind of sacred space: within its boundaries, every significant act should be a causal antecedent, "mythically" prescriptive of what goes on in the profane world of history and time. This is how the story has been read by those who (like Paul) say that because the first Woman opened the door to disobedience, all women do likewise; because the first Man was granted dominion over his wife, all men wield authority over all women for all time; and so on. What happened in the Garden of Eden, in other words, is paradigmatic of all things because the Garden was there at the sacred and absolute Beginning of all things. But this is not unarguably the case: to draw a comparison once more from the Genesis 1 text, we can see that mythical time and space have, to all intents and purposes, no recognisable context, nothing before or around them, and that the mythical creation of the world in the Priestly narrative began at a point where all was *tohu wabhohu*, empty but for a disembodied Presence moving over the face of chaos. The Garden of Eden, on the other hand, is not created *ex nihilo* or even *ex vacuo*; it is planted "in Eden, to the east", a place with which the narrative seems to presuppose some geographical familiarity on the part of the reader. So the Garden has a context, and significantly this context is described partly with reference to the world of the reader—we know exactly where the Tigris and the Euphrates (2:14) are—and partly with reference to an unknown world where the mysterious rivers of Pishon and Gihon (2:11-13) rise. The correspondence between Eden and reality, therefore, has elements both of identity and of otherness, it is a correspondence that occurs somewhere between history and myth, partaking of both worlds simultaneously and giving the Garden the indeterminacy which is entirely appropriate to a *fictional* environment.

Yahweh, then, speaks and acts in a world created not by himself but by a narrator, a manifestly "written" world whose landscape is literary and whose laws are those of language. In his relationship with his human creatures he wields a certain inevitable authority, but this authority is not grounded so much in ontological superiority as in a superior level of experience in the ways of the world, experience which eventually proves only too accessible to the human couple. In his story "The Circular Ruins", Jorge Luis Borges writes of a man who succeeds in dreaming another man and introducing this creature of dreams into the waking world; the dreamer-creator rests fulfilled in his task until the point (at the end of the story) where he finds that he himself is a shadow, the product of some previous dreamer's dream, no more substantial than his own phantom creation.[29] In much the same way, Yahweh creates, animates and instructs the human couple, but to the extent that he puts himself forward as the ultimate and authoritative Source of being, he obscures the fact that he too is the creature of a pre-existent author, and so that he differs from humanity principally in terms of knowledge or fulfilled potential.

There are signs in Gen. 2:4b-3:24 which indicate a strong identity-in-difference existing between Yahweh and the human couple. First, we see Yahweh as more an artisan than a supernatural creator, fashioning *ha-'adam* from *ha-'adamah* in much the same way that an earthly potter would fashion a clay figurine, and appropriately enough the verb used to describe this activity is *yatsar* (2:7 *wayyitser YHWH-'elohim*, "and the LORD God formed....") rather than the more literally "theological" *bara'*. Here, Yahweh shows clear traces of local mythological antecedents, as he follows the Egyptian god Khnum and the Mesopotamian goddess Mami in forming humanity out of clay; indeed, the Hebrew word for "potter" (*yotser*) derives from the verb *yatsar* and provides a particularly strong link between Yahweh and "Khnum, the potter".[30] Similarly, Yahweh's creation of *ha-'ishshah* (2:22) is an act described in human terms—*wayyibhen*, "and he built"; *banah* being (like *yatsar* and *'asah*) a verb used to

---

[29] Borges (1989), pp.72-77.
[30] Cf. Brandon (1963), pp.61, 89, 123.

denote creation in the social world beyond the perimeters of Eden.[31] These terms are appropriate to all Yahweh's creative activity, as there is something decidedly "human" about the way in which he pieces his handiwork together; assessing and adjusting ("it is not good that *ha-'adam* should be alone"), working by trial and error (cf. the first unsuccessful attempt at finding a mate for the earth-creature in 2:18-20) and, most significantly, maintaining only partial control over his creatures and having to take defensive steps to stop them from usurping his power (3:22-23). Yahweh learns from experience and is thus not strictly omniscient;[32] he appears to perceive a potential threat from the human couple and thus cannot be said to be utterly omnipotent; he strolls in the Garden at evening, searching for *ha-'adam* and calling "where are you?", and so his presence must somehow be bounded by time and space. Yahweh's dimensions are, at least in part, human dimensions, and this is reflected in the fact that his medium of communication is human discourse:

> [t]he biblical writers present us with a picture of a personal God who, when addressing humanity, does so in the manner of all human speech,[33]

and in his dealings with humanity, therefore, Yahweh can be said both to differ *and* to inhabit the order of the same, the relationship being one in which understanding is incomplete, interpretation is inevitable, and yet "communion through mutuality"[34] is achieved.

The Garden, however, is a world-within-a-world where mutuality is subordinated to hierarchy, and relationships are conducted according to the exercise of power. A close reading of Genesis 2:8 reveals that the scene of this primal drama is not, in fact, the commonly-termed "Garden of Eden" but *gan-b^e'eden*, "a garden *in* Eden": the Garden is a sectioned-off part of the pre-existent world, its boundaries are constructed and delineate not the sphere of Divine presence-in-communion, but of Yahwist rule—and this rule exhibits all the characteristics of patriarchy. As we have seen, Yahweh's authority is that of the father: exercised as the requirement to obey, and bol-

---

[31] Cf. the creation of the first city: *way^{e}hi boneh 'ir* (Gen. 4:17).

[32] Cf. Zelechow (1992), pp.166-67.

[33] *Ibid.* p.166.

[34] *Ibid.* p.166.

stered with threat. In addition to being hierarchical, it is patrilineal: once the undifferentiated *ha-'adam* has been formed into two gendered individuals, the power and responsibility attendant upon naming rests with *'ish* alone, and notably he identifies *'ishshah* as a subspecies of his own gender ("this shall be called woman, because she was taken out of man", 2:23), names his wife *chawwah* and thus confers upon her a primarily procreative role (she is to be *'em kolchay*, "the mother of all living", 3:20), and the rectitude and propriety of these very significant speech acts is tacitly acknowledged by Yahweh's pronouncement (3:16) which seeks to confirm childbearing and willing obedience to the male as sacred womanly obligations.

Yahweh's authority is also patriarchal in that it is based on the implicit claim to self-evident, "natural" integrity: it is complete and admits no alternative. When Yahweh warns the human couple away from the tree of knowledge, the one question that must not be asked is *why* such a command has been issued, and as long as silence is observed on this point, Yahweh is able to maintain the inscrutable Otherness appropriate to *'elohim*. But events prove that Yahweh's authority, like his speech, is by no means pure or absolute—it can be questioned, subverted and contextualised, as the serpent demonstrates when he reveals the defensive will-to-power operating underneath the decree: rather than being predicated upon "the way things are", Yahweh's command is designed to protect the way he wants things to be. This strategy serves to uphold another mainstay of patriarchal power: the dualistic separation of self/other. I have indicated above that there are various ways in which Yahweh does *not* differ from his creatures, ways in which he belongs to the order of the same, particularly as far as his language and the limits of his power are concerned. But otherness is precisely what Yahweh stresses and seeks to maintain in his relationship with humanity—otherness is what he defends when he forbids Godlike knowledge to *ha-'adam*; otherness is what is significantly threatened when the human couple eat from the tree of knowledge; otherness is what Yahweh fears will be eradicated altogether if *ha-'adam* eats from the tree of life. What principally separates Yahweh from humanity at the beginning of the story is the ability to create, along with individual immortality. The former power is conferred upon *'ish* and *'ishshah* when they become aware of sexual difference and thus realise their potential to engender life;[35] the latter attribute, as the one remaining factor separating Yahweh from his creatures, is to be defended at all costs, and so the way to the tree of life is barred once and for all.

We can see, then, that the Garden, far from being the blank slate of prehistory where knowledge, meaning and intention are "pure" and devoid of any covert social or political interest, is in fact the scene of struggle where language equals interpretation, and meaning requires the exercise of coercive power for its stability. It is a place where authority is wielded by a creator-figure who, while being in many respects of a kind with his creatures, attempts to safeguard his otherness by keeping humanity ignorant of their own Godlike potential. The Garden is the disturbed dream of patriarchy, at once representing the highest degree of patriarchal power, and troubled by a nervous awareness of its own contingent foundations. Within the Garden, creation is effected in solitary splendour by a male God who, in alone possessing the power to engender life, has no need of (or dependence upon) a female consort; indeed, the Female only exists at all as his own handiwork, and both his human creatures are brought into the world as innocent, obedient subjects:

> Yahweh desires the human beings to abide as two naive children....[he] intends to create only two human beings, two children eternally worshipful of their creator.[36]

But a sacred Garden, as the medieval allegorists knew, should be an enclosure within whose walls the unpredictable chaos of nature is subordinated to Divine harmony and order. The Garden of Eden is no such place; the security of its inside/outside structure is under-

---

[35] Cf. Dragga (1992), pp.4-5:

> The significance of the tree of knowledge of good and evil, and specifically its association with sexual knowledge, is obvious only following the human couple's eating of the fruit and their immediate and single discovery of their nakedness, their sexual differences (Gen. 3.6-7). The divine command to abstain from the fruit of the tree of knowledge of good and evil is thus designed to preclude the human discovery of procreativity.

Cf. also Brandon *op. cit.* pp.13-67.

[36] *Ibid.* p.5.

mined by the fact that the law of "outside" holds sway over the "inside", and this is not the law of dualistic patriarchal order but of ambiguity and indeterminacy. When Yahweh's command is disobeyed, the human couple realise that the division between creator and creature, for example, is not a clear one, as they now see that they have the potential to do what Yahweh can do. Their eyes are opened, and Yahweh's punitive response to this betrays the wrathful dismay of the father whose children inevitably grow up to claim his power. The same goes for the good/evil dichotomy: according to the prohibition, "good" signifies obedience and "evil" disobedience, but these moral certainties become blurred when the serpent asks how a deceptive command can be fundamentally "good", and when we wonder how human responsibility and maturity can be completely "evil". Opposing concepts become enmeshed, and the human couple learn to perceive sameness-in-difference: what is perhaps most significant, and paradoxical, is that the dualism of identity/difference itself is disrupted when *'ish* and *'ishshah*, resting comfortably in their common humanity, eat from the tree of knowledge and begin to know sexual difference, that most undecidable of phenomena which both fundamentally divides and substantially unites female and male. It is important to note that none of this deferral is *initiated* by the eating of the fruit of knowledge; it has been, from the beginning of the story, very much a part of Yahweh's creation. Even though Yahweh himself dissembles indeterminacy, and the humans are initially ignorant of it, the serpent—not some kind of supernatural adversary, but one of the wild creatures that *YHWH-'elohim* has made (cf. Gen. 3:1)—happily lives and breathes it, and for this reason above all others he is silenced and cursed by his creator. The Rabbinic commentary on Gen. 3:14, where Yahweh executes judgement on the serpent, elaborates on the idea of the creator being somehow at a loss when directly confronted with his wily creature, and thus having to resort to summary justice. The midrash relates that

> with *'adam* [Yahweh] engaged in dialogue; with *chawwah* he engaged in dialogue, but with the serpent he did not engage in dialogue. Rather, the Holy One (blessed be He) said: "this serpent is wicked; he is an expert at replies. If I say [anything] to him, he will say to me: 'you commanded them, and I commanded them; why did they set

aside your commandment and follow my commandment?'" Instead, [Yahweh] shut him up and cut him off.[37]

The question which the Rabbis here depict Yahweh as wanting to evade is pertinent to say the least, as it is the question which above all others indicates that the structure of meaning in Eden, the "text" in which Yahweh's authority is inscribed, is deeply divided against itself: why indeed did the human couple follow the words of the serpent rather than those of their creator? The answer must have much to do with the fact that Yahweh's words, the Divine *ipsissima verba*, admit interpretation and ambiguity, even when spoken and heard directly against a background of primal silence. The question also leads us inevitably to remember that the woman at least, in her brief argument with the serpent, displays a definite (if unsophisticated) awareness of what she should and should not do in a given situation, an awareness of what is *tobh* (i.e. in perfect agreement with the Divine word) and what is not—a form of knowledge which, as I have noted, should not as yet be part of humanity's ethical repertoire, and which therefore strangely contradicts Yahweh's command even before the question of disobedience arises. Like any author, Yahweh has created a world in which *différance* operates, a world where the significance of words and events can never be final, and where the author's own intentions concerning meaning are subject to the play of infinite counter-readings—and all this because he inhabits a "host-text of pre-existent language"[38] whose possibilities for signification extend far beyond his immediate control.

In the midrash quoted above, the Hebrew expression translated here as "engage in dialogue" is *nasa' wᵉnatan*, literally "take and give", and also carrying the sense of argument, transaction and bargaining. The expression is apposite in this context because it implies that what is at stake in linguistic exchange is not Truth but (to put it perhaps over-simply) vested interest; to engage in dialogue involves various means of persuasion—even "beguiling"—with the end in mind of fixing meaning in much the same way as one would fix a price, i.e. by common agreement. *Nasa' wᵉnatan* also implies that the relationship between interlocutors is one of (ideally) equal

---

[37] *Ber. Rab.* 20:2.
[38] Norris (1982), p.93.

power; less a relationship of writer/reader than one of writer/writer, in accordance with a discursive concept of "take and give" rather than a static one of "give and receive". Yahweh's relationship with his "readers", however, is unequal in that the power to signify rests with him alone, and this power imbalance (as the midrashists realised) is what the serpent, a *ba'al t^eshubhot*, exposes when he challenges Yahweh in 3:4-5 and offers a new reading—a perfectly legitimate one, as it turns out—of the Divine command. Yahweh's authority rests, like all structures of patriarchal rule, on the claim that he is the ultimate source of meaning, that his commands in particular are intrinsically meaning-full and thus demand to be *received* and observed strictly according to the letter of the law. The serpent knows, however, that this kind of power is dependent upon the ability to conceal its own tactics and motives, to disguise its particular strategic assumptions as unquestionable norms; that

> the recourse to a position....that places itself beyond the play of power ....is perhaps the most insidious ruse of power,[39]

but as soon as Yahweh's "textual politics" are exposed, he is shown to be a *literary* figure in every conceivable sense of the word, a participant in discourse and not its Architect. His words lose their inscrutable authority, and in cursing the serpent, Yahweh plays out a kind of vengeful wish-fulfilment which reflects, above and beyond anything else, the malevolent designs harboured by a good many authors upon their more astute critics.

Exactly who or what Yahweh *is* is not clear; his origins are as obscure as the origins of patriarchy itself, and accordingly his power is grounded in the myth of an eternal Presence—his name, according to most translations of Exod. 3:14-15, is I AM, a name which, harnessed to the title *'elohim*, implies that his authority is absolute and that obedience is due to him because this is how things have always been—a classic patriarchal claim if ever there was one. What Genesis 2:4b-3:24 shows us, however, is that Yahweh's claim to the status of *'elohim* is self-defeating, and that its subversion is not an act of criminal intent or perverse nihilism, but simply the inevitable condition of the language in which the claim is made—when Yah-

---

[39] Butler (1992), p.6.

weh speaks, he creates a text, and one of the legitimate possibilities offered by any text is that it can be read as ambiguous and internally divided. In the Garden of Eden story, then, the "Fall" chronicled is one which occurs both before and after the fruit of knowledge is eaten (i.e. whether we know it or not), and it is not so much a Fall as a collapse sideways, the inescapable slide of linguistic certainty into undecideability and interpretation, a movement that threatens above all those who claim ontological primacy and a monopoly on Truth. It is from this understanding that the Garden of Eden story can be read as an ironic critique of patriarchy, a critique which is overtly "feminist" to the extent that the serpent chooses *ha-'ishshah* as his partner-in-subversion, and that she takes the initiative in eating the fruit before *ha-'ish*, but which stops short of valorising the mythical woman-as-Woman or in any other way perpetuating epic-heroic female chauvinism. This critique falls somewhere between "a certain assertion of women" (to use Derrida's term) and the displacement of the essential Female; to put it more simply, it may be "feminist" in intent, but not by definition.

Perhaps the Garden of Eden story's canniest critic is its own earliest casualty, the serpent, and the deconstructive reader could do worse than to pay close attention to what this character represents. There exists an extremely suggestive symbolic parallel between the role of the serpent in the Genesis text and the function of writing as discussed by Derrida in one of his key works. In "Plato's Pharmacy",[40] Derrida provides an extensive commentary on Plato's dialogue the *Phaedrus*, a commentary which touches on many of the issues discussed in these pages, in particular the issue of speech and writing. Plato's principal concern in the *Phaedrus* is to demonstrate the superiority of speech over writing, to show that writing is a lifeless simulacrum, a deceptive and even dangerous substitute for the plenitude and truth inherent in the oral transmission of knowledge. Plato presents his argument in the form of a mythical dialogue: the Egyptian king Thamus is visited by the god Theuth, a god accredited with having invented (among other things) the art of writing. Theuth exhibits his art to the king and declares that it will be eminently beneficial both to himself and to all his subjects ("This discipline,

---

[40] Derrida (1981a), pp.61-171.

my King, will make the Egyptians wiser and will improve their memories"[41]). The King refuses Theuth's proffered gift, arguing that the art of writing, if widely adopted, will in fact result in the *dereliction* of memory and the devaluation of direct (i.e. spoken) instruction:

> This invention will produce forgetfulness in the souls of those who have learned it because they will not need to exercise their memories ....[t]hanks to you and your invention, your pupils will be widely read without the benefit of a teacher's instruction; in consequence, they'll entertain the delusion that they have wide knowledge, while they are, in fact, for the most part incapable of real judgement.[42]

At issue here is the difference between the "real" wisdom which direct speech and instruction are said to impart, and the so-called sophistry engendered by the written word: as we have seen, a logocentric distinction. Derrida's treatment of the story is lengthy and complex; relevant to our purpose here is his discussion of the term *pharmakon*, a word which surfaces at several important points in Plato's (Greek) text. Theuth offers writing as a *pharmakon* for memory and instruction, and writing's efficacy as *pharmakon* is what the King disputes. This word, however, commonly translated as "remedy", in fact has a double, divided sense; it also—and equally—denotes "poison". Derrida points out that translations of the *Phaedrus* which opt (as they invariably do) for the former, remedial sense of *pharmakon* are incapable of conveying the important idea that

> the stated intention of Theuth being precisely to stress the worth of his product....he *turns* the word on its strange and invisible pivot, presenting it from a single one, the most reassuring, of its *poles* ....interrupting, for his own purposes, the communication between the two opposing values.[43]

Theuth, in other words, presents writing as *pharmakon* in only one sense of the word; the King, in his reply to Theuth, indicates that he is aware of the god's duplicity, that Theuth "has passed a poison off

---

[41] The *Cratylus* 274c-e, quoted in Derrida *op. cit.* p.75.
[42] The *Cratylus* 274e-275b, quoted in Derrida *op. cit.* p.102.
[43] Derrida *op. cit.* pp.97-98.

as a remedy".[44] In his suspicion of writing, the King evokes the pejorative denotation of *pharmakon*, and thus he restores the "communication" between the two opposed senses of "remedy" and "poison" within the one signifier. This is ironic, given that the King rejects writing according to a logic which privileges univocity of meaning and which "does not tolerate such passages between opposing senses of the same word".[45] The main point here, however, is that in Plato's text,

> the two interlocutors [i.e. the King and Theuth], whatever they do and whether or not they choose, remain within the unity of the same signifier. Their discourse plays within it, *which is no longer the case in translation.*[46]

Here, Derrida seeks not so much to discredit those translators who have reduced *pharmakon* to only one of its disjunctive senses, as to suggest that (in the words of one commentator)

> what is really "on trial" in these efforts to cope with the *pharmakon* of writing is an ethics of language that has always privileged authentic, self-present speech over the vagaries of textual inscription....there is simply no reckoning, on logocentric terms, with an instance like Plato's *pharmakon* that disrupts the very logic of self-identity, that opens up a play of semantic substitutions beyond all hope of assured conceptual grasp.[47]

I wish to suggest that the serpent in Genesis 2:4b-3:24 is a kind of biblical *pharmakon*, operating in much the same way as Plato's *pharmakon* and presenting much the same problems (or opportunities) for the interpreter. The idea is suggestive partly because we do not have to go as far as Derrida or the twentieth century to find an explicit intertextual link: we already have, in Numbers 21:4-9, a biblical instance of serpents acting both as poison and as remedy for the people of Yahweh. Moreover, as the Israelites in the wilderness, bitten by *hann^echashim hass^eraphim* ("fiery serpents"—or are they angelic? cf. Isaiah 6:2-3) and dying, look to Moses' bronze serpent

---

[44] *Ibid.* p.98.

[45] *Ibid.* p.99.

[46] *Ibid.* p.98 (my italics).

[47] Norris (1987), p.38.

for healing, we can see that there is a sense here in which the authentic, "true" thing kills while its representation gives life. These are ambiguous serpents indeed, sent to cure Israel's poisoned faith by poisoning the people and eliciting their faith in the restorative power of a simulacrum; never did Derrida's comment seem so resonant that "[t]here is no such thing as a harmless remedy. The *pharmakon* can never be simply beneficial".[48]

So too, the Edenic *pharmakon* embodies strange inversions and contradictions. As part of Yahweh's creation, we might reasonably expect the serpent to be fundamentally *tobh*, and yet it is impossible to consider its words and actions without conceding somewhere along the line that the serpent is something other than the agent of unqualified *tobhah*. The serpent is not "good" for the human couple in any absolute sense of the word, or even for itself; the results of the encounter between serpent and humanity are silence, enmity, pain, toil and exile for all concerned. This is not to say, however, that the serpent in itself represents complete discord. As *pharmakon* it plays an undeniable part in poisoning the fruits of Yahweh's creative labour, but at the same time it can be said—as I have argued— to provide a remedy for human moral ignorance, as well as offering a crucial insight into the workings of language and power, and thus "remedying" the injustice perpetrated by Yahweh's duplicitous command. Referring to Plato's *pharmakon*, Derrida writes that translations which render the word "remedy" or "cure", at the expense of its opposite sense,

> produce on the *pharmakon* an *effect of analysis* that violently destroys it, reduces it to one of its simple elements by interpreting it, paradoxically enough, in the light of the ulterior developments it itself has made possible. Such an interpretative translation is thus as violent as it is impotent: it destroys the *pharmakon* but at the same time forbids itself access to it, leaving it untouched in its reserve.[49]

Moreover, when *pharmakon* is translated into only one of its possible meanings,

---

[48] Derrida *op. cit.* p.99.
[49] *Ibid.* p.99.

> what is in question is not just a localized example of semantic insen-
> sitivity, but a need to ignore the problematical effects of a writing that
> nonetheless resists such reduction.[50]

Similarly then, to "translate" the serpent in Genesis into terms which
are morally or in any other way unambiguous (after the manner of,
say, Milton in *Paradise Lost*, who portrayed the serpent as Satan, or
of the medieval and Renaissance iconographers who gave the serpent a woman's face) is to curtail the play of signification, to erase
one side of the dual inscription which can be traced in and through
this most undecideable of characters. As *différance* could be said to
be the *pharmakon* of meaning—poison from the logocentric perspective, cure from a relativist point of view, both at once for those
of us who oscillate precariously between both poles—so the serpent
in Eden represents much that is uncomfortably yet necessarily contradictory in human thought and experience. We might well respond
to such a character both with mixed feelings and with hermeneutical
caution. Many critics have noted—some with dismay—that Milton
gave Satan all the best poetry and made him by far the most dynamic, three-dimensional character in his epic. Satan's gift to literature is neither more nor less than the gift of Theuth to King Thamus,
or the gift of the serpent to the human couple in Eden—a *pharmakon*, a hard cure, perhaps ironically best expressed in the oxymo-
ron familiar to Christian theologians: a *felix culpa*.

   The serpent, then, is not a resolver but an underminer of oppositions, one who mingles dichotomous forces "within the unity of the
same signifier". I have argued that it is in and through the serpent
that good and evil take on a non-identical "sameness", as do truth
and falsity, Edenic harmony and discord, remedy and poison—and it
is important to note that the same agency could be attributed to
Yahweh and the humans; only the serpent, however, accepts and
exploits the undecideable. In the serpent we also see a flickering
back and forth of identity between beast and human (the "wild
creature" speaks and reasons), earthly and Divine (the serpent is
subject to Yahwist rule, and yet privy to intimate knowledge of his
Creator), mortal and immortal.[51] Most significant here, however, is

---

[50] Norris *op. cit.* p.38.
[51] Cf. Brandon (1963), pp.129-32.

the serpent's ambiguous sexual orientation. The pun in Gen. 2:25-3:1 on *'arumim* (describing the naked human couple)/*'arum* (referring to the serpent's subtlety) establishes a strong linguistic link between the themes of sexuality and wisdom, a link which in turn suggests an intertextual connection between the Garden of Eden story and other such ancient Near Eastern myths as the Gilgamesh epic, in which wisdom and sexual experience are closely associated. The mythological background to Gen. 2:4b-3:24 weaves around the serpent a sexuality that is radically undecideable, as resistant to determination as the knowledge the serpent makes available to *'ish* and *'ishshah*. Traditionally associated with fertility cults (and in particular the worship of the Canaanite goddess Astarte[52]), the serpent is well known as a Goddess-icon, but its function as such has to do with the fact that it is a *phallic* emblem. The serpent functions as the phallus and yet it signifies the Female, its metaphorical and its symbolic "beings" ambiguously knit. This makes its role in the Garden of Eden story extremely difficult to determine, certainly much more complex than readings of the text allow which seek to establish strict equations between either evil dissembler/weak woman (the standard patriarchal account) or bringer of knowledge/brave heroine (the reading of Trible *et al*). Derrida, in his discussion of woman and gender in the interview "Choreographies", plays with the idea of "a choreographic text with polysexual signatures", a reading-writing matrix evincing a diffuse discursive "sexuality" which is not so much neutral as plural:

> what if we were to approach....the area of a relationship to the other where the code of sexual marks would no longer be discriminating? The relationship would not be asexual, far from it, but would be *sexual otherwise*: beyond the binary difference that governs the decorum of all codes....I would like to believe in the multiplicity of sexually marked voices. I would like to believe in the masses, this indeterminable number of blended voices, this mobile of non-identified sexual marks whose choreography can carry, divide, multiply the body of each "individual", whether he be classified as "man" or as "woman" according to the criteria of usage.[53]

---

[52] Cf. *ibid.* p.129.
[53] Derrida (1982a), p.76 (my italics).

The serpent could be understood as a figure representing the realisation of this possibility. Referred to in the Genesis text as "he" (and,
in the course of this study, somewhat confusedly both as "he" and
"it" according to context), the serpent would in fact be better designated some kind of loose combination of the male and female pro-
nouns. Far from being asexual, androgynous, hermaphroditic, or in
any other way sexually fixed, the serpent is "sexual otherwise", embodying the movement of a restless dynamic of both sexes. At once
phallic totem and Goddess-representative, symbolising male and
female fertility, the serpent encapsulates the movement of deferral
between sexual designations, a body at once divided and multiplied.
Of course, there is a certain sympathy between serpent and woman
in the biblical narrative which cannot be explained away, but this is
necessitated by a narrative environment—both within the story and
in the ancient society from which it has emerged—in which the text,
the hermeneutical framework, and the accumulation of power to be
deconstructed, are all male-identified. In a story compiled by patriarchal authors and editors, and subject to generations of phallogocentric interpretation, the meaning to be disputed is patriarchal. But
history and culture are subject to change, and appropriately enough
the serpent is a skin-shedder, a character whose sexual orientation
might not be so specific according to a different criterion of usage.
This kind of understanding of gender is a radical one; difficult perhaps to think through because it involves a diffuse concept of biological sex which confounds the idea of a "natural" (i.e. binary) sexual economy that has prevailed for centuries in philosophical, religious, medical and scientific discourses. What could be "more real,
primordial, or prediscursive" than the binary division of bodies into
male and female?[54] Demonstrating that the answer to this question is
not as self-evident as might be supposed has been the project of an
increasing number of feminist theorists, such as Judith Butler and
Elizabeth Grosz. The latter's 1994 study *Volatile Bodies* traces the
attempts of various philosophical figures to show ways in which the
sexed body might be understood as in fact constructed, pliable and
undecideable, rather than as a fixed, pre-cultural "given". In the

---

[54] Grosz (1994), p.154.

context of a discussion of Foucault and the role of power in determining gender, Grosz writes:

> Sex [i.e. biological sex] is a kind of conglomeration of elements of varying consistency and composition—physiological processes, hormonal secretions, muscular activities, wishes, hopes, desires, sensations, attitudes—which have historically been attributed a status as a unified, even natural, entity. The unification of these disparate elements is an effect of a particular investment of power....Is it that there is a sexual continuum—a (quasi-biological or even natural) continuum of (sexual) differences between bodies, which power divides and organizes in historically and culturally variable forms? Or does power help constitute the very biologies, and pleasures, of bodies?[55]

Grosz goes on to suggest that the reason these questions find "no ready answer" has much to do with the way in which sexual difference has rarely been called into question as a grounding principle or fundamental of human experience. There is perhaps no more radical (or difficult) project than that of rethinking or displacing ontologies, but Grosz argues that it is crucial for feminism to do precisely that, with regard to the ontological status attributed to biological sex. The pervasiveness of dualism and its recourse to a male norm (discussed here in chapter 2) depends on the notion that "male"—and, by implication, "female"—can be defined as a fixed, determinate entity, as Derrida has argued:

> when sexual opposition is determined by *opposition* in the dialectical sense....one appears to set off "the war between the sexes"; but one precipitates the end with victory going to the masculine sex. The determination of sexual difference in opposition is destined, designed, in truth, for truth.[56]

To disrupt this deeply-entrenched binary equation is essential for the undermining of patriarchal assumptions, power structures and truth-claims, and so feminism, accordingly, could have much to gain by exploring strategies for the redeployment of binary-oppositional sexual difference and its attendant appeals to metaphysical Truth. What the Garden of Eden story shows us is not only that the undermining of "true" referents has its dangers—e.g. the provocation

---

[55] *Ibid.* pp.154, 156.
[56] Derrida (1982a), p.72.

to the issuing of harsh official counter-directives under the banner of objectivity and hermeneutical neutrality—but also that it offers freedom; the serpent is punished, but not before it has directed the human couple to a world beyond the walls of Eden, a world where circumscribed awareness is exchanged for knowledge, choice and responsibility. In this more complex world, the closest we can come to unadulterated Presence of any kind (sexual, experiential, or Divine) is through a signifying system, a text—stable meaning may be a necessary fiction, but it is a fiction nonetheless, always-already "written". If Genesis 2:4b-3:24 is to be read as an aetiology, a prescriptive myth, then it should be read as such with this understanding in mind, as documenting the way in which logocentrism of all kinds (whether patriarchal or otherwise) must always fall prey to language—which makes the story the most peculiarly "Greek" of tragedies. The Garden of Eden thus provides the setting for a genesis of the uneasy, restless tension that exists between fixed structures of signification and approaches to meaning which allow for

> flux, continuity and phases of alternation, offering [images] not of exclusive realities, nor of final beginnings and endings, but of infinite cycles of transformation.[57]

This tension receives frequent and close attention within the context of feminist discourse, but it operates wherever statically dualistic modes of thought and language are in conflict with ambiguity and change. To imagine any kind of final resolution to this cultural tension, any kind of flight from the "implacable destiny which immures everything for life in the figure 2",[58] is to imagine nothing less than a new language and a new understanding of being. "But where would the 'dream' of the innumerable come from", Derrida asks, "if it is indeed a dream? Does the dream itself not prove that what is dreamt of must be there in order for it to provide the dream?".[59]

---

[57] Baring and Cashford (1991), p.676.
[58] Derrida *op. cit.* p.76.
[59] *Ibid.* p.76.

CONCLUSION

Gayatri Spivak, in an essay on Wordsworth's *The Prelude*—in which she seeks to articulate certain sections of the poem by examining Wordsworth's sexuality, his ideas on poetry and his revolutionary politics[1]—writes at the outset of her study that such a deterministic approach necessarily compromises the force of Derrida's "trace-structure". Spivak—who elsewhere describes herself as a "feminist, Marxist deconstructivist" critic[2]—goes on to say that to "explain" a text in terms of particular authorial characteristics, or of particular historical events, is effectively to fix the movement of signification in a static cause-and-effect structure: Wordsworth's poem is like *this* because Wordsworth and his world were like *that*. To stop there, however, is to ignore the trace of phenomena within other phenomena; to forget that no single origin is definitive, that origins always refer us back to other origins, or sideways in the direction of alternative origins, or forward in time toward the possibility of alternative developments. This trace-structure "disrupts the unified and self-contained description of things",[3] and it reminds us that even the most commonsensical explanations of texts have their fictitious aspect. Derrida puts it bluntly:

> I will go so far as to say that it is *not to read* the syntax and punctuation of a given sentence when one arrests the text in a certain position, thus settling on a thesis, meaning or truth.[4]

Intelligible discourse, however, is impossible without settling at least provisionally for these kinds of misreading, without

> the unity of *something* being taken for granted. It is not possible to attend to the trace *fully*,[5]

---

[1] Spivak: "Sex and History in *The Prelude* (1805): Books Nine to Thirteen" in *In Other Worlds* (1987), pp.46-76.

[2] Spivak: "Explanation and Culture: Marginalia" in *ibid.* p.117.

[3] Spivak: "Sex and History in *The Prelude*" in *ibid.* p.46.

[4] Derrida (1982a), p.69.

because such unimagineably comprehensive attention to an infinite proliferation of significatory minutiae would result in incoherence— the language of God, perhaps, but one spectacularly inconvenient for human purposes.[6] Spivak's dilemma in "explaining" Wordsworth is repeated here: this book is, perhaps more than anything else, the re- cord of an attempt to attend to the trace of misreading in reading (and vice versa) in a manner which is both rigorous and limited, faithful and compromised, which adopts the critical resources of what Paul de Man famously termed "blindness and insight". Ex- plaining deconstruction in conventional philosophical terms—in conformity to the logic of "the unified and self-contained descrip- tion of things"—is rather like demonstrating the finer points of swimming while sitting in a chair by the fire (a metaphor made all the more apt by the fact that water enjoys ambiguous status in West- ern culture as an element both alien and natural, as well as being something you have simply to jump into to understand). Such an undertaking is bound to be self-contradictory, even to an extent self- defeating, and fraught with inconsistencies. In the introduction to this book, for example, I suggested that the would-be deconstructor of these pages might begin by looking at the contradiction between my endorsement of Derrida as the architect of an aesthetics of egalitarian textuality—as one who takes the *author* out of author- ity—and my habitual reversion to him as, precisely and personally, an authority, a master-philosopher whose name can be invoked as a kind of charm to ward off criticism. This incongruity is one of the many perils encountered by those who wish both to practice or study deconstruction and to satisfy at least some of the discursive re- quirements laid down by traditional philosophical reasoning. The demands of epistemological convention, appeals to demonstrative sense and "rules of competence", to say nothing of the language of pedagogy:[7] all these are unavoidable (or at least I have not avoided them for the purposes of this essentially introductory study), and the

---

[5] Spivak: "Sex and History in The Prelude" in *op. cit.* pp.46-47.

[6] Jorge Luis Borges' fictional reflections on the possibility of "perfect" significa- tion are invariably melancholy ones: cf. "The Garden of Forking Paths", "The Li- brary of Babel", "Funes the Memorious" and "The God's Script" in (1989), pp.44- 54, 78-86, 87-95, 203-7.

[7] Derrida (1988), p.146.

best one can hope to do is to walk a fine line between feigning ignorance of such ironies and wallowing in a morass of critical self-
consciousness. It is interesting to note that Derrida—showing the
courage of his convictions, one would like to think—never completed his state doctorate.[8]

Another inconsistency (related to the one above) is apparent in
the way in which I have argued, with equal insistence, both that deconstruction is a *specific* programme, inseparable from its particular
applications, and that it forms an "approach" to reading, or a
"reading strategy"—these latter phrases, and others like them, are all
part of the attempt to avoid labelling deconstruction as a "method"
or a "concept", and while they are to some degree useful in this respect, they still, to my mind, carry unwelcome typological connotations. Again, I believe that this dilemma should be weighed prag-
matically against the demands of a certain kind of argument, and yet
at the same time the resulting compromises must be acknowledged,
largely because they provide a good illustration of how the serious
political implications of deconstruction—in this case implications
for how knowledge is required to be understood, processed and disseminated within the academy—are never far from its more apparently innocuous activity as literary/philosophical criticism. The difference between deconstruction as a reading strategy and deconstruction as something more obviously political is principally a
function of where one chooses to stop. One can begin, for example,
by reading deconstructively the patriarchal "meaning" inscribed
within the narrative boundaries of Genesis 2:4b-3:24, but such a
reading will inevitably lead to the realisation that this so-called
original inscription is a cultural product, not a kernel of truth to be
disputed but an interpretation of the text to be reworked, as is one's
own deconstruction. The idea that the Garden of Eden story's
meaning lies in its interpretation leads to the consideration of which
interpretations have been traditionally held as legitimate, why they
have been deemed so, which interpretations might have been re-
pressed and by whom, and so on. Almost before we know it, what is
being interrogated is no longer a comfortably familiar bible story,
but the biblical canon, the workings of power within religious insti-

---

[8] Cf. Norris (1987), pp.12-15.

tutions, the function of religion in society, and other issues which
can lead alarmingly rapidly to visions of the wholesale deconstruction of language, history and culture. That way madness lies, and we
take refuge back in literary criticism, where we may now be sur-
prised at the complaints of those who argue that deconstruction fails
to "respect the text"—I would say that the power attributed by deconstruction to the text and to literary language is granted in decidedly respectful measure, and furthermore that those who believe the
study of literature begins and ends with formal codes of expression
grievously underestimate the discourse they defend.

The problems posed by these contradictions between what deconstruction logically, inexorably, remorselessly "is" and what we
more humbly make of it are perhaps rooted in the fact that we call it
"deconstruction", and thereby ground it in the work of one thinker
and one putative school of thought. Deconstruction is too often mis-
understood as an activity which is *applicable to* structures of meaning, necessitating a facility of sleight-of-hand to be learned from a
master illusionist. It is better, I have argued, to think of deconstruction as something which is at work *within* structures of meaning, necessitating more a kind of perception than a box of critical tricks.
One commentator on Derrida recommends that his introductory
guide to the French philosopher be understood as "a ladder to be un-
ceremoniously kicked away once it has served its purpose",[9] and
there are many points in the texts of Derrida himself at which he
similarly disclaims pretensions to critical mastery or authoritative
wisdom. Derrida has (with heavy and necessary reliance on Plato,
Rousseau, Hegel, Husserl, Nietzsche, Heidegger and others) pointed
out various things concerning language, culture and history; to label
all those who appropriate or develop these insights as "deconstructionists" is misleading to the extent that it implies both a critical
homogeneity and a quality of discipleship, neither of which is always in evidence. Those who read with a deconstructive perception
exhibit not so much a necessarily Derridean affiliation as an awareness of certain aspects or characteristics of signification. The awareness which deconstruction demands and fosters is an awareness of
the differential nature of language, of the constructed nature of

---

[9] *Ibid.* p.17.

meaning, of the tendency of our dominant Western philosophical tradition to ignore or sideline these paradoxes *and* of our need to maintain both the awareness and the ignorance.[10] This matrix gives scope to an infinitely varied number of critical styles and strategies which range from (it must be admitted) jargonistic cultural catastrophe theories to more conventional-looking approaches; again, the difference between both poles is a matter not of how authentically deconstructive one or the other is, but of where one wishes to arrest one's exemplary slide into linguistic "play" and buy into the more conveniently familiar structures of logocentrism. The conventional approach errs on the side of irony or logical ambiguity, the radical on the side of incoherence; ambiguity and incoherence alike are what deconstruction argues for as legitimate linguistic/philosophical possibilities, "phenomena" which are as "natural" or "essential" to all signifying structures as are univocity and stable sense.

The preceding pages constitute, basically, the attempt to forge strong links between deconstruction, feminism and biblical interpretation, and it cannot by any means be expected that the move to bring these three fields together will please all feminists, deconstructionists or exegetes—now as always, "there is a war on, and he who ventures into no-man's-land brandishing cigarettes and singing carols must expect to be shot at".[11] Opposition may well arise to the fact that the links I wish to forge depend very much on the provisional legitimacy of paradox, of ambiguity and incoherence. The kind of feminism I have put forward as redemptive within an ailing culture is that which undermines the identity/difference dualism (a construct which underlies common sense and perception at its simplest level) in patriarchal thought and society, and which subverts the logic of rationality and objectivity in favour of more diffuse, undecideable structures of value and meaning. Particularly in feminist

---

[10] Cf. Drucilla Cornell:

> Deconstruction reminds us of the limits of the imagination, but to recognize the limit is not to deny the imagination. It is just that: the recognition of the limit. The political need to heed the limit, as well as to imagine, stems from the danger that any imagined scheme comes to be seen once again as the only truth.

Beyond Accommodation: Ethical Feminism, Deconstruction and the Law (Routledge, New York 1991), p.169. Quoted in Butler (1993), p.6.

[11] Kermode (1983), p.7.

theology, "coherence" as a yardstick for legitimate discourse about God is seen as upholding "the false abstractions and overly rational- istic conceptualisations"[12] of patriarchal theology, and the less quan- tifiable areas of intuition, subjectivity and experience are affirmed as valuable fields for exploration and experimentation. Similarly in biblical interpretation, the "meaning" of the text, both from a femi- nist and a deconstructive perspective, is as much as anything else a function of the subjectivity and experience of the reader: frag- mented, divided, unstable and yet possessing a conventional (and vulnerable) cohesiveness. This tension between the necessity to mean and the undecideability of meaning, I believe, lies close to the heart of religious experience, in that it reflects the desire both to make profound sense of the world and to acknowledge the risk and uncertainty, the openness to meaninglessness, that faith demands. It is this tension to which I would draw the notice of those who hold that feminism and deconstruction have little to do with each other, and even less to do with "devoted" biblical interpretation. For feminism and for deconstruction, as for the religious individual, the centre cannot hold, and yet its invocation is a necessity. The *diffé- rance* of this difference shakes the structures of patriarchal thought and logocentrism, and opens on to possibilities for their reconfigu- ration, for "a dismantling that enables a more intimate kind of knowing",[13] for a way of envisioning humanity, society and truth which acknowledges the workings of power and the political impli- cations of what we believe.

Where this dismantling might end, or what this "more intimate kind of knowing" might involve, is inexplicable according to the semantic logic of our received epistemologies; patriarchal and logo- centric concepts alike are deeply sedimented in that language, and so to rewrite them in any far-reaching way necessitates recourse to a new understanding of signification, a new language whose structures and dynamics cannot be adequately delineated in currently familiar terms. That this rewriting is necessary (in the moral or ethical sense of the word) is the foundational imperative of feminism; that it is necessary (in the sense of inevitability, of being always-already the case) is a deconstructive axiom: the fact that these necessities appear

---

[12] King (1989), p.167.
[13] Lentricchia (1980), p.209.

to contradict social norms on one hand and common sense on the other is an indictment not upon feminism or deconstruction, but upon the pervasiveness and persuasiveness of "phallogocentric" logic, which sees rewriting or radical interpretation not as the affirmation of "play" but as the perversion of truth. That this tension has an immediate bearing on biblical interpretation is manifest in the argument that determinations of meaning have a strongly theological programme attached to them; Derrida writes that "the intelligible face of the sign remains turned toward the word and face of God....[t]he sign and divinity have the same place and time of birth",[14] and it is no coincidence that reading strategies like deconstruction which pay full respect to the *unintelligibility* of the sign are often branded by biblical scholars as atheistic. Between the myth of perfect intelligiblity, of full Presence, and the chaos of nonsignification, lies a crisis whose form and implications can, as yet, be only vaguely perceived:

> Here there is a kind of question....whose *conception, formation, gestation,* and *labour* we are only catching a glimpse of today. I employ these words, I admit, with a glance toward the operations of childbearing—but also with a glance toward those who, in a society from which I do not exclude myself, turn their eyes away when faced by the as yet unnamable which is proclaiming itself and which can do so, as is necessary whenever a birth is in the offing, only under the species of the nonspecies....[15]

So wrote Derrida in 1966; the degree of pertinency which his comments hold today for biblical interpretation testifies to the fact that appeals to determinate Truth are still very much alive and well, and reinforcing the official discourse of exegesis. Where this notional Truth sanctions patriarchy and sexist oppression is where feminist biblical interpretation must read the text against itself. The points of conflict between the bible's patriarchal or sexist "nature" and its calls for justice provide the *aporia* where this deconstruction becomes not just a methodology, not just an interpretative strategy, not just an unsettling literary-critical gesture but an imperative, a movement away

---

[14] Derrida (1976), pp.13-14.
[15] Derrida (1978), p.293.

from the margins of an unjust society in the direction of creative re-definition.

BIBLIOGRAPHY

Alcoff, Linda, "Cultural Feminism vs. Post-structuralism: The Identity Crisis in Feminist Theory" in *Signs* 13:3 (1988), 405-36.

——, "The Problem of Speaking for Others" in *Cultural Critique* (Winter 1991), 5-22.

Alexander, Philip S., "Quid Athenis et Hierosolymis? Rabbinic Midrash and Hermeneutics in the Graeco-Roman World" in Davies and White (1990), 101-24.

Alter, Robert, *The Pleasures of Reading in an Ideological Age* (Simon & Schuster, New York 1989).

——, and Frank Kermode (eds.), *The Literary Guide to the Bible* (The Belknap Press of Harvard University Press, Cambridge, Mass. 1987).

Altizer, Thomas J.J. *et al*, *Deconstruction and Theology* (Crossroad, New York 1982).

Aristotle, *Categories & De Interpretatione* trans. J.L. Ackrill (Oxford University Press, London 1963).

Aschenasy, Nehama, *Eve's Journey: Feminine Images in the Hebraic Literary Tradition* (University of Philadelphia Press, Philadelphia 1986).

Ash, Beth Sharon, "Jewish Hermeneutics and Contemporary Theories of Textuality: Hartman, Bloom and Derrida" in Modern Philology 85 (1987), 65-80.

Atkins, G. Douglas, *Reading Deconstruction/Deconstructive Reading* (The University Press of Kentucky, Lexington 1983).

Auerbach, Erich, *Mimesis: The Representation of Reality in Western Literature* trans. Willard R. Trask (Princeton University Press, New Jersey 1953).

Bach, Alice (ed.), *The Pleasure of Her Text: Feminist Readings of Biblical and Historical Texts* (Trinity Press International, Philadelphia 1990).

Baring, Anne & Jules Cashford, *The Myth of the Goddess: Evolution of an Image* (Viking Arcana, London 1991).

Beauvoir, Simone de, *The Second Sex* trans. M. Parshley (Jonathan Cape, London 1972).

Becher, Jeanne, *Women, Religion and Sexuality* (WCC Publications, Geneva 1990).

Bernstein, Richard J., *Beyond Objectivism and Relativism: Science, Hermeneutics and Praxis* (Basil Blackwell, Oxford 1983).

Bloom, Harold *et. al.* (eds.), *Deconstruction and Criticism* (Routledge & Kegan Paul, London and Henley 1979).

——, and David Rosenberg, *The Book of J* (Grove Weidenfeld, New York 1990).

Boman, Thorlieff, *Hebrew Thought Compared With Greek* (SCM Press Ltd., London 1960).

Borges, Jorge Luis, *Labyrinths* (Penguin Books, London 1989).

Bos, Johanna H., "Out of the Shadows: Genesis 35; Judges 4:17-22; Ruth 3" in *Semeia* 42 (1988), 37-67.

Brandon, S.G.F., *Creation Legends of the Ancient Near East* (Hodder & Stoughton Ltd., London 1963).

Brenner, Athalya, *The Israelite Woman: Social Role and Literary Type in Biblical Narrative* (JSOT Press, Sheffield 1985).

Bruteau, Beatrice, "The Image of the Virgin-Mother" in Plaskow and Arnold (1974), 93-104.

Burnett, Fred W., "Postmodern Biblical Exegesis: The Eve of Historical Criticism" in *Semeia* 51 (1990), 51-80.

Butler, Judith, *Gender Trouble* (Routledge, New York and London, 1990).

——, and Joan W. Scott (eds.), *Feminists Theorize the Political* (Routledge, New York and London, 1992).

——, "Poststructuralism and Postmarxism" in *diacritics* 23:4 (1993), 3-11.

Cannon, Katie Geneva, "The Emergence of Black Feminist Consciousness" in Russell (1985), 30-40.

——, "Slave Ideology and Biblical Interpretation" in *Semeia* 47 (1989), 9-23.

Cantarella, Eva, *Pandora's Daughters: The Role and Status of Women in Greek and Roman Antiquity* trans. Maureen B. Fant (Johns Hopkins University Press, Baltimore & London 1987).

Caputo, John D., *Radical Hermenutics: Repetition, Deconstruction and the Hermeneutical Project* (Indiana University Press, Bloomington and Indianapolis 1987).

Castelli, Elizabeth, "Les Belles Infidèles/Fidelity or Feminism? The Meanings of Feminist Biblical Translation" in *Journal of Feminist Studies in Religion* 6:2 (1990), 25-39.

Christ, Carol P. & Judith Plaskow (eds.), *Womanspirit Rising: A Feminist Reader in Religion* (Harper & Row, New York 1979).

Clines, David J.A., *What Does Eve Do To Help? and Other Readerly Questions to the Old Testament* (JSOT Press, Sheffield 1990).

Cohn-Sherbok, Dan (ed.), *A Traditional Quest: Essays in Honour of Louis Jacobs* (JSOT Press, Sheffield 1991).

Collins, Adela Yarbro (ed.), *Feminist Perspectives on Biblical Scholarship* (Scholars Press, Chicago 1985).

Cooey, Paula M., "Emptiness, Otherness and Identity: A Feminist Perspective" in *Journal of Feminist Studies in Religion* 6:2 (1990), 7-23.

Coward, Harold and Toby Foshay (eds.), *Derrida and Negative Theology* (State University of New York Press, Albany 1992).

Craig, Kerry M. and Margret A. Kristjansson, "Women Reading as Men/Men Reading as Women: A Structural Analysis for the Historical Project" in *Semeia* 51 (1990), 119-36.

Crosby, Christina, "Dealing With Differences" in Butler and Scott (1992), 130-43.

Crossan, John Dominic, "Difference and Divinity" in *Semeia* 23 (1982), 29-40.

Culler, Jonathan, *On Deconstruction: Theory and Criticism After Structuralism* (Routledge and Kegan Paul, London 1987).

Cunningham, Adrian, "Psychoanalytic Aproaches to Biblical Narrative (Genesis 1-4)" in Cohn-Sherbok (1991), 113-22.

Daly, Mary, *Beyond God the Father: Toward a Philosophy of Women's Liberation* (Beacon Press, Boston 1973).

——, "Theology After the Demise of God the Father: A Call For the Castration of Sexist Religion" in Plaskow and Arnold (1974), 3-19.

——, *Gyn/Ecology: The Metaethics of Radical Feminism* (Beacon Press, Boston 1978).

——, *Pure Lust: Elemental Feminist Philosophy* (Women's Press, London 1984).

Daube, David, "Rabbinic Methods of Interpretation and Hellenistic Rhetoric" in *Hebrew Union College Annual* 22 (1949), 239-64.

Dauber, Kenneth, "The Bible as Literature: Reading Like the Rabbis" in *Semeia* 31 (1985), 27-48.

Davies, P.R. and R.T. White (eds.), *A Tribute to Geza Vermes* (JSOT Press, Sheffield 1990).

Derrida, Jacques, "Différance" in *Speech and Phenomena, and Other Essays on Husserl's Theory of Signs* (Northwestern University Press, Evanston 1973), 129-60.

——, *Of Grammatology* trans. with an introduction by Gayatri Chakravorty Spivak (Johns Hopkins University Press, Baltimore & London 1976).

——, *Writing and Difference* trans. Alan Bass (Routledge & Kegan Paul, London 1978).

——, *Spurs: Nietzsche's Styles* trans. Barbara Harlow (University of Chicago Press, Chicago 1979a).

——, "Living On: Border Lines" in Bloom *et. al.* (1979b), 75-176.

——, *Dissemination* trans. Barbara Johnson (The Athlone Press, London 1981a).

——, *Positions* trans. Alan Bass (The Athlone Press, London 1981b).

——, "Choreographies: An Interview with Jacques Derrida" trans. Christie V. McDonald in *diacritics* 12:2 (1982a), 66-76.

——, "White Mythology: Metaphor in the Text of Philosophy" in *Margins of Philosophy* trans. Alan Bass (The Harvester Press Ltd., Sussex 1982b), pp.207-71.

——, *The Ear of the Other: Otobiography, Transference, Translation* trans. Peggy Kamuf (Schocken Books, New York 1985).

——, *Limited Inc.* trans. Samuel Weber (Northwestern University Press, Evanston 1988).

——, "How to Avoid Speaking: Denials" trans. Ken Frieden, in Coward and Foshay (1992), 73-142.

Detweiler, Robert, "What Is a Sacred Text?" in *Semeia* 31 (1985), 213-30.

——, "Speaking of Believing in Gen. 2-3" in *Semeia* 41 (1988), 135-41.

Dragga, Sam, "Genesis 2-3: A Story of Liberation" in *Journal for the Study of the Old Testament* 55 (1992), 3-13.

Eagleton, Terry, *Literary Theory: An Introduction* (Basil Blackwell, Oxford 1986).

Edwards, Bruce L. and Branson L. Woodard, Jnr., "Wise As Serpents, Harmless As Doves: Christians and Contemporary Critical Theory" in *Christianity and Literature* 39:3 (1990), 303-15.

Edwards, Michael, "The Project of a Christian Poetics" in *Christianity and Literature* 39:1(1989), 63-76.

Evans, James H., Jnr., "Deconstructing the Tradition: Narrative Strategies in Nascent Black Theology" in *Union Seminary Quarterly Review* 44:1-2 (1990), 101-19.

Felperin, Howard, *Beyond Deconstruction: The Uses and Abuses of Literary Theory* (Clarendon Press, Oxford 1985).

Fewell, Danna Nolan, "Feminist Reading of the Hebrew Bible: Affirmation, Resistance and Transformation" in *Journal for the Study of the Old Testament* 39 (1987), 77-87.

Fewell, Danna N. and David M. Gunn, "'A Son Is Born To Naomi!': Literary Allusion and Interpretation in the Book of Ruth" in *Journal for the Study of the Old Testament* 40 (1988), 99-108.

——, "Boaz, Pillar of Society: Measures of Worth in the Book of Ruth" in *Journal for the Study of the Old Testament* 45 (1989), 45-59.

Finley, C. Stephen, "Hermeneutic and Aporia: Beyond Formalism Once More" in *Christianity and Literature* 38:1 (1988), 5-17.

Fiorenza, Elisabeth Schüssler, *In Memory of Her: A Feminist Theological Reconstruction of Christian Origins* (SCM Press Ltd., London 1983).

——, *Bread Not Stone: The Challenge of Feminist Biblical Interpretation* (Beacon Press, Boston 1984).

Fisch, Harold, "The Hermeneutic Quest in *Robinson Crusoe*" in Hartman and Budick (1986), 213-35.

Flax, Jane, "The End of Innocence" in Butler and Scott (1992), 445-63.

Foucault, Michel, *The Order of Things: An Archaeology of the Human Sciences* (Tavistock Publications Ltd., London 1970).

——, *Language, Counter-Memory, Practice: Selected Essays and Interviews* ed. Donald Bouchard (Blackwell, Oxford 1977).

——, *The History of Sexuality, Volume 1: An Introduction* trans. Robert Hurley (Allen Lane, London 1979).

——, "Nietzsche, Genealogy, History" in Rabinow (1984), 76-100.

Fowler, H. N., *Plato, with an English Translation* (William Heineman, London 1926).

Fuchs, Esther, "Who Is Hiding the Truth? Deceptive Women and Biblical Androcentrism" in Collins (1985), 137-44.

Fulkerson, Mary McClintock, "Contesting Feminist Canons: Discourse and the Problem of Sexist Texts" in *Journal of Feminist Studies in Religion* 7:2 (1991), 53-73.

Gardner, Anne, "Genesis 2:4b-3: A Mythological Paradigm of Sexual Equality or of the Religious History of Pre-Exilic Israel?" in *Scottish Journal of Theology* 43:2 (1990), 1-18.

Gilkes, Cheryl Townsend, "'Mother To the Motherless, Father To the Fatherless': Power, Gender and Community in an Afrocentric Biblical Tradition" in *Semeia* 47 (1989), 57-85.

Goldberg, Arnold, "The Rabbinic View of Scripture" in Davies and White (1990), 153-66.

Gottlieb, Lynn, "The Secret Jew: An Oral Tradition of Women" in Heschel (1983), 273-77.

Green, William Scott, "Romancing the Tome: Rabbinic Hermeneutics and the Theory of Literature" in *Semeia* 40 (1987), 147-68.

Greenstein, Edward L., "Deconstruction and Biblical Narrative" in *Prooftexts: A Journal of Jewish Literary History* 9:1 (1989), 43-71.

Griffin, Susan, *Woman and Nature: The Roaring Inside Her* (Harper & Row, New York 1978).

Grosz, Elizabeth, *Sexual Subversions* (Allen & Unwin, Sydney 1989).

——, *Volatile Bodies: Toward a Corporeal Feminism* (Allen & Unwin, Sydney 1994).

Halivni, David Weiss, *Peshat and Derash: Plain and Applied Meaning in Rabbinic Exegesis* (Oxford University Press, Oxford and New York 1991).

Hampson, Daphne, *Theology and Feminism* (Basil Blackwell, Oxford 1990).

Handelman, Susan, *The Slayers of Moses: The Emergence of Rabbinic Interpretation in Modern Literary Theory* (State of University of New York Press, Albany 1982).

Haney, Eleanor Humes, "What Is Feminist Ethics? A Proposal For Continuing Discussion" in *The Journal of Religious Ethics* 8:1 (1980), 115-24.

Hartman, Geoffrey H. and Sanford Budick (eds.), *Midrash and Literature* (Yale University Press, New Haven and London 1986).

Hayman, A.P., "The Fall, Freewill and Human Responsibility in Rabbinic Judaism" in *Scottish Journal of Theology* 37:1 (1984), 13-22.

Heschel, Susannah (ed.), *On Being a Jewish Feminist* (Schocken Books, New York 1983).

Jabes, Edmond, "The Key" trans. Rosmarie Waldrop, in Hartman and Budick (1986), 349-60.

Jefferson, Ann and David Robey (eds.), *Modern Literary Theory: A Comparative Introduction* (B.T. Batsford Ltd., London 1986).

Jobling, David, "Writing the Wrongs of the World: The Deconstruction of the Biblical Text in the Context of Liberation Theologies" in *Semeia* 51 (1990), 81-118.

Joy, Morny, "Equality or Divinity: A False Dichotomy?" in *Journal of Feminist Studies in Religion* 6:1 (1990), 9-24.

Kamuf, Peggy (ed.), *A Derrida Reader: Between the Blinds* (Harvester Wheatsheaf, New York and London 1991).

Kee, Alistair, *Domination or Liberation: The Place of Religion in Social Conflict* (SCM Press Ltd., London 1986).

Kermode, Frank, *Essays on Fiction 1971-1982* (Routledge & Kegan Paul, London 1983).

King, Ursula, *Women and Spirituality: Voices of Protest and Promise* (Macmillan Education Ltd., London 1989).

Kristeva, Julia, "Woman Can Never Be Defined", trans. Marylin A. August, in Marks and de Courtivron (1981), 137-41.

——, "Stabat Mater" in Suleiman (1986), 99-118.

LaFargue, Michael, "Are Texts Determinate? Derrida, Barth and the Role of the Biblical Scholar" in *Harvard Theological Review* 81:3 (1988), 341-57.

Lanser, Susan S., "(Feminist) Criticism in the Garden: Inferring Genesis 2-3" in *Semeia* 41 (1988), 67-84.

Lawton, David, *Faith, Text and History: The Bible in English* (Harvester Wheatsheaf, London 1990).

Leavey, John P., "Four Protocols: Derrida, His Deconstruction" in *Semeia* 23 (1982), 43-57.

Lentricchia, Frank, *After the New Criticism* (The Athlone Press, London 1980).

Lerner, Gerda, *The Creation of Patriarchy* (Oxford University Press, New York and Oxford 1986).

Lloyd, Genevieve, *The Man of Reason: "Male" and "Female" in Western Philosophy* (Methuen & Co. Ltd., London 1984).

Loades, Anne (ed.), *Feminist Theology: A Reader* (SPCK, London 1990).

——, and Michael McLain (eds.), *Hermeneutics, the Bible and Literary Criticism* (MacMillan Academic & Professional Ltd., London 1992).

Long, Burke O., "The 'New' Biblical Poetics of Alter and Sternberg" in *Journal for the Study of the Old Testament* 51 (1991), 71-84.

McFague, Sallie, *Metaphorical Theology: Models of God in Religious Language* (SCM Press Ltd., London 1983).

Mackey, Louis, "Slouching Towards Bethlehem: Deconstructive Strategies in Theology" in *Anglical Theological Review* 65:3 (1983), 255-72.

Macksey, Richard and Eugenio Donato (eds.), *The Structuralist Controversy: The Languages of Criticism and the Sciences of Man* (Johns Hopkins University Press, Baltimore 1972).

Magonet, Rabbi Dr. Jonathan, "The Biblical Roots of Jewish Identity: Exploring the Relativity of Exegesis" in *Journal for the Study of the Old Testament* 54 (1992), 3-24.

Maitland, Sara, "Ways of Relating" in Loades (1990), 148-57.

Marcus, Sharon, "Fighting Bodies, Fighting Words: A Theory and Politics of Rape Prevention" in Butler and Scott (1992), 385-403.

Marion, Jean-Luc, "Metaphysics and Phenomenology: A Relief for Theology" trans. Thomas A. Carlson, in *Critical Inquiry* 20:4 (1994), 572-91.

Marks, Elaine and Isabelle de Courtivron (eds.), *New French Feminisms* (Schocken Books, New York 1981).

Mehlman, Jeffrey, "The 'floating signifier': from Levi-Strauss to Lacan" in *Yale French Studies* 48 (1972), 10-37.

Merchant, Carolyn, *The Death of Nature: Women, Ecology and the Scientific Revolution* (Wildwood House, London 1982).

Meyers, Carol, *Discovering Eve: Ancient Israelite Women in Context* (Oxford University Press, New York 1988).

Miscall, Peter D., "Jacques Derrida in the Garden of Eden" in *Union Seminary Quarterly Review* 44:1-2 (1990), 1-9.

Moi, Toril, "Feminist Literary Criticism" in Jefferson and Robey (1986), 204-21.

Neusner, Jacob, *Genesis Rabbah: The Judaic Commentary to the Book of Genesis— A New American Translation Vol.1* (Scholars Press, Atlanta 1985).

Norris, Christopher, *Deconstruction: Theory and Practice* (Methuen, London and New York 1982).

——, *Derrida* (Fontana Press, London 1987).

Ochshorn, Judith, *The Female Experience and the Nature of the Divine* (Indiana University Press, Bloomington 1981).

Plaskow, Judith, *Standing Again at Sinai: Judaism From a Feminist Perspective* (Harper Collins, San Fransisco 1991).

——,and Joan Arnold (eds.), *Women and Religion* (Scholars Press, Missoula, Montana 1974).

Plato, *Cratylus* in Fowler (1926), 1-191.

Poovey, Mary, "Feminism and Deconstruction" in *Feminist Studies* 14:1 (1988), 51-65.

Rabinow, Paul (ed.), *The Foucault Reader* (Pantheon, New York 1984).

Ramsey, George W., "Is Name-Giving an Act of Domination in Genesis 2:23 and Elsewhere?" in *The Catholic Biblical Quarterly* 50:1 (1988), 24-35.

Ranke-Heinemann, Uta, *Eunuchs For Heaven: The Catholic Church and Sexuality*, trans. John Brownjohn (Andre Deutsch Ltd., London 1990).

Raschke, Carl A., "The Deconstruction of God" in Altizer *et al* (1982), 1-33.

Rich, Adrienne, *On Lies, Secrets and Silence* (Norton, New York 1979).

Ruether, Rosemary R., *New Woman/New Earth: Sexist Ideologies and Human Liberation* (The Seabury Press, New York 1975).

——, "Motherearth and the Megamachine: A Theology of Liberation in a Feminine, Somatic and Ecological Perspective" in Christ and Plaskow (1979), 43-52.

——, "Feminist Interpretation: A Method of Correlation" in Russell (1985), 111-24. _

——, "Re-Contextualizing Theology" in *Theology Today* 43 (1986), 22-27.

Russell, Letty M. (ed.), *Feminist Interpretation of the Bible* (Basil Blackwell, Oxford 1985).

Sakenfeld, Katherine D., "The Bible and Women: Bane or Blessing?" in *Theology Today* 32:3 (1975), 222-33.

Salmon, Rachel and Gerda Elata-Alster, "Retracing a Writerly Text: In the Footsteps of a Midrashic Sequence on the Creation of Male and Female" in Loades and McLain (1992), 177-97.

Saussure, Ferdinand de, *Course in General Linguistics* (eds. Charles Bally and Albert Sechehaye) trans. Wade Baskin (Peter Owen Ltd., London 1960).

Schneidau, Herbert N., *Sacred Discontent: The Bible and Western Tradition* (Louisiana State University Press, Baton Rouge 1976).

——, "The Word Against the Word: Derrida On Textuality" in *Semeia* 23 (1982), 5-28.

Scott, Joan W., "Deconstructing Equality-Versus-Difference: or, The Uses of Poststructuralist Theory for Feminism" in *Feminist Studies* 14:1 (1988), 33-50.

Setel, T. Drorah *et al,* "Feminist Reflections on Separation and Unity in Jewish Theology" in *Journal of Feminist Studies in Religion* 2:1 (1986), 113-30.

Shulman, Gail, "A Feminist Path to Judaism" in Heschel (1983), 105-9.

Spivak, Gayatri Chakravorty, *In Other Worlds: Essays in Cultural Politics* (Methuen, New York and London 1987).

Steiner, George, *Real Presences* (Faber & Faber, London 1989).

Stern, David, "Moses-cide: Midrash and Contemporary Literary Criticism" in *Prooftexts* 4 (1984), 193-204.

——, "Midrash and Indeterminacy" in *Critical Inquiry* 15 (1988), 132-61.

Suleiman, Susan R. (ed.), *The Female Body in Western Culture: Contemporary Perspectives* (Harvard University Press, Cambridge/Massachusetts/London 1986).

Thomson, David, "Deconstruction and Meaning in Medieval Mysticism" in *Christianity and Literature* 40:2 (1991), 107-21.

Tolbert, Mary Anne, "Protestant Feminists and the Bible: On the Horns of a Dilemma" in Bach (1990), 5-23.

Trible, Phyllis, "Depatriarchalizing in Biblical Interpretation" in *Journal of the American Academy of Religion* 41:1 (1973), 30-48.

——, *God and the Rhetoric of Sexuality* (Fortress Press, Philadelphia 1978).

Warner, Marina, *Alone of All Her Sex: The Myth and the Cult of the Virgin Mary* (Pan Books, London 1985).

Weedon, Chris, *Feminist Practice and Poststructuralist Theory* (Basil Blackwell, Oxford 1987).

Wolosky, Shira, "Derrida, Jabès, Levinas: Sign-Theory as Ethical Discourse" in *Prooftexts* 2 (1982), 283-302.

Zelechow, Bernard, "God's Presence and the Paradox of Freedom" in Loades and McLain (1992), 162-76.

INDEX OF NAMES

INDEX OF BIBLICAL REFERENCES

BIBLICAL INTERPRETATION SERIES

ISSN 0928-0731

1. VAN DIJK-HEMMES, F. & A. BRENNER. *On Gendering Texts*. Female and Male Voices in the Hebrew Bible. 1993. ISBN 90 04 09642 6
2. VAN TILBORG, S. *Imaginative Love in John*. 1993. ISBN 90 04 09716 3
3. DANOVE, P.L. *The End of Mark's Story*. A Methodological Study. 1993. ISBN 90 04 09717 1
4. WATSON, D.F. & A.J. HAUSER. *Rhetorical Criticism of the Bible*. A Comprehensive Bibliography with Notes on History and Method. 1994. ISBN 90 04 09903 4
5. SEELEY, D. *Deconstructing the New Testament*. 1994. ISBN 90 04 09880 1
6. VAN WOLDE, E. *Words become Worlds*. Semantic Studies of Genesis 1-11. 1994. ISBN 90 04 098879
7. NEUFELD, D. *Reconceiving Texts as Speech Acts*. An Analysis of I John. 1994. ISBN 90 04 09853 4
8. PORTER, S.E., P. JOYCE & D.E. ORTON (eds.). *Crossing the Boundaries*. Essays in Biblical Interpretation in Honour of Michael D. Goulder. 1994. ISBN 90 04 10131 4
9. YEO, K.-K. *Rhetorical Interaction in 1 Corinthians 8 and 10*. A Formal Analysis with Preliminary Suggestions for a Chinese, Cross-Cultural Hermeneutic. 1995. ISBN 90 04 10115 2
10. LETELLIER, R.I. *Day in Mamre, Night in Sodom*. Abraham and Lot in Genesis 18 and 19. 1995. ISBN 90 04 10250 7
12. TOLMIE, D.F. *Jesus' Farewell to the Disciples*. John 13:1-17:26 in Narratological Perspective. 1995. ISBN 90 04 10270 1
13. RYOU, D.H. *Zephaniah's Oracles against the Nations*. A Synchronic and Diachronic Study of Zephaniah 2:1-3:8. 1995. ISBN 90 04 10311 2
14. PORTER, S.E. & J.T. REED. *The Book of Romans*. A Grammatical-rhetorical Commentary. In Preparation. ISBN 90 04 09908 5
15. SELAND, T. *Establishment Violence in Philo and Luke*. A Study of Non-Conformity to the Torah and Jewish Vigilante Reactions. 1995. ISBN 90 04 10252 3
16. NOBLE, P.R *The Canonical Approach*. A Critical Reconstruction of the Hermeneutics of Brevard S. Childs. 1995. ISBN 90 04 10151 9
17. SCHOTTROFF, L.R & M.-T. WACKER (Hrsg.). *Von der Wurzel getragen*. Christlich-feministische Exegese in Auseinandersetzung mit Antijudaismus. 1996. ISBN 90 04 10336 8
18. BECKING, B. & M. DIJKSTRA (eds.). *On Reading Prophetic Texts*. Gender-Specific and Related Studies in Memory of Fokkelien van Dijk-Hemmes. 1996. ISBN 90 04 10274 4
19. BRETT, M.G. (ed.). *Ethnicity and the Bible*. 1996. ISBN 90 04 10317 1

20. HENDERSON, I.H. *Jesus, Rhetoric and Law*. 1996. ISBN 90 04 10377 5
21. RUTLEDGE, D. *Reading Marginally*. Feminism, Deconstruction and the Bible. 1996. ISBN 90 04 10564 6